NINE WARTIN

James Hinton, Professor Emeritus at the University of Warwick, has published widely on the social history of twentiety-century Britain. His early work in labour history included *The First Shop Stewards' Movement* (1973) and *Labour and Socialism* (1983). A spell of intense political activism in the 1980s anti-nuclear movement was reflected in *Protests and Visions: Peace Politics in Twentieth-Century Britain* (1989). More recently he has published monographs on two contrasting groups of active citizens during the Second World War: *Shop Floor Citizens* (1994), and *Women and Social Leadership* (2002). Following his work on the Mass-Observation diaries, he is now engaged on a full-scale history of Mass-Observation.

Praise for *Nine Wartime Lives*

'A compelling account that presents much that is unexpected about the lived experience of the war.'

Penny Summerfield, *BBC History Magazine*

'The life stories are moving and beautifully described.'

Vernon Bogdanor, *New Statesman*

'Skilfully synthesising a dense conceptual literature on themes of modernity, identity and the self, Hinton makes a powerful case for the value of diary-writing to the historian. . .an immensely enjoyable read.'

Helen McCarthy, *Reviews in History*

'Elegantly written and subtle in its analysis, this book will offer much to those interested in the social history of the war, those new to using personal sources, and more generally to those interested in existential questions about life.'

Hester Vaizey, *Times Higher Education*

'[An] absorbing and sophisticated exploration of how the public demands of war intruded into the private sphere and moulded new identities.'

Literary Review

'[A] welcome, scholarly and illuminating instalment in the story without end of the "People's War". '

Juliet Gardiner, *Financial Times*

NINE
WARTIME
LIVES

MASS-OBSERVATION
AND THE MAKING
OF THE MODERN SELF

JAMES HINTON

OXFORD
UNIVERSITY PRESS

OXFORD
UNIVERSITY PRESS

Great Clarendon Street, Oxford OX2 6DP
United Kingdom
Oxford University Press is a department of the University of Oxford.
It furthers the University's objective of excellence in research, scholarship,
and education by publishing worldwide. Oxford is a registered trade mark of
Oxford University Press in the UK and in certain other countries

© James Hinton 2010

The moral rights of the author have been asserted

First published 2010
First published in paperback 2011
Reprinted 2013

Published in the United States of America by Oxford University Press
198 Madison Avenue, New York, NY 10016, United States of America

British Library Cataloguing in Publication Data
Data available

Library of Congress Cataloging in Publication Data
Data available

ISBN 978-0-19-960515-6

Preface

I first visited the Mass-Observation archive at the University of Sussex in 1979 when my research interests turned to the social history of the Second World War. Like other historians of the period I found, and used, much interesting material in the files accumulated by Mass-Observation on particular wartime topics. But I was also aware of another huge body of material, diaries sent in by hundreds of volunteers, millions of mainly handwritten words. At intervals during the next twenty years I dipped into the diaries, fascinated by the intimacy of their revelations, terrified by their quantity, puzzled about what—if one ever had the time—one might be able to do with such a treasure trove. Academic life being what it is, it was not until I decided to escape into so-called retirement, that I dared to engage seriously with the war diaries. This book is the result.

I have used a selection of the war diaries to write biographical essays about nine of the diarists. Most of them wrote hurriedly, posting the material off to Mass-Observation without any opportunity to revise the text. In quoting from the diaries I have corrected grammar, spelling, and punctuation where necessary to convey the sense. I have also added notes with direct quotation from the diarists, but for the sources of assertions made on the basis of the Mass-Observation material without direct quotation the reader is referred to my notes, indexed and digitally searchable, available from the Mass-Observation archive.

An earlier version of Chapter 9 was published as 'Middle-class socialism: Selfhood, democracy and distinction in wartime County Durham', *History Workshop Journal*, 62 (Autumn 2006).

Apart from the diarists themselves, my primary debt is to the Mass-Observation trustees for permission to use this material and to the archivists: Dorothy Sheridan, Fiona Courage, Jessica Scantlebury, and Karen Watson who did so much to facilitate my research. Lucy Allwright, a wonderfully reliable research assistant, helped me with the reading of the diaries, funded by a grant from the British Academy. Bob Malcolmson, Mathew Thomson, and Dorothy Sheridan read drafts of the text and gave me invaluable feedback, as did OUP's three anonymous readers. Others who have contributed in various ways include Alison Hancock, Rita Lawson, Jen Purcell, Ronald Sands, Laurie van Someren, and my colleagues in the Warwick History Department with whom I learned how to reflect on the historian's craft. Finally, as always, my gratitude to Yvette Rocheron, not only for her critical readings, but also for sharing with me a life of writing, friendships, walks, and love.

JH
Rhyd-y-Sarn

February 2009

Contents

List of Illustrations

List of Abbreviations

AEU	Amalgamated Engineering Union
ARP	Air-Raid Precautions
CAB	Citizen's Advice Bureau
DR	Directive Replies (Mass-Observation)
ICAA	Invalid Children's Aid Association
ILP	Independent Labour Party
MO	Mass-Observation
NAAFI	Navy, Army, and Air Force Institutes
NCC	Non-Combatant Corps
NCO	Non-Commissioned Officer
NCW	National Council of Women
PPU	Peace Pledge Union
WAAF	Women's Auxiliary Air Force
WEA	Workers' Educational Association
WI	Women's Institute
WVS	Women's Voluntary Services
YMCA	Young Men's Christian Association
YWCA	Young Women's Christian Association

Our knowledge of man is still far too rudimentary to allow wide generalisations...To say that the ways of man are mysterious is to make a scientific, not a religious statement. I have therefore deliberately left my arguments and my suggestions in juxtaposition, rather than tying them all up in a specious causal web. Instead of a theory, I offer an attitude...

Theodore Zeldin, *France 1848–1945: Politics and anger* (Oxford 1979), p. xv

I

Introduction

This book is an experiment in historiography. Time and again, discussions of the social ills of contemporary Britain look back nostalgically to the years of the Second World War, when Britain, it is said, was united against Nazism and its citizens uncommonly active in pursuit of the common good. Sixty years on, the memory of the war years, worked and reworked in a never-ending flow of memoirs, diaries, and popular historical works, continues to occupy the centre ground of British national identity. Despite the best efforts of critical historians to debunk the more starry-eyed accounts of national unity, a positive image of dutiful citizens in wartime continues to provide a seemingly irresistible foil to the selfish individualism characteristic of our own times.

As a historian concerned with the use and abuse of the past, I wanted to take a close look at this apparent contrast between wartime citizenship and contemporary individualism. In my own previous work on the social history of the war I had written about two very different groups of wartime activists: shop stewards anxious to boost production in wartime factories, and middle-class women doing their bit as organizers of voluntary social service.[1] In both cases the research exploded any simple equation between active citizenship and patriotism, revealing wartime 'national unity' as a site of conflict, a place where different interest groups jockeyed for social prestige and political advantage. But this work, cast in the mould of social history, left unanswered deeper questions about the motivation of the individuals involved. What made people into active citizens? How did their private lives affect their public activities, and vice versa? What records existed that would allow one to explore such questions?

There was one source crying out to be used—the wartime diaries preserved in the Mass-Observation archive at Sussex University. Formed in 1937 from the cross currents of 1930s radicalism, Mass-Observation (MO) set out to document popular life and belief in ways that would contribute to the democratization of sociological knowledge: 'an anthropology of ourselves'. One of their innovations was the establishment of a national panel of volunteer observers, briefed to write occasional reports on their everyday lives and to respond to regular questionnaires ('directives'). When war broke out members of the panel were invited to send in 'war diaries' recording their activities and observations. About 400 people responded to this invitation, some very briefly, but more than 100 writing over several years, a few throughout the war and beyond.[2]

Mass-Observation had been founded not only to document and give voice to the values expressed in the private lives of ordinary people, but also as 'an elementary piece of human organisation and adaptation' designed to foster a genuinely democratic public sphere capable of resisting the twin evils of top-down political manipulation and popular political apathy.[3] By soliciting the opinions of 'ordinary' people, summarizing them honestly, with no axe of its own to grind, and circulating their findings through its own publications and the mass media, MO hoped to build a barrier against the demagogic exploitation of irrational anxieties, and to promote realistic, enlightened, and scientific attitudes in social and political life. Most of those who volunteered as mass observers shared these goals. They were people on a quest, looking for a meaning and purpose in their lives beyond the mundane satisfactions of everyday life, feeling a need to participate in society not only as members of families and friendship networks, consumers, and workers, but also as active citizens making a voluntary contribution to the greater social good. Indeed their readiness to write for Mass-Observation was itself symptomatic of such a commitment.[4]

The nine diarists discussed in the body of this book—six women and three men—were all people who, at one time or another, were active in public life. Between them they span a wide range of wartime active citizenship: political parties (Conservative, Labour, Communist and the short-lived Common Wealth party); voluntary work (Women's Voluntary Services, and other charities); the women's movement (Women's Institutes, the National Council of Women); adult education (the Workers' Educational Association, informal discussion groups); pacifist organization (the Peace Pledge Union); churches (Anglican, Quaker); and a humanist group (the Birmingham Ethical Society). Three of them lived in (or near) London, three in the industrial north, two in the West Midlands and one, a young man in the army, was moved around from camp to camp before being sent overseas in the autumn of 1944. All, except the young man, were, or had been, married: three were in their fifties, five in their late thirties. All nine diarists thought of themselves as middle class, but in fact they span a wide social range, from a woman married to a garage mechanic, via people in professional jobs, to the wife of a man on track to becoming managing director of one of Britain's largest electronics companies. In all but one case I have used their real names, with the approval of those descendants that I have been able to track down. I also decided to refer to them, most of the time, by their first names; an anachronistic impertinence, but one which felt more natural to my twenty-first century sensibility than the more formal address which they would have expected in their own time.

The war diaries provided extraordinarily rich material. In asking panel members to keep diaries Mass-Observation made it clear that they were as interested in the diarists' observation of their own feelings and behaviour as in the behaviour of others. As members of the national panel they received the monthly directives, many of which invited critical self-examination on intimate issues of snobbery, sexual behaviour, marriage, friendship, death, and religious belief. Once a year panel members were asked: 'What effects, if any, do you feel the war is having on your mind and general outlook on life?'[5] During 1944–5 MO conducted its own enquiry into belief, on behalf of the secularist Ethical Society, and this encouraged the diarists to look as deeply as they could into the sources of their own selfhoods, as they struggled to respond coherently to such questions as: 'Do you consider you have any "aims in life" clearly enough formulated to put in writing?'[6] Regular diary writing fostered the diarists' capacity to respond to such questions by articulating the ambiguous, unresolved, contradictory nature of the thoughts and feelings involved in their own ongoing projects of self-fashioning.

Selfhood

The last thirty years have seen an explosion of writing, across many disciplines, about the sources of the modern self. Historians have become increasingly interested in the ways in which individuals have used available cultural resources to weave meaningful narratives of their personal identities. Modernity has been seen as a process involving the radical disembedding of individual subjectivity from received sources of meaning.[7] In pre-modern times, it is argued, the individual was anchored in hierarchical social structures underwritten by cosmological chains of being. Although Western individualism has deep roots in the remoter past, it was seventeenth-century science and the eighteenth-century Enlightenment which laid the basis for the central historical drama of modernity, the world-transforming dynamism of industrial capitalism and the democratic upheavals launched by the American and French Revolutions. Deprived of secure anchorage and ready-made systems for understanding the meaning of life, modern selfhood had, of necessity, to be constantly remade in the face of unceasing upheavals in the social order and in the understanding of man's relation to the natural world, including his own nature. In mid-twentieth-century Britain, this meant grappling not only with domestic social and political change (social mobility, family limitation, democracy, the interventionist state, working-class organization, consumerism, mass media, etc.); not only with the international context of an era of unprecedented violence; but also the working through of the revolution in self-understanding wrought by the new sciences of man—sociology, anthropology, psychology. Confronted by the ever-repeated shock of the new, the modern individual was to an unprecedented degree his or her own invention. In a world which, for an increasing number of people, appeared to offer alternative possibilities for self-invention, selfhood was not a given, but a quest.[8]

Not, of course, a quest in a void. However disembedded the modern individual might be from pre-modern categories of being, the isolated individual free to choose his or her own destiny had more to do with the fantasies of modernity than its reality. 'Somewhere,' remarked Norbert Elias, 'he has people he knows, trusted friends and enemies, a family, a circle of acquaintances to which he belongs...'[9] Selfhoods are constructed as much from the outside in as from the inside out. *Who we are* is determined more by *who we are with*, than it is by those apparently deep-laid personal characteristics which, on examination, turn out to be less a coherent whole than a range of often mutually incompatible potentialities. We find ourselves in practical cooperation with other people—family, friends, colleagues—and in making masks appropriate for the performance of our various roles, we make ourselves.[10] Many relatively unchanging factors contributed to the making of a self—gender, ethnicity, class, material conditions of existence, the need to earn a living, inescapable ties of family, deep-laid personal characteristics, formative experiences, and memories. Nevertheless living in modernity required each individual to negotiate selfhood in a world of rapid change which repeatedly threatened to disrupt whatever ground he or she might have found to stand upon. The self was always under construction, never a fixed state of being.

Historical sources bearing directly on the construction of selfhood are limited, and many of those which exist (autobiography, oral history) provide retrospectively crafted narratives which may do as much to obscure as to reveal the processes shaping an individual life. 'Remembering' how we became *who we are now*, involves a process of narrative construction in which, often, we forget or rewrite earlier stories about *who we were then*. Oral historians have come to understand the ways in which personal memories are rearranged and reshaped to conform to publicly available narratives, nowhere more so than in relation to a period so present in British culture as the Second World War.[11] It is the diary, by its nature free from teleology, that provides the privileged source for the historical investigation of selfhood.

One fruitful way of understanding diary writing is as 'the room behind the shop' in which the diarist reflects on and prepares his or her performance, mask, persona. If our self-fashioned selves are produced in performance to others, we nevertheless struggle to maintain them against the internal chaos, the fluctuations and animal passions within us, the insecurities, the unknown unconscious.[12] In this struggle, the diary functions, alongside other technologies of the self (confession, letter-writing, meditation, occult practices, photograph albums, prayer, psychotherapy, yogic exercises, etc.) as a means of keeping the show on the road; the diarist using the room behind the shop to relax, to drop the mask temporarily the better to act it out in front of house. Where the 'real' self is to be found—in the deep interior or in the performances—is a question best left to philosophers.[13] We should remember, however, that the diary is itself a performance—not only to the imagined audience at Mass-Observation but also to the 'self' being addressed by the 'self' who writes. In this sense all writing is performance, as we are reminded by the mass observer who explained a two-week gap in her diary by an emotional upheaval which she did not intend to disclose but which left her disinclined to 'put . . . myself down on paper' until she felt better.[14] Putting oneself down on paper is itself a sign of a degree of composure, a certain self-possession.

Diaries present their own problems of interpretation, and cannot be treated as transparent windows on the soul. While few activities are more private than the writing of a diary, the MO diaries were all written with an imagined audience in mind, conditioning what the diarist saw as significant, or embarrassing, or not worth recording.[15] Mass-Observation offered a discipline and a context which transcended the purely private, meeting a need to frame individual quests in relation to larger public purposes. In the ten years following 1937 Mass-Observation published more than twenty books analysing its findings on subjects ranging from war production to religion, and it was frequently referred to in the press and on the radio. Though guaranteed anonymity, individual observers were proud to find their opinions quoted, and they drew satisfaction from the belief that they were contributing to a scientific project; to the enhancement of democratic life; to the creation of a historical archive. Many of them kept going out of a sense of duty and the discipline supplied by the regular posting to MO. This sense of audience, however, does not diminish the authenticity of the diaries. If anything, the probing demands of MO's monthly questionnaires encouraged the diarists to explore and reveal their feelings with a directness and honesty lacking from diaries produced (or edited for publication) with other audiences in mind.[16] Secure in their anonymity and the fact that their diary entries were posted off to MO rather than left lying around the house, the diarists were often prepared to tell things to Mass-Observation that they did not discuss with their partners or the closest of their friends.[17]

The MO diaries contain material in various stages of being shaped. Some wrote every day. Others kept notes and wrote—or typed—the diary when they could, every few days, once a week, irregularly.[18] Regular diary writing created a space alongside the exigencies of everyday living in which the diarist could experiment, more or less playfully, with possible selfhoods. Depending on the conditions of production, the diaries reflect different stages in the processing of raw experience into selfhood: some diarists recorded every nuance of feeling, day by day; others sent in retrospective accounts, more worked-upon and shaped. The diary helped the writer to manage the tensions of daily life and relationships; to mediate old self and new self, rational and emotional self, private and public self, ordinary self and higher self. The diary reader, eavesdropping on a conversation about the meaning of a life, can take nothing at face value. Meanings shift from day to day, mood to mood, crisis to crisis. It is precisely this fragmentary, raw, experimental, unedited nature of the diary, that makes it so revealing of the processes by which narratives of selfhood are produced.[19] The more introspective of these diaries take us as close as a historian can hope to get to observing selfhood under construction, making it possible to explore the strategies employed to sustain the singularity of a self, the meaning of a life.

The personal is political

Gradually, as I immersed myself in the diaries, the focus of my enquiry shifted. I had started out looking for the sources of active citizenship in wartime Britain. But wider themes emerged. I found that what I was reading about, particularly in the women's diaries, were individual struggles for personal autonomy. An investigation which had started from a trajectory of moral decline, a negative contrast between our own times and the presumed social cohesion of the war years, was twisting around, pointing instead to a more optimistic account of recent social evolution. Close attention to the interplay between the private and public lives of wartime active citizens suggested a reading of twentieth-century history altogether more hopeful than that embodied in the familiar contrast between contemporary antisocial individualism and the presumed public spirit of wartime Britain.

Sometime in the twentieth century 'human character changed'. Virginia Woolf, spokeswoman of the upper class avant-garde, placed it early, and precisely, 'on or about December 1910'—when London's first post-impressionist exhibition opened new ways of seeing, and cook came into the drawing room to borrow the printer's strike sheet, the *Daily Herald*.[20] More popular turning points include 1916—17, when the trenches devoured imperial masculinity and Lenin's bravado etched the dream (or nightmare) of a workers' state onto the modern consciousness; the People's War of 1939—45, when 'the British people came of age' and laid the foundations of a welfare state offering genuine citizenship to all;[21] or the cultural revolution of the 1960s which opened the floodgates for a new age of personal autonomy, women's liberation, and, so pessimists observe, antisocial individualism.

Anyone can play at this game. By choosing different turning points, or attributing different meanings to the same turning point, one denotes divergent trajectories. The Somme, Auschwitz, Hiroshima—or, in another register, the 'fall of public man', 'bureaucratic individualism', 'the narcissistic society'—fulfilled the most despairing anticipations of twentieth-century modernity. Critics of modern society have analysed the hollowing out and bureaucratization of the public sphere, the sapping of social solidarity by antisocial competitive individualism, and a retreat into private life which has left the individual anxious and alone with nowhere to turn beyond a narcissistic sphere of intimacy incapable of sustaining the expectations placed upon it.[22] Attention to the Mass-Observation diarists, however, suggests a more optimistic reading, in which the twentieth-century appears as an era of democratization. Despite continuing oppression, inequality, and exploitation, later twentieth-century Britain was becoming a less deferential society, one in which people came to see themselves less in terms of where they were placed within functional hierarchies, more as autonomous individuals aspiring to relate to one another in egalitarian ways. Much of this shift originated not in public life but in the changing relationships between men and women in the intimate sphere.

When historians influenced by the 1970s women's movement started to write the history of twentieth-century female self-assertion they puzzled about the apparent gap between the wining of the suffrage early in the century, and the renewed campaigning for women's liberation in their own era. Did the vote, incorporation into conventional partisan politics, and improvements in everyday life consequent on rising living standards and a falling birth rate, divert two generations of women from more radical questioning of sexual inequality? Did the overwhelming presence of war and the threat of war create such a psychological need for the comfort of home and hearth that women drew back from challenging the patriarchal structures underpinning the 'compensatory domesticity' which, as wives and homemakers, it was their role to provide? Was emancipation only available for spinsters, marginal figures in a moral economy that placed marriage and motherhood at the apex of female self-fulfilment?[23] Such speculations, however, soon gave way to exploration of the subtler ways in which married women, in the years between the militancy of the battle for the suffrage and the 1970s, sought to establish greater personal autonomy: negotiating more democratic arrangements in the private sphere; asserting their authority as mothers, homemakers, and consumers; claiming status in the public world of female associational life and voluntary work, if not in paid employment.[24] The Mass-Observation diaries, the men's as well as the women's, help to document such stratagems, providing a snapshot of intimate relationships during the mid-century rich in detail and variety, the eddies and the backwaters as well as the main forward flow. However much an 'ideology of domesticity' might seem to constrict and constrain women's lives, closer inspection revealed cracks and contradictions and, beneath the surface, ongoing processes of democratic change which were eventually to explode in the transformation of women's lives during the closing decades of the century.

The slogan that the 'personal is political' was coined by 1970s feminism, but it was an idea that informed much twentieth-century thinking, often in reaction against the cold, detached, masculine instrumental rationality driving economic life, wartime mobilization and statist welfare reform. Examples of such thinking include 1890s socialists like Edward Carpenter and his friends, seeking to live the fellowship of the 'new life' in the here and now, convinced that any genuine political democracy would have to be rooted in 'a personal democracy of feeling' and setting the agenda (as one historian of companionate marriage has suggested) 'for the remaking of personal relationships in the twentieth century'.[25] Or Virginia Woolf, in 1938, locating the root cause of militarism in the psychological brutalities of the patriarchal family, and its cure in the creativity of women experimenting in private life to transform gender relations:

the public and private worlds are inseparably connected...the tyrannies and servilities of the one are the tyrannies and servilities of the other...we are not passive spectators doomed to unresisting obedience but by our thoughts and actions can ourselves change [patriarchal culture].[26]

Or the Christian Socialist philosopher John Macmurray, challenging the gendered sundering of reason and emotion in the name of an 'emotional reason' attuned to the 'the primacy of the personal nexus of community over the functional nexus of organized society'.[27] For Macmurray 'community' was where people related to one another with the whole of themselves, acknowledging individual personhood as an end in itself, to be served by, not subordinated to, the impersonal disciplines of the formal social order: 'Society exists for the life of personal relationship. Personal life does not exist for society.'[28] Writing at much the same time as Virginia Woolf, Macmurray agreed that the relationship between the sexes was 'the most important of all the problems which this generation is called upon to face'.[29] And it was women, demanding the right to personal autonomy and self-realization, who were the driving force, setting in train a transformation of the intimate sphere that, as Anthony Giddens has argued, potentially provided the key to the realization of genuine democracy in the public sphere.[30] This has been the biggest social change in my own adult lifetime (I was born in 1942), contributing in a multitude of ways to the more general de-legitimation (if not, yet, dismantling) of authoritarian hierarchies.[31] If, as feminists have pointed out, authoritarian political structures are commonly legitimated by reference to the 'natural' hierarchy of the patriarchal family, then any challenge to the latter will also weaken the power of the former.[32] The democratic revolution remains radically incomplete, whether in the interstices of the family or the routines of public life, but in the course of the twentieth century the processes of democratization gathered a momentum which, in a time marred by more than its fair share of horrors, did more than anything else to keep alive the hope that human beings might yet progress to ways of living capable of unlocking their full creative capacities.

But here, as elsewhere, we are confronted by uncomfortable ambiguities. Built into the deepest sources of modern Western selfhood there was a tension between a classical tradition which located human dignity primarily in the public exercise of citizenship, and a Christian sensibility which saw the cultivation of a more private communion with God as the core of personhood.[33] A leading characteristic of the citizenship tradition, whether acted out in the Athenian forum, the Renaissance city, the eighteenth-century coffee house, or the civic culture of the Victorian city, was its elitism. The individuals whose rational discourse and free cooperation was deemed to constitute the public sphere were sustained and serviced by other, lesser people, women and workers excluded by their labours from the exercise of citizenship and, thus, from their full development as human beings.[34] In formally democratic societies many aspired to universalize active participation among the citizens, stalwarts of the Women's Institute no less than socialist agitators; and others paid lip service to this goal. But participatory democracy proved elusive; and, in the meantime, activists were all too likely to regard themselves as people of a special kind, marked off from the 'apathetic' masses by their devotion to public duty. At the same time inequalities of gender and class continued to structure the public sphere. The active citizens of Second World War Britain tended to be men whose capacity for public work depended on the service of wives, or middle-class women whose voluntary work depended on a continuing supply of domestic servants. We cannot read the active citizenship of either men or women as a straightforward manifestation of democratic relationships in the private sphere: indeed it might often have rested on the subservience of those excluded from the public realm.

The Christian tradition, by contrast, was available to all. However thoroughly the Church lent itself to the maintenance of social hierarchy and the cruelties of power, it could never entirely escape the original egalitarian vision: all men are equal in the sight of God. And women too. The Reformation made explicit an affirmation of ordinary life (domesticity, work as a vocation) as a source of individual fulfilment that had always been implicit in the Christian tradition, contesting the classical restriction of fully human status to members of the polis.[35] Of course, these two traditions interacted and, over the centuries, frequently found embodiment in the same individual. The historiography of the Victorian age, for example, is replete with evangelical women operating in the public sphere and Christian gentleman whose domestication matched their civic virtue.[36] But the tension remained, and in so far as women found a satisfactory selfhood in the private sphere, or men in their jobs, this could exercise a pull against seeking purpose and meaning through participation in public life.

Context of war

Whatever was happening in the longer term, the wartime context is omnipresent in the diaries, and it would have been easy to plunder them for illustration of more familiar themes. The war, it is argued, fostered a sense of national unity and purpose embodied at every level of British society from neighbourly community in the face of bombing to a vastly extended state apparatus capable of gigantic feats of planning and mobilization. On the back of these achievements broad currents of opinion—memorably described by Richard Titmuss in the first serious social history of the war, published in 1951, as 'the war-warmed impulse of people for a more generous society'—looked forward to the construction of a post-war New Jerusalem, planned, humane, and mildly socialistic.[37] At no other time in British history had the pressures been greater on individuals to shape their lives as dutiful citizens, providing a context in which people already

endowed with the public spirit characteristic of the mass observers could
be expected to flourish. The Second World War saw a late flowering of
Victorian values of altruism, character, and service, in which a rational
public sphere, a society united by a coherent sense of purpose had, perhaps,
never been more imaginable or closer to realization. Several of the diarists
bear witness to the reality of this reading of the wartime experience.

Much recent historical writing has been concerned to dismantle this
celebratory account. Despite the rhetoric of the People's War, the active
citizens who, in Angus Calder's words, 'surged forward to fight their own
war, forcing their masters into retreat' were only a small minority of the
population.[38] The visions of participatory democracy which inspired many
of these activists were checked, again and again, by the indifference or
the cynicism of those they aspired to lead towards the New Jerusalem:
and such frustrations served to reinforce the belief in their own personal
superiority to the apathetic masses harboured more or less shamefacedly
by even the most democratically minded of active citizens.[39] Far from
encouraging more people to become active citizens, the longer-term effect
of wartime mobilization may well have been to provoke a retreat into the
private sphere. During the war people did what they could to preserve
the integrity of their private lives against the relentless disruptions of
war—evacuation, military and industrial conscription. Most people did
not 'surge forward to fight their own war'. More or less reluctantly they
were conscripted into the national war effort: and even those taking up
voluntary work were often driven less by patriotism than by the desire
to avoid being drafted into less desirable activities. At the end of the
war, whatever hopes they may have entertained for social reconstruction,
most people's aspirations were focused most urgently on the restoration of
ordinary life—family, privacy, a job. Six years of compulsory participation
in the national war effort probably did more to enhance the appeal of
the private sphere than to strengthen the desire of individuals to pursue
their search for self-fulfilment in the public sphere. Even though the Mass-
Observation diarists were predisposed to such participation, they were not
always immune to the temptation to turn their backs on citizenship in
pursuit of a selfhood realized in friendship and family life. At such times
the personal could become all too thoroughly *apolitical*.

Celebratory accounts of wartime national unity also commonly overlook
another awkward fact. No reflective individual could escape the knowledge
that the wartime triumphs of cooperation and community were directed

towards one single all-pervasive goal: death and destruction to the enemy.
Once the threat of invasion was over, nothing could hide the fact that
the informing purpose of the national effort was mass murder. It was
not primarily as creators of a new and better world, as social reformers,
or as revolutionaries, that the British discovered their talismanic modern
national identity, but as paid-up participants in the industrialized violence
of modernity's dark side. Although none of the diarists were combatants
directly implicated in the killing, they all wrote with an uneasy awareness
that the unity of the nation was inextricably linked to a murderous violence
incompatible with the deepest values they sought to preserve. However
necessary it was to pursue military victory over Nazi Germany, it was
difficult to be optimistic that the limitless violence involved could lay
the foundations for a peaceful world. Despite efforts to link wartime
patriotism to the promise of post-war social reconstruction, most notably in
Beveridge's report on social security, profound doubts about the viability
of 'progress' remained.[40]

   Pacifistic sentiment had been widespread in pre-war Britain and it did not
simply vanish when war came. Popular pessimism about the post-war future
may have reflected not only the memory of betrayal of hopes for a better
society after 1918, but also, less consciously, a kind of war guilt: 'a . . . diffuse
underlying belief that collectively and individually the sin of war has to
be expiated'.[41] This paradox of wartime national unity has been largely
absent from its endless nostalgic recycling in post-war British culture as a
comfort zone from which to face, or evade, the challenges of a globalizing
modernity. The nostalgia set in very early, during the war itself: 'the myth
of the blitz'—the cheerful, stoic Cockney 'seeing it through'—assiduously
promoted by official propaganda, was willingly embraced by a population
desperate to find something positive to hold onto, more or less consciously
participating in the myth-making as a way of shoring up sanity against the
maelstrom.[42] In this way the myth became part of the reality, and Titmuss
could recycle it for posterity in an attempt, highly successful, to defend
optimistic social democratic narratives against more pessimistic accounts
emerging in the later 1940s of what war had done to the human spirit.[43]
Titmuss had read Elizabeth Bowen's 1949 novel of suspicion, treachery, and
anomie in wartime London, *The Heat of the Day*, and had (one imagines)
found it so disturbing that he unconsciously lifted her phrase 'the war-
warmed impulse' from its sardonic context—it is said in the novel by a
pro-Nazi traitor explaining his disgust at wartime myth-making—and used

it to project his own vision of a positive relationship between war and
social progress.[44] At the time, that relationship had seemed rather more
problematic. The context of violence was deeply felt by all the diarists.
Although two of the three men started the war as conscientious objectors,
coming to terms with the necessity of violence played a significant part
in their quest for an acceptable selfhood. And while none of the women
explicitly endorsed the link proposed by Virginia Woolf between domestic
patriarchy and international violence, all of them, even the most patriotic,
found gendered ways of distancing themselves from the killing.[45]

Transcendence

> Men's curiosity searches past and future
> And clings to that dimension. But to apprehend
> The point of intersection of the timeless
> With time, is an occupation for the saint...
> For most of us, there is only the unattended
> Moment, the moment in and out of time,
> The distraction fit, lost in a shaft of sunlight,
> The wild thyme unseen, or the winter lightning,
> Or the waterfall, or music heard so deeply
> That it is not heard at all, but you are the music
> While the music lasts.
>
> T. S. Eliot, 'The Dry Salvages', 1941[46]

There were meanings to be found in life beyond fulfilment in the intimate
sphere, in work, or in the performance of one's duty as a citizen. Confronted
by the maelstrom of modernity at its most destructive, the Mass-Observation
diarists felt a need for something to hold on to, something to dignify and
lend meaning to their lives beyond the disappointments of intimacy, the
frustrations of public life, or the fickle promises of history. They looked for
sources of nourishment impervious to time.

For many the key to transcendence was to be found in religion.
The death of Christian Britain has been persistently predated: it was not
until after the Second World War, in the 1960s, that Britain become a
predominantly post-Christian society.[47] While regular church going was
a minority activity, private religious belief remained widespread in mid-
twentieth-century Britain, and it helped to frame the ways in which people

tried to make sense of the catastrophe through which they were living.[48] Many of the diarists believed they possessed a selfhood continuous beyond death, an immortal soul striving for communion with God. For a few of them, prayer made such communion an everyday reality, and through it they sought the full realization of selfhood at 'the point of intersection of the timeless with time', Eliot's 'still point of the turning world'.[49] One mass observer (not one of those discussed in this book) wrote of:

a feeling indefinable but very certain that there is a personality in me, far above and beyond anything I can know; something which rules and directs me, but quite beyond my imagination or anything in my conscious world. There are no words for it. Nothing I do affects it; no sorrow and no joy reaches it. It is above it all and has its existence on another plane than this, but it is the real ME.[50]

Alongside do-it-yourself versions of Christian theology, Mass-Observation's own investigations revealed a widespread belief in astrology, spiritualism, the occult, reincarnation, and the transmigration of the soul in successive embodiments.[51] Coexisting with secular rationality, the diaries, particularly those of the less well educated, reveal a mental hinterland of magical and/or apocalyptic beliefs which might be seen as pre-modern survivals, precursors of later twentieth-century New Age thinking, or, perhaps, a necessary counterbalance to the spiritual poverty of modernity.

But the supernatural was not the only available source of transcendence. For some, the modern substitute for religion was to be found, as the philosopher Charles Taylor has argued, in art:

Art has come to take a central place in our spiritual life . . . The awe we feel before artistic originality and creativity place art on the borders of the numinous . . . It is now what realizes and completes us as human beings, what rescues us from the deadening grip of disengaged reason . . . It is the key to a certain depth, or fullness, or seriousness, or intensity of life, or to a certain wholeness.[52]

While the centrality Taylor attributes to high culture may have more to do with his own spiritual autobiography than with empirical observation of more popular sources of selfhood, many of the mass observers insisted on the importance of music, painting, novels, poetry, or film in their lives, believing, with Taylor, that engagement with the arts put them in touch with imaginative and creative aspects of their own natures, nurturing sources of selfhood inaccessible by other means.[53] Music—the purest, least contextual of the arts—held a special place, providing moments out of time, intimations of immortality, 'a means of focussing the spirit on its real objective by cutting it loose from the entanglement of living'.[54]

Moreover, the capacity of human beings to make meaning for themselves in a disenchanted universe could itself be a source of awe and wonder.[55] Some found this in the Enlightenment ideal of the disengaged intellect, the self as the *cogito*, freed from the pull of irrational emotion, master of the lower self of the passions, living a life bathed in the light of reason. Others might identify with a Romantic view of nature, including human nature, as itself a source of the good. Contemplating the beauty of the landscape, with Wordsworth, one was infused with elevated thoughts; believing, with Rousseau, in the innate innocence of mankind, one understood that true self-possession required, not the mastering of the passions by reason, but the recognition and unleashing of the genius of nature within. These stances—of the reasoner or the romantic—were available to anyone living in modernity; and they were by no means mutually exclusive.[56] The self-reflexivity of the diary writer, observer of his or her own inner being, could be seen as an attempt to combine them both. Putting oneself down on paper offered a kind of transcendence, a way of dignifying existence by standing apart, beyond the flow of mundane events. Making space in a busy life to write up the diary, the mass observer claimed a metaphorical—sometimes a literal—'room of one's own'; a place in which to reflect on life and, in so doing, to translate the everyday scramble to cope with the pressures of modernity into a self conscious quest for a meaningful selfhood.

Representativeness

The wartime diaries preserved in the Mass-Observation archive represent one of the largest collections of life-writing ever accumulated.[57] But their use by historians has, to date, been limited. A few of the diaries have been opened up to the general reader through full or partial publication.[58] Extracts from other diaries have appeared in a number of compilations.[59] Much of the pleasure to be gained from these books lies in their ability to capture something of the lived experience of individual people in the past: their joys, passions, anxieties, and idiosyncrasies. Despite the richness of the diaries, however, historians have been puzzled about how to make use of them. Intimidated by the sheer bulk of the material and worried about its representativeness, they have found little to do with the diaries beyond trawling them for vivid illustration of conclusions already reached from other sources.[60] It is only in recent years, with the growth of interest in the history of 'the self', that it has become possible to approach the diaries in search, not of snippets illustrative of more general experiences, but for what cannot be discovered elsewhere: the ways in which individuals sought to construct a coherent sense of their own identities.[61]

Nine individuals could not possibly be representative. But nor could ninety. 'At this degree of intimacy,' wrote Tom Harrisson, puzzling about the scientific value of the diaries, 'the word "typical" is no longer suitable. No one is privately typical of anyone else.'[62] Individual subjectivity is always more complex than generalizations about the life of the group. No one is typical and every person does it differently; and the more one knows about any particular individual, the less they can be used to illustrate some more general experience or theme. This book is not about 'everyman's' experience of war, but about a handful of people originally selected because their diaries enable me to explore, in a number of different social contexts, the interplay of public and private in the lives of active citizens. I chose these individuals not because they were in any way typical of their sex, class, or region, but because each of them combined an unusual degree of participation in the public sphere as active citizens with a still more unusual discipline of recording on paper their day-to-day experiences, feelings, and thoughts. Even among the Mass-Observation diarists they were atypical in writing at such length and in revealing so much of their inner lives. The only way in which they might be seen as representative is in the radically non-statistical sense that, as exceptionally self-reflective people, they can provide us with access to a cultural world that others inhabited with less self-awareness.[63]

Be that as it may, historians have long worked with individual cases, believing that each part holds a microcosm of the whole, teasing from unique stories insights into more general historical processes. This is what I have endeavoured to do in this book, moving backwards and forwards between trying to make sense of each individual life and the wider themes sketched out above. These themes have influenced the way in which I have told the individual stories and the individual stories have, in turn, enriched and extended the themes from which I started. Sociologists reared on prescriptions of scientific method derived from the physical sciences may find such a procedure frustratingly unmethodical, but, as the growing use of life-history work in the social sciences continues to demonstrate,

'the luminosity of single cases' can provide a 'point of discovery' and a
'starting point for inferences about social structure'.[64] Historical process can
be illuminated from the contemplation of individual life histories because it
is, in the end, the choices made by individuals which drive those processes
forward. So I have used the diaries to write biographical essays, showing
how, in their different ways, each of these nine individuals, in seeking to
make the best of their own lives, contributed to the making and remaking
of the culture. Nothing can be proved from a handful of individual cases,
but if these essays help to enrich our understanding of the impact of war
and the broader processes of democratization in twentieth-century Britain,
then they will have succeeded in their purpose.

I have not approached the diaries in search of intimate revelation for
its own sake, or in the belief that the closer we can approach to the dark
Freudian interior the closer we will be to understanding the 'real' self.
Despite Auden's 1940 tribute, it was not yet true that Freud had created 'a
whole climate of opinion/Under [which] we conduct our different lives';
not, at least, outside the avant-garde.[65] While psychological ideas were
broadly diffused, the 'practical psychology' popular at the time had less
to do with the insights of psychoanalysis than with the re-articulation in
modern, scientific language of values and attitudes associated with Victorian
ideas of self-improvement, character, service, and the ethical life, values
which, as we shall see, were close to the hearts of many of the Mass-
Observation diarists.[66] A few respondents saw what they were doing in
psychoanalytical terms, and some diaries contain hints, suggestive for the
psychoanalyst, about childhood experiences. But there is nothing to be
done with that information in the absence of the living adult: it would be
pointless and not a little macabre to play the therapist with dead diarists.[67]
All the diaries, however, are rich in social context, enabling the historian to
map the social spaces inhabited by their authors, and the ways in which they
interacted with their milieus. It is as a social historian, not as a speculative
psychoanalyst, that I have approached this material, seeking to locate these
individuals in their social context, and to understand how, in constructing
their own selfhoods, they contributed to larger patterns of continuity and
change.

In the late twentieth century, post-modern theorists were to demote
selfhood from a quest to an illusion. The notion of the individual human
subject as historical agent had, Foucault told us, no more substance than
'a face drawn in the sand at the edge of the sea'.[68] The power to

make meaning, decentred from the individual, was now to float free in a world of disembodied discourse. Cultural histories written under the influence of such ideas tended to present accounts of the discursive formation of identity—the ways in which gender, nationality, class, or any other collective attribute were imagined and represented in newspapers, books about contemporary problems, advice manuals, academic writing, novels, films, etc.—as though they were writing the history of actual subjectivities, rather than of some of the raw materials from which real individuals constructed their own unique selfhoods. By thus collapsing subjectivity into discourse, historians risk neglecting the moment in which culture was confronted by experience; the creative moment in which an individual, struggling to make sense of him- or herself in the world, will bend, select, recombine, amend or transform sources of meaning available in the public culture.[69] We now have, partly thanks to the cultural turn in historical scholarship, an extensive literature on the resources available to mid-twentieth-century individuals in their quests for meaning in their lives, spanning everything from the discourses of politics or patriotism to those of sex advice manuals, and I have made full use of this work in seeking to locate the individuals whose wartime lives I discuss. But analysis of public discourse cannot by itself reconstruct the ways in which individuals struggled to decide—as one self-reflective woman writing in the 1930s had put it—'which of the conflicting exhortations of a changing civilisation was appropriate to my needs'.[70]

A focus on how individuals put the elements of a culture together may enable us to dig deeper into the complexities of human behaviour and meaning-making than analysis conducted solely at the level of discourse. The biographical essays that follow are frequently suggestive of broader themes and, where appropriate, I have tried to draw out their implications for existing debates about gender, marriage, religion, and other sources of identity during the war years. I could have trawled more widely in the diaries for evidence of the power of discourse across individual lives: but that would have been to neglect the richer harvest to be reaped from a biographical approach which, as Michael Roper puts it, 'allows us to see the assimilation of cultural codes as a matter of negotiation involving an active subject'.[7] The focus is on the site of agency, where individuals are present at their own making.

Life bursts the bounds of this or any other analytic framing and loose ends proliferate—invitations for further work and alternative readings. I have tried to tell each wartime story with full regard for its uniqueness. These are biographical essays, not 'case studies' narrowly designed to sustain a particular theory or test a particular hypothesis. I have been concerned not, in T. S. Eliot's phrase, to 'fix' these diarists 'with a formulated phrase', but to present their lives respectfully, as provocations for further scientific work.[72] Hopefully one can return from such excursions into the biographical not only with new theoretical challenges to confront but also with a reinforced sense of the richness and complexity of ordinary lives, and the resilience, suffering, joy, guilt, fulfilment, and frustration involved in creating meaning in a life.

Figure 1. Nella Last with her son Arthur, 1940.
Courtesy of the Mass-Observation Archive.

2

Nella Last: Nation before husband

Nella Last is the best known of the Mass-Observation diarists. An edited version of her wartime diaries *Nella Last's War: A mother's diary* was first published in 1981, and republished in 2006, following an acclaimed TV drama based on the diaries, with a new subtitle *Housewife 49*—49 being her age when war broke out.[1] Neither subtitle does justice to the scope of Nella's writing. While motherhood and housewifery were both central to her identity, she was also a woman engaged in the public sphere, a sometime Conservative Party activist and a wartime voluntary worker.[2] Often struggling to make ends meet as the wife of a not very successful tradesman, Nella saw herself as part of a small-town provincial middle-class elite, sharing with the women she associated with in public life, many of them much better off than herself, a sense of cultural isolation and political embattlement in the remote, Labour-dominated shipbuilding town of Barrow in Furness. Motherhood, voluntary work, and the diary writing itself enabled her to build up a sometimes fragile sense of self and to find a measure of fulfilment despite being trapped in a disappointing marriage. Unshaped by formal education, her writing is vivid, funny, sad, intensely personal, and often moving. Nella's diaries provide a compelling account of a woman's struggle for autonomy within a patriarchal culture, a record both of emancipation and of the limits to personal growth in the circumstances of wartime Britain.

Marriage and motherhood

Nella often looked back in her diaries to earlier phases of her life. An accident, aged five, had left her with a broken thigh and pelvis. Crippled and needing successive operations until she was 13, her schooling was severely disrupted. Her father, a railway audit clerk, could have afforded private tuition, but thought it a waste of money to educate girls; but he did encourage her to read. Sheltered from the distractions of school and childish sociability she read widely, although this did not prevent her from seeing herself throughout her life as ignorant and ill-educated. Arithmetic frightened her—she shied away from any task involving figures—and she believed that her daily struggle with pencil and paper to give precise expression to her feelings reflected, not the hard graft of literary creativity apparent to readers of her diaries, but a peculiar inability to manipulate the written word. If only she had had a better education, she felt, she could have written books; which, as it turned out, she did, posthumously, with the help of some rigorous editing.

She had married young, aged 21, seeking escape from a domineering father whom she loved but feared, and a mother she remembered as 'a rather vague lonely shadow' who had never ceased pining for a previous husband and daughter, both dead years earlier.[3] Nella's marriage was problematic from the start. Will Last, a joiner working in his father's shop-fitting business, was a shy, moody man who had little in common with his more outgoing wife. As Nella saw it, he had married her for her gaiety but then wanted to keep it for himself alone. Throughout the diaries she complains about Will's refusal to socialize, his coldness with anyone who called in, his refusal to go visiting and his resentment if she went out without him. As a result she had few friends and little social life.

Temperamental incompatibility was exacerbated by cultural difference. Both sets of parents had opposed the marriage, and her relations with Will's family, who reacted against what they called her 'fine lady ways', were bleak from the outset:

I married into a different 'class' . . . perhaps I was a bit of a prig to be so shocked at their ways—indifferent table manners, dress—or rather undress—in the house, gossiping at doors, neighbours running in and out . . .[4]

For many years they lived among shipyard workers in a dark and sunless terraced house in the town centre, across the street from her uncongenial in-laws. There was a brief escape towards the end of the First World War when Will was drafted to naval work in Southampton. She spent two happy years living in the New Forest and came back to Barrow with reluctance. It was not until 1936 that Nella finally succeeded in persuading Will to move to a semi-detached house in a 'nice little estate' newly built on the northern fringes of Barrow, a middle-class neighbourhood which housed, she remarked with satisfaction, 'a large percentage of [Barrow's] doctors'[5] as well as wealthy traders and the chief constable. But she still felt out of place among the wives of tradesmen like her husband and yearned for the company of 'educated people with a dignified sense of themselves'.[6] Nella managed to combine an abiding sense of educational inferiority, with a firm belief in her own, unfulfilled, capacity for higher things.

While her husband read nothing but the occasional thriller, and irritated Nella with his insistence on the lightest of entertainment on the radio or at the cinema, Nella, though emphatically insisting that her tastes were not 'highbrow', thrived on travel literature (feeding a fantasy wanderlust encouraged by her father's stories of seafaring ancestors), and the family sagas of Galsworthy and Hugh Walpole whose novels were set in the Lake District, which she knew and loved. Before her marriage her admirers had included a friend of John Ruskin's ex-secretary, who told her stories about the great man's practices as a writer. (Ruskin, who died in 1900, had lived during his later years beside Coniston lake.) Unlike her mother, Nella was not one to dwell on irretrievable loss, although she did once introduce this old flame to her younger son as 'the man who might have been your father'.[7] The happiest part of Nella's childhood had been time spent with her maternal grandmother on an isolated farm between Barrow and the Lakes, and her most regular source of spiritual renewal in the 1940s were Sunday trips to Coniston lake where Will would stay in the car and do his invoices while she sat against a favourite larch tree absorbing the beauty and tranquillity of the landscape. They were an ill-matched pair.

It was motherhood that made married life tolerable. Her two sons— Arthur (1913–67) and Cliff (1918–91)—became her project, their upbring-ing her proudest achievement. Money was tight. The shop-fitting business, which Will ran with his brother Frank, never employed more than five workers, and what Nella considered an unfair proportion of the profit was taken by their father, who had retired early—leaving Nella to manage on 'a workman's wage with the position to keep up of a master's wife and the cold determination my boys should have their chance in every way'.[8] For a brief moment, following her father's premature death in 1920 (her mother had already died four years earlier) Nella believed she had the resources necessary to launch the boys on professional careers. But the value of her inheritance, £3,000-worth of shares invested in a Belfast shipyard, collapsed in the post-war slump, and she had to scrimp, save, and take in sewing and baking to pay for the music, dancing, and elocution lessons she deemed essential to making her sons into civilized professional men, and to support them in full-time education after they won grammar-school scholarships. As the boys grew up she kept open house for their friends, delighting in the merriment of intelligent, idealistic, and argumentative young people. Arthur, who was studious, left home in 1930 to train as a tax inspector, though his work brought him back to Barrow for a couple of years later in the 1930s. He became her closest confident, someone to whose education and capacity for logical thought she was happy to defer.[9]

Cliff was more problematic. He had thrown up school aged 16 to join the family business, but quickly realized his mistake when confronted by his father's combination of conservatism, inefficiency, and incapacity to express any appreciation of his workers' efforts. With Nella he was solicitous, affectionate, even flirtatious, commenting on her make-up and clothes (for which she professed indifference) and even, one birthday, buying her a wildly unsuitable siren suit: 'the maddest most amusing thing a sedate matron of 50–51 ever possessed!' Early in the war she played along with his fantasy that the two of them would set up a country pub together: to keep her 'young and lovely', he said, ruffling her hair. Will, who had taken little interest in his children's upbringing, complained that 'neither of the boys are like other people's lads', to which she retorted: 'well so what, hasn't that always been the battle cry of your folks about me?'[10] Having succeeded in turning his boys into the 'educated people with a dignified sense of themselves' whose company she had always craved, she saw no need to apologize. Motherhood gave her a project, something to fight for against Will's reclusive timidity, and allies when she overcame what the boys called her 'weak streak' sufficiently to stand up for her own interests and well as theirs. What pleased her most of all was that Arthur and Cliff treated her not only as the mother they loved, and but also as a friend who, they told her, they *liked*.

For Cliff, as much as for Nella, the coming of war was to provide a welcome escape. Conscripted shortly before war broke out, he was drafted initially as a machine gunner, and then spent a year as a PT instructor before volunteering to train for service abroad. He was sent to the Middle East in June 1942 and took part in the invasion of Italy where he was seriously wounded in November 1944, spending the next ten months in and out of hospital. Nella, despite seeing a good deal of him in the early years of the war, regretted their loss of intimacy. Cliff was gay, and although she never says so explicitly (homosexuality was, of course, illegal), there are hints in the diary to suggest that Nella may have been aware of this. She disliked most of his male friends, distrusted their influence on him, disapproved of his plans to share a flat with one or other of them after the war. Worrying about Cliff's plans in 1943 she hoped he would abandon the idea of going into business with a friend running a clothes shop who she described as 'that Downs "man" selling dresses. I do like a *man*.'[11] A year later she remarked, in response to an MO directive:

we have had a little bother in the family and it's shown me how 'sex' can be such a keystone of life. It seems to have opened windows in my mind giving me views and understandings I did not hitherto possess . . . somehow I grow more sorry for 'sex misfits'.[12]

This, of course, may have had nothing to do with Cliff, although an incident she recorded in May 1945 suggests some wary mutual acknowledgement. Arthur, who was studying psychology in his spare time, lent Cliff a book by Havelock Ellis on homosexuality. When Cliff tried to prevent his mother from looking at it, she responded: 'Don't be silly, I read Freud, Jung, and Havelock Ellis before you were born'—an unlikely story, given what she says elsewhere about her reading habits and her sexual ignorance as a young wife, but she clearly felt the need to keep her end up.[13] But they could not discuss his sexuality openly, and she felt reduced in his eyes to the role of 'a music hall mother' who—as he woundingly told her shortly after this incident—he loved but 'somehow didn't like . . . as much' as he used to:[14]

If Cliff knew how clearly I saw things, his way of thinking and acting, the worthlessness of so many of his 'friendships', I feel something would go. It's better I should let him think I'm sweet and dumb, seeing and understanding only what he thinks fit, knowing nothing but what he thinks fit to tell me. He forgets—or ignores—that talk and gossip filters through.[15]

Despite this knowledge, and Cliff's insistence that he would never marry, she still hoped he would find a woman to settle down with, perhaps Margaret, the girl next door, who had spent a lot of time in the house during the war when she more or less adopted Nella as a substitute mother. Cliff did not return Margaret's affections, but whether to please his mother or because he himself was uncertain about his future, he told her of various other liaisons and even, he reported, proposed marriage to a WAAF in the autumn of 1945. Playing 'sweet and dumb', however, could not restore her relationship with Cliff. After the war he discovered his metier at art school in London, and in December 1946 emigrated to Australia where he had a successful career as a sculptor. The inability of mother and son to communicate openly about his sexuality had contributed to a souring of their relationship starkly revealed in the deeply negative account of his childhood that Cliff gave in an interview published after Nella's death.[16]

'Are you a slave or a free born Briton?'

There has been a long-running historical debate about the apparent association between war and female emancipation. In both world wars feminists welcomed the mobilization of women as a precursor of female emancipation. By proving in wartime their capacity to undertake work previously restricted to men, women would demonstrate the irrationality of existing gender roles and lay the basis for greater equality between the sexes. The extension of the suffrage after the First World War seemed to bear this out. But it was as housewives and mothers, rather than as citizens on an equal footing with men, that the political parties chose to address the new voters, and both between the wars and in the 1950s the language of domesticity dominated public discussion of the position of women, pushing equal rights feminism to the sidelines. This reflected not just a male backlash against women's wartime advances, but, more fundamentally, the ambiguous meaning of wartime mobilization itself. War might require women to step temporarily into masculine roles on the home front, but, at the same time, it served to re-emphasize the gendered distinction between the warrior and the homemaker, and to put a premium on women's role as providers of the private shelter of home in a violent and comfortless public world. It is arguable that, on balance, the omnipresence of war during the first half of the twentieth century did as much to hold back as to encourage female emancipation.[17]

Individual life stories elicited by oral historians, which often testify to the liberating effects of war, should be treated with caution. The narrative linkage of war and emancipation quickly became established in popular memory, and it was easy for individuals, looking back, to perceive their experience of a particular life stage—a young woman's first wage packet, for example, or a middle-aged housewife's escape from full-time child-care into part-time work—as a consequence of war, rather than something that would have occurred at that stage in her life, war or no war. Some of these ambiguities are apparent in Nella's case. Her story has been seen as an example of the emancipating impact of war work (in her case voluntary work) on women's lives. In fact a previous history of public engagement, the departure from home of her youngest child (itself, admittedly, war-related), and the intervention of an enlightened doctor had as much to do with her capacity to flourish during the war as did the demands of war itself.

There is no doubt that Nella's involvement in wartime voluntary work helped her to establish greater autonomy and a more secure sense of her own worth than she had previously enjoyed. After two years of war, during which her diary recounts successive confrontations with Will, she was able to look back on her pre-war life as 'the slavery years of mind and body . . . the years when I had to sit quiet and always do everything he liked, and never the things he did not'.[18] The 'slavery years' is a striking phrase, nicely encapsulating optimistic feminist readings of the impact of war. Read in context, however, it was clearly a polemical remark; and it overdraws the contrast between the pre-war housewife and the wartime public woman. Nella's wartime liberation rested on firmer foundations than a pre-war life confined to domestic 'slavery' could possibly have supplied.

During the First World War, when she had spent two years living near Southampton, Nella had helped out in a Welfare Centre and done hospital visiting. When they returned to Barrow she inherited her dead mother's position in the 'Ladies Aid', co-opted by the public assistance committee to run soup kitchens and distribute blankets and clothing to the unemployed: 60 per cent of the shipyard workforce had been laid off by 1922.[19] It was ill-health—a year convalescing after an operation (probably for a prolapsed uterus), followed by months spent nursing Will through a major illness—that put an end to this phase of her public life. Sometime later in the 1920s she joined the Conservative Party, and was, for two years, chair of her local ward. In this capacity she fought local elections and the 1931 general election which successfully ousted the sitting Labour MP, working full time during the last week of the campaign while a cousin moved in to look after Will and the boys. Later in the 1930s her political activity declined, but she was kept in touch by Arthur and Cliff who both made their mark as public speakers in local Conservative politics. In 1935 Cliff co-founded a Junior Imperial League in the town, and later served as the first chair of the right-wing Economic League.

Although it was not literally true that her husband prevented her from undertaking any independent activity outside the home, Nella's perception of 'the slavery years' certainly reflected a reality in her relationship with Will, particularly her lack of a social life. What brought matters to a head, however, was not the war, but a nervous breakdown three years earlier and the intervention of a remarkably enlightened doctor. Nella's health had remained fragile. The move to the suburbs in 1936 had been prompted, in part, by medical advice when she had heart trouble following an appendix operation (the doctor had actually proposed a rather more drastic change—emigration to Australia). But her chronic problems remained: periodic nervous collapses, 'a baffled feeling of intense frustration', and 'spells of sickness—vomiting—when it was impossible for me to digest food at all for days on end'. Various medical interventions failed and in the winter of 1937–8 she broke down completely, loosing coordination in her feet and barely able to walk. One consultant diagnosed multiple sclerosis, but it was her GP who got to the root of the problem. In March 1938 the *Lancet* published a groundbreaking article on the 'suburban neurosis', in which symptoms like Nella's were ascribed to psychosocial causes. We cannot know whether Dr Millar, her GP, had read this article, but he clearly came to much the same conclusions:

He used to talk and talk to me and ask all kinds of questions and one day he told me I had nothing whatever wrong with me, that considering the several operations and the amount of sick nursing and worries I'd had for my family, I was really a 'remarkable woman', mentally and physically.[20]

Visiting her at home, the doctor turned on Will: 'Do you know the meaning of repression? . . . What would happen to a kettle if you put a cork in the spout and tied the lid down tight and yet kept it at boiling point?' His prescription for Nella was to go out and buy 'a new dress and hat ... and to get amongst friends more and to get over the silly idea that my husband couldn't eat a meal—even prepare it for himself—if I was not in on time'. Protesting that she already had a dress and a hat that she'd scarcely worn, she put them on to show him:

'Why did you choose dark brown?'

'Because my husband does not like me in conspicuous colours.'

'Hell roast us!' the doctor exploded: 'Are you a slave or a free born Briton?'

'And then', Nella recalled, 'we both laughed. He said a lot of unforgettable things and after that I got better quickly...'[21] She remained profoundly grateful to Dr Millar, referring to him frequently in her diaries, and saw his intervention as a major turning-point in her life.

At first Nella did not find it easy to follow the doctor's prescription. She had few friends of her own, and, in any case, the norms of middle-class female sociability—coffee drinking, whist drives, and cinema matinees—were not sufficient to hold her interest. Nor could family fill the empty spaces in her life. With the move to the suburbs she had (thankfully) cut herself off from the in-laws; Arthur had again left home; and Cliff's apprenticeship in his father's business caused her more anxiety than satisfaction. She started writing for Mass-Observation at the time of her breakdown, resolving in March 1938 to make things easier for her readers by learning to type (she never did). Little survives of her pre-war writing, and there is no clue as to how she was initially recruited, although the opportunity MO directives gave her to initiate conversations with strangers seems to have been one its attractions.[22] It was not until the outbreak of war that MO became part of her daily routine, by which time Women's Voluntary Services (WVS), which she had joined in February 1939 shortly after its foundation in Barrow, was enabling Nella to find new meaning and purpose in her life.

WVS played a central role in Britain's wartime mobilization. By 1943, under its charismatic and dictatorial leader, Lady Reading, WVS had recruited around a million volunteers, mostly housewives, to help in organizing evacuation, billeting troops, dealing with bombed-out civilians, and the administration of a bewildering variety of wartime social-welfare innovations. Although WVS itself was a war-related improvisation, it was built on a long history of middle-class female philanthropic effort, and, particularly since the granting of the suffrage to older women in 1918, the burgeoning inter-war growth of separate women's organizations in town

and countryside.[23] Nella's earlier involvement with the 'Ladies Aid' and
the women Conservatives—the largest single women's organization of the
inter-war years—placed her squarely within these traditions. Her initial
commitment was to Hospital Supply—'the Centre'—where by the early
months of the war she was spending three afternoons a week with up to
eighty other women making blankets and other necessities for the local
hospital, and reconditioning old clothes for the seamen's mission. Following
the Barrow blitz in May 1941, she took on a second job working in a WVS
canteen. And from August 1942, alongside her other activities, she took
the initiative in establishing a charity shop to raise money for Red Cross
parcels for prisoners of war. By the end of the war the shop had raised over
£6,000, fulfilling a long held desire 'to have a shop and work with people',
an ambition which Nella ranked second only to motherhood and writing
books.[24]

In her work with the WVS, Nella was able to discover new talents and
redeploy existing ones. Invited to act as advisory cook for the canteen, she
reflected that wartime austerity had turned rather shameful private habits
into public virtues: 'I am realising more each day what a knack of dodging
and cooking and managing I possess, and my careful economies are things
to pass on, not hide as I used to!'[25] Mrs Waite, who ran Hospital Supply,
was quick to discover that there were better ways to use Nella than have
her sitting at a sewing machine. The closest Nella had to a hobby was
making rag dolls to sell for charity: 'I . . . stitch . . . my thoughts, my hopes,
my fears, into them—no wonder that no two ever look alike!'[26] These
sold well, and the proceeds were used to buy wool and other raw materials
for Hospital Supply. Discovering an unexpected gift as a fund-raiser, Nella
branched out, begging items to raffle among the women at the Centre
and she soon acquired a reputation of being able to raffle anything. In
June 1940 she organized a fund-raising Garden Party, and other events
followed: 'It's funny how little gifts . . . can be used in war work. I never
thought when planning parties for the boys that it would be of use in
Hospital Supplies!'[27] In fact it was her father, in his spare time a promoter
of Barrow's music hall, who had first spotted her talent for 'making things
go', encouraging his daughter to 'cultivate [her] gift of laughter' and 'play
the fool': to which end he sent her to a local professional for instruction in
stand-up comedy.[28] As part of her charity work after the First World War
she had joined a Concert Party touring local chapels, churches, and clubs: 'I
could not sing but could get the audience singing and [tell] jokes and think

up silly stunts . . .'.[29] At the Centre she deployed the same talents and her clowning and jokes (carefully memorized from radio shows and *Tit-Bits*) became part of the daily routine, helping to relieve the tedium of sewing and to create an atmosphere which encouraged the volunteers to return week after week. Twenty years later she was gratified, meeting a friend from the war years, to be remembered as 'an old time music hall star!'[30]

Within two months of the outbreak of war she had been appointed to the Centre's committee, its youngest member. Although she felt something of a Cinderella among women married to a retired Borough Treasurer, the editor of the local newspaper, and senior managers in the shipyard, her inability to donate her own money was compensated by her achievements as a fund-raiser. And she was at one with her colleagues in her distaste for what they called the 'new rich', the feckless wives of shipyard workers glorying in their new found prosperity, dolled up in newly acquired fur coats and diamond rings, foolishly squandering their wartime wealth rather than putting anything aside for the lean years that, in a town so dependent on naval spending, were bound to follow. These women were Nella's chief clients in the charity shop, and she had no scruple in raiding their overflowing purses for the cause with overpriced knick-knacks, while making fun of them behind their backs. Through the WVS work she was able to revalue herself—not the 'odd', 'uneducated' woman she had often been made to feel by in-laws and others, but as Doctor Millar had said, 'a remarkable woman', with a unique contribution to make to the wider community.[31]

Nella's diaries give a vivid picture of life in the female voluntary sector, enlivened by her often acid commentary on her colleagues. As in many predominantly working-class towns, the WVS was run by Tory middle-class women who felt themselves embattled against a local political establishment run by the labour movement. Although the Conservatives held the parliamentary seat in all the inter-war elections except in 1924 and 1929, the Labour Party with deep roots among the well-organized skilled workers in the Vickers shipyard which dominated the local economy, had established a solid grip on municipal power since the mid-1930s.[32] The Labour council had been obstructive when the WVS was established, and were reluctant to give the organization any significant responsibility during the war.[33] Confronted with such stand-offs, the national WVS leadership did its best to build bridges, especially by recruiting Labour women to leading positions. In Coventry, for example, the WVS was led by a Labour activist respected for her competence and forcefulness by leaders of the middle-class women's movement.[34] But no such symbiosis could be imagined in Barrow, where WVS remained firmly in the hands of Conservative women throughout the war, and the Council's hostility to WVS was fully matched by the volunteers' contempt for the 'uneducated and ignorant Labour people' in charge, a nest of 'conchies' and communists who made council meetings a laughing stock: 'when the scum of the town get to their feet and bray', wrote Nella, 'decent people of all political opinions blush.'[35] When a new Mayor—'a draggle tailed orator who used to splutter and mouth at street corners and upset any meetings with wild remarks'—promised that he would stand for the National Anthem and go to church on Mayor's Sunday, Nella and her WVS colleagues delighted at the Conservative response: 'God will be relieved... particularly if the blighter washes his neck and puts a collar on!'[36] The rhetoric of class war was unrestrained, and the WVS women saw no need to hide their political sympathies, happy to lend a meeting room to the anti-union Economic League when it was refused access to premises controlled by the council; and Nella, remembering Cliff's pre-war involvement with the League, offered to put up visiting speakers. In 1945, when the sitting Tory MP was defeated in an exceptionally large swing to Labour, 'we simply could not believe it... everyone who came in this afternoon spoke of "the complete slide"'. Mrs Higham, whose husband was high up in the shipyard, could not understand why Nella took it so calmly: 'Don't you realise we may be on the brink of revolution?' The elderly wife of the editor of the local newspaper 'personally feared riots and uprisings in the civil population... with her poor old voice rising in hysterics' and had to be calmed down with two aspirins and the dregs of a bottle of sherry kept in the Centre for medicinal purposes.[37] The next day the WVS leader in Barrow, wife of a wealthy jeweller, told Nella that 'all was lost' and 'England was done for now'.[38]

Nella, though a Tory, was more philosophic about the Labour landslide than most of her WVS colleagues. Even as a ward chairman in the 1930s she felt she had lacked 'the real bigotry' needed for political work: 'I was a sad "wobbler" and had no hard and fast conviction...'.[39] As the wife of a small businessman she had a conventional hatred of cooperatives, controls, and nationalization; like other progressive Tories she approved of Beveridge and secondary education for all; and her resentment at stories of vested interest blocking all-out mobilization in the earlier years of the war sometimes made her sound more radical than she really was. What she disliked was not the substance of Conservative politics, but the 'rancour and narrow bitterness' of the partisan mind-set, typified for Nella by Mrs Finlay, one of the few Conservative members of the local council and secretary of the Women Conservatives.[40] Early in the war Finlay had ambitions to take over Hospital Supply but was rebuffed for her high-handed behaviour, including a spat with Nella (recorded with gusto in the diary: Nella could give as good as she got). Nella, who had always been sympathetic to the more progressive wing of the local Conservatives, saw Finlay as little better than the Labour councillors she so despised: 'a silly ignorant woman, badly educated and incapable of learning from life . . . narrow minded, bigoted and prejudiced to a degree.'[41]

Following the 1945 election, despite fears that the drying up of WVS work would leave her at a loose end, Nella refused to fulfil a promise she had made early in the war to return to active politics. She had no stomach for the adversarial politics represented by Mrs Finlay, or indeed by Churchill whose partisan rhetoric during the election disgusted her. Respecting Attlee, she thought the new Labour Government should be given a chance to show its paces. As late as January 1947, when things were going badly for Labour, she still could not summon up the necessary partisan loyalty, believing that the government was:

trying to work to a goal, where no one will be hungry, and all will have work to do. I've a deep admiration for their ideals and aims. If I began to speak or work for the Conservatives, I feel I'd have just that sympathy to opponents that would make anything I said or did of little value.[42]

This did not mean that she had ceased to be a Conservative. But she had never expected post-war reconstruction to be easy and she was prepared to follow the advice of the WVS national leader, Lady Reading, and put country before party during the reconstruction period.[43]

Hospital Supply

Among the contributions which Nella saw herself as making to WVS was her capacity to appease conflict among the volunteers, defusing tension with a timely joke. Nevertheless, she could hold her own in everyday infighting. Mrs Waite, the septugarian who ran Hospital Supply, had taken

Nella under her wing from the start and, at first, Nella returned Waite's trust and affection with a fierce loyalty. Waite, who had run a similar programme during the First World War, resented the fact that WVS—an upstart organization as she saw it—claimed ownership of Hospital Supply. When the woman appointed as leader of WVS in Barrow, Agnes Burnett, tried to muscle in, Nella—newly appointed to the committee—rushed to Waite's defence, warning Burnett off with a threat that reveals assumptions about racial purity that were probably normal in her milieu.

Burnett had referred in a meeting to one of the volunteers as 'a person of no breeding whatever', to which Nella responded, with devastating effect:

Breeding is such an elusive word Mrs Burnett...I can never define it or decide how many generations make a person well bred...Our eyes met and she knew that I knew.[44]

Agnes, it seems, had 'a bit of the tar-brush in her',[45] and Nella possessed photographic evidence of its source: their grandfathers had know each other as sea captains trading with the East, and Agnes' grandfather had married the daughter of an Indian tea merchant. Nella relished the power she gained from knowing this shameful family secret:

Wish I'd put the fear of death into that loud mouthed windbag years ago. I must have a bully streak—I love to see the wary way she speaks to Mrs Waite with one eye swivelled round to see where I am![46]

She was confident that her blackmail would enable her to 'keep [Agnes] from bullying dear old Mrs Waite...if I was catty I could raise a laugh in Barrow that would sweep her off committees where her money and husband's position had put her'.[47] Such, apparently, was the disgrace involved in having an Indian grandmother. According to a fellow committee member, Mrs Waite's affectionate nickname for Nella—'pussy'—took on a new meaning following this encounter: 'you turned from a gentle gay little woman into a creature who could scratch and fight'.[48] In another context, tearing a strip off a flighty married woman who she blamed for diverting Cliff's attention from Margaret, Nella confessed that she was capable of 'a spirit of calculating downright cruelty and delight in flaying the hide off anyone who incurs my wrath. Luckily it's a rare feeling, it's not pleasant.'[49]

The blitz, when it came to Barrow in a week of intense bombing in May 1941, revealed further Nella's strengths. Reading of the London bombing, she had wondered whether she would be able to cope when her turn came, but in fact she rose to the occasion. Contemplating the damage to her much-loved (and recently redecorated) house—windows out, ceilings down, walls cracked—she marvelled at her detachment. Much of Barrow fled each night to the safety of the countryside, but Nella, whose rural relatives would have made her welcome, was determined to follow official instructions and 'stay put', scornful of the selfishness of neighbours who expected her to protect their houses from incendiaries while they slept in peace out of town. With much of the WVS leadership, including Mrs Waite, bombed out or collapsing with shattered nerves, Nella took it upon herself to reopen Hospital Supply, to the fury of Waite's second-in-command who felt herself usurped. Nella's pride in this achievement was further enhanced when a regional office investigation of WVS reactions to the blitz ended with the resignation of Agnes Burnett.[50]

While Nella flourished in adversity, Mrs Waite declined, her age catching up with her, and relations between the two women became increasingly strained. Waite—'the naughty old thing',[51] wrote Nella—was childishly jealous of her protégé's post-blitz involvement with the WVS canteen; but affectionate exasperation gave way to real fury when Waite tried to close down the Red Cross shop, fearing that its success would distract Nella and other stalwarts from Hospital Supply. In defence of what she saw as 'my baby, my dear child', Nella was quick (once again) to 'discover claws and fangs', but it was now Waite's turn to feel 'the acid, biting edge of my tongue'.[52] 'Whatever Mrs Waite does or does not,' she wrote at the end of 1942, 'I'm through with her, no liking, no loyalty, no toleration is left.'[53] At other times she felt sad for Waite, whose domineering spirit had alienated both family and friends: 'She went through life like a tank and wonders why no daisies grow round her feet . . .'.[54] Waite had always been dictatorial in the way she ran the Centre and, in retrospect, Nella was astonished at the degree to which the 'grown and capable' women on the committee had allowed themselves to be pushed around. When Waite, raking up old battles fought during the First World War with the mother of the new WVS leader, threatened to 'cut loose and . . . *damn* the WVS', Nella and her colleagues made it clear that they would resist any such move, confident that the great majority of volunteers in the Centre would follow them rather than Waite if it came to a showdown. In the interests of harmony Nella tried to avoid open conflict and earned compliments from colleagues for her prowess in 'managing the old battle axe'.[55] But by 1943 the 'calm', 'well-balanced', 'darling "young" woman of 72'[56] who Nella had been so thankful to work for at the beginning of the war, had become

a peevish and disagreeable old woman, who abused her position to help
herself to sugar from the Centre's supplies or underpay for items in the Red
Cross shop, and displayed an intolerance and ignorance of the younger
generation which Nella found shocking in a woman who continued, as a
magistrate, to sit in judgment on others. No doubt Waite had changed,
but so had Nella and she no longer allowed Waite's flattering view of
her as the indispensable 'sunshine' of the Centre to blind her to the older
woman's faults.

Looking back from the end of 1943, Nella felt that her war work was
having 'a really amazingly good effect' on her health:

I'm a very nervy woman and circumstances rather kept me down. I have found
a surprisingly lot of little talents I did not realise I possessed and I have grown to
feel I really can help...It's removed a feeling of frustration and taken me into
company who never think I'm odd—or if they do they don't mean it as a rebuke.
It's made life more enjoyable, if harder. I don't mind work.[57]

But her contentment was fragile, her devils seldom far from consciousness,
and she *had* to work hard to keep them at bay. She was subject to fits of
wild sobbing while she slept, waking, exhausted and limp, her face wet
with tears. She used the diary to describe, perhaps to exorcize, the 'black
suit of misery' which 'wraps and chokes me', the moments of utter despair:

I made my reluctant fingers stitch, my back-bone stayed straight up, and my lips
tight closed. I felt I could have collapsed like an empty sack on the rug, and let
the tide of desolation and misery flow over me and swamp me...I felt as if the air
was full of whirling, baffling wings—all black. Wings that, without touching or
hurting me, brought cold draughts of icy air buffeting me. The whirling montage
grew faster and faster...[58]

Her misery fed on the fear that she might break down again as before
the war, and on the ever-present anxiety about the safety of her son Cliff:
'a cold stone' deep down in consciousness, 'which only grows heavier,
with no gaiety or warmth for more than a fleeting hour'.[59] She wrote
about a feeling of doubleness—'down at the...Centre they think I'm
a "mental tonic"...I must be a very good actress, for I don't feel gay
often'—wondering which was the real Nella: the comedienne with jester's
licence to boost morale, or the ageing woman, 'tired, beaten and afraid'
who had learned how to use bright red lipstick to paint a smile on lips
which would not of themselves turn up at the corners.[60] 'Only the heart
knoweth its own bitterness', she wrote, quoting the Bible, and wondered if

'everyone we see and mix with' had the same disjunction between outward appearance and inner reality.[61] But it was not so much a question of which was the real Nella, more a struggle to inhabit the mask of cheerfulness sufficiently to 'keep away black thoughts [that howl] like wolves in the night'.[62]

From the outset she had been 'grateful for my work at the WVS Centre...When my sewing machine is whirring it seems to wrap me round with a rhythm, as music sometimes does, and keeps me from thinking about my Cliff in the Machine Gun Corps.'[63] The Centre functioned as a therapeutic community, providing not only the narcotic of work and the satisfactions of service, but also the 'companionship and unexpected laughter and gaiety, understanding and sympathy' that helped to 'keep back the bogeys that wait to pounce on mothers and wives'.[64] Nella was gratified by her own part in constructing this refuge, feeling that they were all 'my dear children', and wishing she could 'shield them from the heartaches ahead':

I look round the big room at faces I've known and loved for over four years. My heart aches and, even in that small circle, the bravery and courage, the 'going on' when only sons have been killed, when letters don't come, when their boys are taught to fight like savages...trained...to go and kill other women's lads, to wipe all the light from other mother's faces.[65]

There was a kind of displaced mothering in the meaning that Nella found in her WVS work. When Cliff was conscripted she had been heartbroken at the thought of her gentle child with his long sensitive fingers being trained 'to kill boys like himself—to hurt and be hurt'.[66] At the same time, however, she made a vow that she would consider herself to be a soldier as long as he was one. This had a satisfying simplicity, but it hardly did justice to the complexities of the impact of war on her sense of who she was. Like most of the Mass-Observation diarists, her feelings about the war were complicated.

'One cannot touch pitch without defilement'

The closest Nella came to being a soldier was in the autumn of 1941, when a chance encounter led her into an adventure worthy of a Graham Greene spy story. Overhearing defeatist talk on a bus she went to the police who, it turned out, already had their eyes on the woman concerned and spun Nella a colourful tale of the suspect's sexual liaisons with Canadian fascists and continental royalty. Needing a positive identification they seized on Nella's imaginative proposal that she should go to the woman's house to offer her services as a fortune teller. Two months later she bumped into the same woman working in the Sailors' Mission (for which Nella collected old clothes), ideally placed to pick up details of Atlantic shipping movements. Fearing for her own safety, Nella went back to the police and shortly afterwards the woman disappeared from view, only to surface in 1943 when, rather mundanely, she was jailed for stealing flag-day money she had collected. Nella, who had been both thrilled and terrified by her encounters with what she took to be pure evil, was disappointed to learn from the police that, despite continued surveillance, they had been unable to find any evidence of Fifth Column activity.

It was, however, not the heroism of counter-espionage, but the exercise of the spirit of service in her voluntary work that enabled Nella to fulfil her pledge to be a soldier. Profoundly distressed by the killing and the chaos of war, her instinct was to provide care and succour for its victims. About the prosecution of war itself she was more ambivalent. But her patriotism was unquestioning. Her immediate reaction to the outbreak of war had been euphoric. Neville Chamberlain's words 'it is an evil thing we will be fighting':

seemed to strike a chord in my inner mind. It was not a withered old man broadcasting to a nervy highly-strung middle aged woman but in some way spirit spoke to spirit and I knew the meaning of the words 'leave all and follow me'.[67]

Chamberlain may have been an improbable Messiah, but some of Churchill's speeches later in the war had a similar impact. Most of all she responded to the vivid red poster issued by the Ministry of Information in September 1939 which proclaimed: 'YOUR COURAGE, YOUR RESOLUTION, YOUR CHEERFULNESS, WILL BRING US VICTORY.' This poster has been much criticized as implying a condescending separation between the 'US' who ran the country and the 'YOU' who merely endured, a point made forcefully at the time by Mass-Observation itself, evaluating the poster in its first wartime commission from Whitehall.[68] But Nella was oblivious to any such reading, and, deeply moved, she long remembered her reaction:

I had had such a baffled wistful feeling till then but [the poster] seemed so personal, so direct. I stood and looked at it and felt myself swept away on a wave of faith and exaltation. As I 'asked' for those simple virtues—and health—to go on to the 'end of the road', I made my vow. To be a soldier till the war ended, to play the game and never grumble and never ask anything else, except that my boys could be guarded and live their life fully.[69]

Faith and exaltation, however, could not hide from Nella the evils of war. When acquaintances talked of the anticipated opening of the second front as the beginning of the end of the war, Nella felt her 'bones turn to water' at the thought of the horrors that allied victories would unleash. She anticipated risings of the oppressed and 'a massacre of all Germans who are keeping whole countries subdued by terror, a mass murder which will not all be on one side, but which will turn inwardly and rend and destroy'.[70] Horrified by the London blitz she had for a time felt revengeful, ready to return evil for evil. But after having experienced bombing herself, she felt ashamed at the allied raids on German cities, proud that her sons were as shocked as she was by those who gloated over the slaughter of the innocent, and confused about the need for such barbarism, convinced that, even if it served to shorten the war it would sow the seeds of new catastrophes. She despaired at 'the utter futility of it all, the uselessness...people seem to feed on cruelty and rouse hate and a longing for revenge'.[71] How could the cycle of violence be broken? 'One cannot touch pitch without defilement', and the allies' high ideals went by the board when they fought evil with evil. 'There is no glamour and glitter now in war—only the butchery of the shambles. When all the fighting is over what kind of wild beasts will be left in the mad chaos?'[72] In the 1930s she had dismissed Arthur's belief that civilization was doomed as a youthful folly, but now she was inclined to agree that civilization might survive only in Australia and America. At best, she believed, it would take several generations for real peace, the slow growth of tolerance and decency, to return to Europe. Because of her pessimism Nella was sometimes accused of being defeatist, or even, on one occasion, a pacifist when, moved by natural sympathy for cold and hungry men, she was friendly to a group of conscientious objectors, normally cold-shouldered by the canteen workers. Pacifism she denied, but her earlier hostility to the 'conchies' had given way to a puzzled tolerance:

we have all been sucked into the cortex of 'destiny'...all have our private perplexities and worries...a pleasant word or smile cost nothing—all kinds of 'threads' shuttled and broke and twisted in my mind, so hard to explain...[73]

While the prospect of the second front distressed her immeasurably, the escape of much of the British Expeditionary Force from Dunkirk in June 1940 had been the emotional highpoint of Nella's war:

This morning I lingered over my breakfast, reading and rereading the accounts of the Dunkirk evacuation. I felt as if deep inside me was a harp that vibrated and sang . . . I forgot I was a middle aged woman who often got tired and who had backache. The story made me feel part of something that was undying and never old . . . [74]

What so thrilled her about Dunkirk was that it was a story of young men rescued. It spoke to the Nella who yearned to shield the women at the Centre from their losses; who, seeing horror at what they were being trained to do in the eyes of young soldiers in the canteen, wished she could 'gather [them] up and hold [them] safe'; who wanted Cliff to come back alive and not too bruised and hardened by his exposure to barbarism.

Struggling to make sense of the war, Nella looked to the supernatural. The Nazis were not just evil men, but evil itself, perhaps the Anti-Christ prophesied in the Book of Revelations. As the war spread she wondered whether Armageddon was at hand, and, if so, whether she was living through the birth pangs of a new religion. Could it be that Communism represented an unconscious striving 'to reach back to the fundamental teaching of the dawn of Christianity'?[75] Though forced to go to church by her father, Nella had been 'defiantly not a Christian'[76] ever since, aged 14, she thought things out for herself, rejecting the divinity of Christ, the resurrection, the threat of eternal damnation, or the promise of a heaven, which sounded to her like an infinitely long church service—more punishment than bliss. While she believed in life after death, it was as a 'going on', a reincarnation to a hopefully less troubled and more fulfilling existence: 'no heaven or hell . . . no rewards and no revenges, just consequences and a beginning afresh, a chance to learn and grow and grow'.[77] Spiritualism did not attract her and she was dismissive of astrological prophecies, but she had an abiding sense of 'a Force and Power that is "just around the corner" and is ours for the reaching'.[78] She believed that she had an 'uncanny' gift for fortune telling and had frequently entertained the boys and their friends by reading the cards or the tea leaves; but in the grim circumstances of war she preferred not to look into individual futures that it might be kinder to leave in obscurity, and was inclined to resist requests to exercise what, with part of her mind, she feared were Satanic powers.

Christianity might be dead, but Satan lived and so did God. Nervous that her fortune-telling parlour games might be the devil's work, she never doubted the power of prayer. Not that she presumed to curry favour, ask for special protection, or 'bombard God with requests and demands'. If God wanted to strike Hitler dead, as her neighbour prayed for him to do, Nella could not 'help thinking . . . that he would not have waited till Mrs Helm asked him'.[79] Rather she prayed 'for patience and courage and strength to work and keep smiling', and did so daily, in the pause when Big Ben struck for the 9 o'clock news, as did millions of others observing a ritual proposed by the 'Big Ben Minute Association', an interdenominational group established in 1940.[80] What Nella knew of God she had learned as a child from her grandmother, a widowed Quaker whose philosophy of life Nella inherited and passed on, she hoped, to her own children: 'I find my life shaped by her maxims, her faith, and never failing kindness, and a goodness that was part of her very fibre. If Gran said a thing, you could steer by it.'[81]

At the core of this philosophy was a fatalistic acceptance that 'what must be, will be'.[82] Behind the apparent chaos of the world, God has a plan, a plan in which our individual lives, mere grains of sand as they are, have a meaning and a purpose. But we cannot hope to see the pattern, to grasp how our struggles and suffering contribute to the fulfilment of God's plan, nor by prayer and asking can we do anything to alter the plan or to hurry things along. Fall into the rhythm of things, take each day as it comes, 'and as for the next—Sayonara':[83]

I try not to think too much ahead and to 'put my hand into the hand of God and go out into the darkness'. It's rather a queer feeling to be having to refuse to think of things till they come along—but it brings me quiet peace and lets me get on with my job . . . It's a blessed feeling for a scatty nervy woman to attain—one who sits and thinks too much.[84]

Each day filled with work and service put another brick in the wall that protected her against the brooding and the terror. As 'an ambitious but rather baffled' youngster Nella had, appropriately enough, been infuriated by her grandmother's insistence that real contentment came from 'making

the best of what was to hand': 'But Gran, I want to *be* something—I want
to travel—to see all these places we read about—to *do* things—to *have*
lovely things.'[85] By the 1940s, however, 'age and bitterness of mind...the
realisation of how quickly life and things pass, of storm and calm, defeat and
loss' had schooled her in fatalism.[86] Acceptance of 'the hand that shapes our
Destiny' brought the promise of peace and serenity, and an understanding
of what her Gran meant by her favourite saying: 'We must do the best we
can—and pass on.'[87]

Aftermath

Having found her feet during the war, Nella was apprehensive when the
coming of peace threatened to put an end to her voluntary work. The Red
Cross shop was first to close, in June 1945; Hospital Supply soldiered on
into the autumn; and the canteen survived until June 1946. During the war
she had longed for more time to read, but found it difficult to concentrate
now that she had the time; and the prospect of an endless round of whist
drives held no attraction for her. 'My heart's ease and feeling of being
worthwhile in the scheme of things passed', she wrote in September 1945,
'when our dear tatty Red Cross shop closed its doors.'[88] There seemed
little opportunity for peacetime voluntary work, and what there was would
be 'pounced on by women like myself who have learned the real joy of
service and working together'.[89] One of her WVS friends was keen to
recruit her to the Social and Moral Welfare Committee, but Nella, who
was relatively non-judgemental in sexual matters, found its members 'dull,
not to say sour'.[90] Paid work for women was scarce in Barrow and she did
not think it right to compete with those who really needed it; in any case
Nella was not qualified for any work appropriate to her social status. In this
situation, what she feared most of all was that she would find herself again
weakly submitting to Will's plaintive demands: 'I don't want any company
but yours', or 'when the war was over, I thought you would always be in
at lunchtime...Must you go?'[91]

WVS had provided Nella with legitimate reasons to follow Dr Millar's
advice and assert her autonomy. Not that this had been achieved without
friction. Her wartime diaries are peppered with tirades—some spoken
aloud, some just letting off steam in the diary—rejecting 'that unspoken,
but very plain Victorian-Edwardian accusation: "I feed and clothe you don't

I? I've a right to say what you do." '[92] In March 1940, for example, she had written:

I reflected tonight on the changes the war had brought. I always used to worry and flutter round when I saw my husband working up for a mood; but now I just say calmly, Really dear, you *should* try and act as if you were a grown man and not a child of ten, and if you want to be awkward I shall go out—ALONE!'[93]

She gave him a packed lunch when she was at the Centre all day, and sometimes did not have his tea quite ready when he came home from work:

He told me rather wistfully I was 'not so sweet' since I'd been down at the Centre, and I said, 'Well! Who wants a woman of fifty to be sweet, anyway? And besides, I suit *me* a lot better!'[94]

Towards the end of 1941, at his initiative, they moved into separate bedrooms and this seemed to 'snap the last tie of intimacy'—not sex, in which, hints in the diary suggest, they had both lost interest years earlier—but 'that last-minute discussion before going to sleep ... when little things could be talked out'.[95] At first she regretted the loss, but quickly came to appreciate her new freedom to go on writing her diary as late as she liked, or to put on the light and read if she woke in the night. 'Tonight I looked at him', she wrote two years later, 'and could *not* think of *any* kind of intimacy, mental or physical.'[96]

Indignant, during the London blitz, about the authorities' failure to provide deep shelters, and infuriated by Will's patronizing insistence that as a mere housewife she could hardly expect to understand the complexities of such matters, Nella discovered in herself 'a militant suffragette streak ... I could shout loudly and break windows and do all kinds of things—kick policemen perhaps—anything to protest.'[97] A few days later, hassled by a gang of youths in the street, she amazed herself by kicking one of them very hard on his shin. As the war came to an end she was determined not to allow Will's 'repressions' to drive her back to the 'frayed and battered' state from which Dr Millar and the WVS had rescued her. Rightly or wrongly, what she had gained from the doctor's diagnosis was a self-understanding in which it was her husband's unreasonable demands, rather than any intrinsic weakness in herself, that explained her susceptibility to nervous breakdowns. Now she was determined that 'no one would ever give me one again, *no* one'.[98]

But the defiant tone revealed her uncertainty. Growing up in the shadow of Victorian patriarchy, 'over ruled by first my father and then [my] husband', she doubted her capacity to sustain her wartime independence.[99] Despite everything, there was still affection between Nella and Will: he occasionally surprised her with his solicitousness, and she sometimes drew back from saying hurtful things, regretting her new 'hardness' and impatience. Marvel as she might 'at the way [Will] had managed to dominate me so for all our married life, at how, to avoid hurting him, I had tried to keep him in a good mood, when a smacked head would have been the best treatment', she knew that it was now too late to change him.[100] Radical changes in gender relations were going to come, but for future generations, not for her own. Young women, like Margaret next door, would demand careers and refuse domestic servitude; and she congratulated herself on bringing her sons up with 'no false ideas of lordly superiority toward women'.[101] Deep down, however, she remained convinced not only that men had the better time of it—'all the responsibility and effort, all the colour and romance'—but also that there was something essential in their make-up that explained this.[102] At the time of the Munich crisis, she had written: 'Wish I knew a clever man who would tell me his views. Clever woman would be no use, women's views limited to welfare of loved men—whether grown up or tiny.'[103] Concern for the welfare of others might make her profoundly ambivalent about the prosecution of the war, but she put this down to the weakness, rather than the wisdom, of her sex, denigrating her own horror of violence as reflecting a feminine incapacity 'to be able to visualise "big" things—things like Victory and smashing blows...My mind seems so limited—I wonder if it's because I am a woman.'[104] While she could lecture her men folk about the unrecognized value of the unpaid work performed by wives and mothers (and was deeply grateful to Beveridge for giving official recognition to such work), she remained distrustful of women in public office—'we have quite a number of women councillors and with one exception I'd swap the lot for a sensible level headed man in his 50's'—and was content to defer to 'clever men' to plan the war and organize reconstruction.[105] Whatever gains Nella had made in establishing greater personal autonomy, her own selfhood remained deeply marked by the patriarchal attitudes characteristic of her generation.

The diary

Like most people, Nella lived with a persistent sense of unfulfilled potential. In place of the young girl's dreams and aspirations—to travel, to
be a writer, to have the freedoms that only men have, to live among
cultured and educated people—she found herself shackled to a depressive
and life-denying husband; with little social life and few, if any, friends
she considered her intellectual equals; afflicted with ill-health and delicate
nerves; and trapped in a remote provincial town with little to stimulate her imagination. The fatalistic religion that she had learned from
her grandmother helped her to cope with life's disappointments. But,
adjusting aspirations to possibilities, she also found positive sources of contentment, fulfilment, and happiness—motherhood and the moulding and
shaping of her boys; social service, which used her talent for spreading
gaiety around her in a worthy cause and gave her a sense of a useful
existence unavailable from her other adventure into public life, Conservative politics; and the more mundane pleasures of cooking, days out
in beautiful countryside, reading the novels and travel literature which
took her out of Barrow at least in her imagination, and, of course, her
writing.

Nella believed that her diary writing served some larger public purpose,
although she seems to have been at a loss to explain quite what this was. She
had started the diary at the outbreak of war partly because the *Daily Express*
columnist William Hickey, had stressed, she said, 'that the Government
would find MO valuable. Never can see just how, but although not clever
am "bright" enough to trust people who are!'[106] Sometimes she wondered
how her 'endless scribbles' could possibly be of use to anyone, but she
was reassured by appreciative letters from MO and by Arthur, one of
those 'clever' men in whom she put her trust, who assured her that her
record of an 'ordinary woman's viewpoint and routine' was just what MO
wanted.[107] As well as keeping the diary, she conscientiously responded to
MO directives throughout the war, sent in various ephemera for MO's
War Library and, when MO requested letters from servicemen, brought
herself to part with Cliff's aerograms from the Middle East despite the fact
that 'they seem all I have left of my laughing lad'.[108]

It was not just her promise to MO that kept the diary going. The hour or so she spent last thing every night writing up her day provided a kind of meta-existence, a space in which she could reflect, evaluate, and monitor her life. In the diary she could manage her responses to conflict and tension—in WVS, with her husband or with Cliff, with the difficult relatives and friends who tended to sponge on her emotionally, articulating the things she couldn't say to their faces, rehearsing the things she had said (or, a reader might sometimes suspect, wish she had said). She often looked back over her life, thinking about how the war was changing her, working with the religious language she had learned from her grandmother and the psychological insights supplied by Dr Millar to make sense of her life. The diary allowed her to contemplate her own doubleness, the mask of cheerfulness and the misery within, and to articulate a Nella who was both and neither of these women. Even the almost daily accounts of cooking served to articulate a baseline sense of worth as a careful, competent, imaginative homemaker.

But the writing was also an end in itself. She was sensitive to language, playful with metaphor, self-consciously literary, and even experimental. Recording reactions to the end of the war in Europe, she concluded with a theatrical image worthy of Virginia Woolf (who Nella had almost certainly never read): 'and all the audience looked at each other, uncertain of the next move—and then they too had slowly dispersed.'[109] She found words to describe her mind on the edge of breakdown the air filled with 'a whirling montage' of black 'baffling wings'.[110] One can see her in the diary working up an account of a long-remembered dream in which she recognizes herself as a 'frayed and battered leaf' struggling against the flow in an immense river of leaves, shaping and reshaping the dream for literary effect.[111] Her intemperate use of inverted commas to mark individual words or phrases sometimes seem to be there to register her awareness that she is using a word in an idiosyncratic, possibly incorrect, way, reflecting an insecurity derived from her interrupted schooling. Sometimes she seems to be indicating that she hasn't quite found the perfect expression for her thought, as any writer might do as an aide memoire for a process of revision which Nella, scribbling in pencil late at night and posting off the text at the end of the week, never in fact undertook. At other times, as one commentator has suggested, she uses inverted commas to establish an anthropological distance from the 'tribal dialect' of her milieu, appropriate to her role as a mass observer.[112] Alternatively her use of them could be seen as registering the liminal nature of her writing, poised on the borderline between recording the language of everyday life and the creative shaping of experience into literary form. While her editors, perhaps rightly, have seen the inverted commas as an obstacle to pleasurable reading and edited them out of the published diaries, they certainly demonstrate the sensitivity to language that produced the following surprising response to an MO directive which asked observers to 'write, as the spirit moves you, on PEACE':

Words have always fascinated me—take War, Strife, Kill; shout, mutter, cry or sing them however loud and they 'finish abruptly'. Words like Love, Pity, Peace—no longer words, [but they] linger on the air, echoing and re-echoing.[113]

For more than twenty years after the war Nella continued to write her diaries. In February 1966, aged 76 and feeling ill, she sent in her final entry, wondering if her writing was ever read and 'if the need for it is past now'.[114] She died two years later. Through the later 1940s she had kept up her association with a much-depleted WVS, serving on its committee, and a willing attender at meetings called to revive the organization. On one such occasion she offered to help in organizing a scheme of hospital visiting.[115] By the mid-1950s, however, any active participation in WVS seems to have ceased, and a selective reading of her voluminous diaries during the 1950s and 1960s reveals 'a saddened and broken woman, increasingly devoid of purpose'.[116] There can be little doubt that, alongside the satisfactions of motherhood, it was Nella's participation in wartime voluntary work that gave her the most fulfilling years of her life.

Figure 2. Gertrude Glover, 1911.
Courtesy of the Mass-Observation Archive.

3

Gertrude Glover: Moral guardian

G ertrude Glover, 53 years old when war broke out, belonged, like
Nella, to the army of middle-class housewives who exercised social
leadership through voluntary work in towns and villages across mid-
twentieth century Britain. But while Nella's social identity was shaped
by the narrow contours of middle-class life in an isolated working-class
town, Gertrude, positioned rather higher up the social scale and involved
in the leadership of women's organizations in both town and country, was
able to develop a broader social vision. Her outlook on life, altogether
more optimistic, less fatalistic, than Nella's, reflected not only the greater
security of her middle-class status, but also a private life which made
relatively little demand on her time and imposed few restrictions on her
freedom. If Nella's diaries testify to the continuing power of patriarchal
values, Gertrude's show that it was possible in the mid-twentieth-century
for a relatively conventional middle-aged, middle-class married woman to
establish a large measure of personal autonomy. To an unusual degree, she
found the roots of her identity not in the domestic sphere of marriage
and motherhood but in her varied and tireless activity as a voluntary social
worker.

By making themselves indispensable, women like Gertrude did much
to shore up middle-class authority against the potentially egalitarian and
democratizing impact of the war, thereby helping to preserve the continuities of class in the social fabric of mid-twentieth-century Britain. It was, I
have argued elsewhere, the impact of affluence and consumerism during the

global capitalist boom of the third quarter of the twentieth century, rather than the impact of war, that proved decisive in disrupting the values represented by confident middle-class women who believed that social leadership was the duty they owed to those less privileged than themselves.[1] Gertrude's diaries reveal these qualities of leadership, but they also suggest how doubts about the relevance of the values they stood for were beginning to emerge among female social leaders well before the cultural revolution of the 1960s.

In contrast to Nella's purely rhetorical relationship to feminism, Gertrude Glover had actually taken part in the suffragette movement, and regularly gave talks on her experiences to women's groups. Born and brought up in a middle-class family in London, she had trained as an infant teacher, and participated in the fight for the vote as one of Christabel Pankhurst's 'humble satellites'.[2] In 1912, aged 25, she married Sam Glover, a Coventry engineer who she had met three years earlier during a cycling holiday in Brittany. During the early years of her marriage she ran a private school in Coventry while spending weekends and holidays on the Glover family farm nearby. After the birth of her first and only child in 1915, a son, and the conscription of her husband a year later, she gave up the school and took over the running of the farm. After the war Sam became works manager at a small Coventry engineering firm, and by the mid-1920s Gertrude was helping to set up the National Council of Women in the city. Although she lived in a sixteenth-century farmhouse five miles outside Coventry, the NCW gave her access to the educational, social, and campaigning activities of the urban middle-class female public sphere, providing a base from which, during the Second World War, she took an active role in the Ministry of Information's local advisory committee where she came in contact with representatives of Coventry's assertive trade unionism. As NCW representative on the executive of the local Young Women's Christian Association (YWCA), Gertrude was also involved in setting up hostels for young women drafted into the Coventry war factories.

The central focus of Gertrude's public activism, however, lay among rural women. She was a long-standing member of the executive of the Warwickshire federation of Women's Institutes (WIs), and, during the war, served as one of a group of volunteers helping to set up new Institutes and sort out problems in established ones. More importantly the WI provided an outlet for her artistic creativity. As county drama adviser she was an inexhaustible promoter of village plays, sketches, concerts, pageants, and—her special passion—mimes. She ran a postal library of plays; toured the county, producing, directing, acting, and stimulating others to do the same; and wrote her own short plays, one of which won a national WI competition and was published in 1937.[3] This rural context included not only agricultural areas, but also the mining villages of the North Warwickshire coalfield; and, in particular, her neighbouring village of Keresley where the pit had opened in 1917, pulling in miners from the depressed areas during the inter-war years, trebling the local population.[4] This social transformation, occurring on her doorstep just across the parish border, provided fertile soil for Gertrude's civic energies. She organized village concerts, helped to run the local girls club, put in time at the infant welfare clinic, and took her 'natural' place in the leadership of the Keresley WI.

Gertrude Glover's busy public life crossed frontiers between three very different local social structures—South Warwickshire rural feudalism, a North Warwickshire mining village, and the archetypal modern industrial city of Coventry. As she travelled from meeting to meeting, sometimes as many as four in a single day, she jotted down issues to pursue in a special notebook—'one end NCW, other end WI. Acts as liaison between two, also between them and anywhere else I am.'[5] Networking across these different strands of the women's movement, she was well placed to reflect on changing cultural patterns and the role of social leaders like herself. Firmly anchored in a rural hierarchical social structure, Gertrude was nevertheless well aware that modernity—represented by Coventry's booming industry, high wages, and the promiscuity of youth—presented challenges to the standards and values that the various organizations to which she belonged existed to uphold.

The household

If her public life encouraged reflection on the contrast between the deferential social relations of the mining village and the class segregation and anarchic modernity of wartime Coventry, the structure of Gertrude's private household provided no less a stimulus to speculation about changing social roles. Sam, son of a Coventry watchmaker, had grown up with seven siblings 'reared in two adjoining cottages amid chaos and muddle . . . no method, no organisation, no tools but the most archaic'. Gertrude tells us little about her own childhood, except that it involved being 'shuttlecocked' between her

parents, an aunt, and boarding school 'never staying anywhere long enough
to feel anything but an outsider and a visitor'. This left her wanting to set up
a home, but 'without the foggiest idea of what it meant'. When they married Sam aspired to 'a tidy, comfortable, artistic home, with no wash day',
fondly imagining that this could be combined with his desire for 'at least six
children'.[6] In the event there was only one child, who Gertrude brought
up while working on the farm, running a business (unspecified in the diary:
perhaps a revival of the private school) in Coventry, and keeping house for
Sam. As a young mother she found this regime exhausting, and it contributed to two miscarriages. Eventually a modus vivendi emerged: with the child
at school, a regular cleaning woman, the business in Coventry abandoned,
the farm handed over to a niece and her husband, Gertrude had the time to
devote herself to the women's movement. She kept housework to a mini-
mum, sending the washing to a laundry, emancipating herself from 'the fag
ends of Victorian house-pride'.[7] Both she and Sam were indifferent to home
improvements, content with an outside lavatory and a daily strip wash in the
scullery: 'a bathroom', she remarked, having been brought up without one,
'is a place to be kept clean and therefore a nuisance'. They did not feel the
need to maintain the domestic standards normally expected of their class,
partly because they never invited people in for meals, apart from family.

Sam had grown up seeing 'womenfolk doing things all day long,
seven days a week', and never himself lifted 'the littlest finger' in the
house. Nevertheless, in the sharp contrast to Nella's Will, he was entirely
sympathetic to his wife's priorities, and never disputed her right to 'go
where I like, do what I like without question'.[8] This freedom to devote
herself to public work was only possible because there were others to share
the burden of housework. In the autumn of 1941, when her MO diary
begins, the war deprived Gertrude of her cleaner, but it had also produced
a replacement in the shape of Mrs Simms, 72-year-old mother-in-law of
one of Sam's brothers, who came to live in the farmhouse after her own
house was destroyed, and her husband killed, in the Coventry blitz. The
blitz also drove Sam's 88-year-old mother to seek shelter in the farmhouse.
Grateful though she was for Mrs Simms' devotion to the housework,
Gertrude never ceased to wonder at the restricted home-bound lives
accepted by the old ladies; and they, in their turn, found Gertrude's
marital arrangements incomprehensible. Despite their 'awed respect for my
"brainwork" as they term it...they don't really class it with "work"',[9]
and there were domestic crises in which Gertrude had to be firm with

herself to resist unspoken family pressures to 'to drop everything and stay at home'. Only Sam, a remarkably accommodating husband, 'would expect to consider my movements and . . . adjust himself cheerfully'.[10]

Crucial to Gertrude's autonomy was her possession of a room of her own, her bedroom, where she wrote her plays, prepared her talks, took refuge in the evenings from inane conversation with the old ladies or the interminable repetitions of the radio news, and wrote up her daily diary entries. When fuel shortage prevented her lighting a fire in her bedroom the diary fell behind.[11] Not least of the advantages of having her own bedroom was that it enabled her to start and end each day with private religious observation. But the woman who knelt at the bedside every night, and went to church twice on Sundays, remained open minded about the meaning of life, unafraid of unorthodoxy, intellectually curious.

The Women's Institute

Formally, the WI was a thoroughly democratic organization and its membership cut across social barriers in a way that was not possible in class-segregated urban society: in practice, however, local leadership tended to follow pre-existing patterns of social hierarchy.[12] In Keresley Gertrude served as one of three vice-presidents, alongside the wives of the colliery's chief engineer and the village schoolmaster, under the presidency of Mrs Fenn, wife of the colliery manager. She ran monthly meetings, which included organized games and sing-songs, but also more ambitious cultural events: 'We try to get a little poetry down their throats . . . '.[13] A talk on Shakespeare misfired: 'completely over women's heads'.[14] But, in a more typical session, Gertrude read them 'The Lady of Shallot' and Kipling's 'Trawlers', plus some limericks, followed by a play reading: 'The miners' wives do well and enjoy it.'[15] Alongside the regular meetings Gertrude directed plays and other entertainments. Despite the constant disruptions of village sociability caused by the pit shift system, which prevented the miners' wives from attending regular rehearsals, Gertrude loved this work:

These women are delight to work with. No trouble with conceit and jealousy which one is warned against in every book on play production. They think they know nothing about anything and humbly carry out orders meticulously.

A similarly deferential attitude governed the WI's impeccably conducted elections.

Following the 1942 AGM Gertrude noted that:

there was only one 'village' member [out of fifteen people] on [the] Committee.
No one's fault that I can see. 'Village' women outnumber the rest of us and could
easily vote themselves in if they liked.[16]

In theory Gertrude was keen to replace these 'remnants of feudalism' with
'new values of personality and individuality', and she was appreciative of
the few 'village' women who were able to assert themselves in the county
federation. In practice, however, she believed that the WI 'is as nearly
democratic as can be managed with the present state of mentality and
education... there may be equality at some remote date, but at present
the crying need is leaders'.[17] Presented by her husband with evidence
that some of the miners' wives preferred the left-wing Women's Co-
operative Guild and refused to join the WI 'because they won't be any
more under thumb of [the] Colliery than [they] can help', Gertrude
was dismissive: 'Quite unjust, but can't be helped.'[18] Facilitating the
establishment of a new WI in another mining village she remarked:
'Colliery managers' wife voted President out of eight nominations. Good
choice.'[19]

    In the county federation she accepted the dominance of the South
Warwickshire gentry on the grounds that, despite the occasional duffer,
'the county families... have kept culture and learning as things of great
price, and have shared with the humbler members their gardens, time,
money and culture. Town agitators', she added, 'have no idea at all
of the immense value of these traditional leaders.'[20] This respect for
the gentry in no way qualified her own delight, in the autumn of
1942, in being elected to the county executive 'over [the] heads of
some uppers'. In the more industrialized parts of North Warwickshire,
where social leadership belonged to the middle class rather than the
gentry,[21] Gertrude deferred to Mrs Fenn: the colliery manager's wife with
a car (and petrol) at her disposal clearly outranked the wife of a works
manager who travelled by bus, train, and bicycle. Nevertheless the two
women worked closely together, not only in Keresley but also at county
federation meetings in Royal Leamington Spa where they would often
lunch together and spend the afternoon at the pictures. When factionalism
among the miners' wives threatened unpleasantness in the local WI,
Gertrude and Mrs Fenn listened patiently to the inchoate complaints of
the contending parties confident that 'lots of yapping will air it all and

clear it away', as indeed it did.[22] Leadership in the WI, Gertrude remarked on another occasion, required the 'wisdom of serpents and gentleness of doves'.[23]

In the spring of 1944 a dispute arose in the village about the exclusion of black American troops billeted in the district from dances at the Colliery Social Club, where the WI also held its meetings. Gertrude, lobbied by some of the members, and herself disgusted by the American colour bar, found herself at loggerheads with Mrs Fenn who approved it, and whose husband had imposed the ban. Handling the potential conflict with some delicacy, Gertrude persuaded Fenn to absent herself from the next WI meeting so that the issue could be discussed without the miners' wives feeling that they had to 'mind their "p"s and "q"s'. Being herself unrestrained by authority structures at the pit—'I am a free lance and they can't do a thing about me whatever I do'—she decided to start the meeting with a short talk on the 'origin of negro population in USA'. To spare embarrassment for the president she would avoid any resolution being put. In the event:

I was really astonished at depth of feeling against any discrimination against blacks. They all said white and black, both or neither in clubs, pubs, dances, etc. No dissidents ... In fact, dislike of white Americans really bitter, but none of darkies. Several said husbands felt just the same. Had to stop discussion at end of an hour for time's sake, as we wanted some singing.[24]

Singing, the usual way to end a WI meeting, no doubt helped to defuse any resentment that might have been directed at the president or her husband. While the unanimity of the village women served to strengthened Gertrude's own hostility to the colour bar, any such fault lines in the structures of deference remained marginal to her understanding of village life.

In her work with the WI Gertrude found little to challenge her belief that 'the crying need is for leaders' drawn from the upper layers of rural society. The village women, much like the two old ladies at home, seemed to Gertrude infuriatingly hidebound in their refusal to contemplate more efficient ways of accomplishing their housework. Following a discussion of housing at the local Institute she remarked:

Nothing illuminating. The new world envisaged as a replica of the old plus some labour-saving devices. Central heating and communal washing not wanted ... Of the complete change in ideas and practice which the next fifty years will bring, there is no inkling.[25]

In a similar vein, she was convinced that miners' strikes must be 'engi-
neered by agitators...I live among miners. Slight and always endemic
dissatisfaction, but left to themselves very few move an inch out of rut, or
want to.'[26]

Coventry

However appropriate such condescension may have been in Keresley,
Gertrude made no such assumption about the innate docility of Coventry's
factory workers. As representative of the National Council of Women on
the Ministry of Information's advisory committee in Coventry, Gertrude
was well informed about industrial unrest in the city, particularly during
the crisis months of the winter of 1941–2 when discontent in the Coventry
factories fuelled a powerful shop-steward movement that was remarkably
successful in pinning the blame for the inadequacies of war production on
the inefficiency and restrictive practices of the employers.[27] As the wife of
a works manager one might have expected her sympathies to lie with the
employers. More often than not, however, she found herself appreciating
the workers' point of view. While sympathetic to Sam's problems in
handling the restless and competitive push for higher wages characteristic
of the Coventry workforce—he dared not 'praise a man however good, as
he immediately asks for more money, and that sets whole shop by ears'[28]
—she believed that he and his fellow employers had only themselves to
blame. Instead of rewarding loyalty and providing non-wage incentives to
their workers, Coventry employers had treated them as disposable assets
to be hired and fired at will. When labour shortages hit early in the war
it was the employers' competitive bidding for individual workers that had
'started the fancy wages ramp'.[29]

Listening to Sam's regular conversations with his brother-in-law
George—who held a staff position in a much larger Coventry factory,
Alfred Herbert—what impressed her was their lack of imagination and
their double standards. Despite having worked his way up from the shop
floor, Sam 'now automatically works on some sort of assumption that
there is one standard for workmen and another for him'. The men must
be at work by 8 o'clock, but Sam and George 'get to work at nine in
a car instead of a crowded bus to which they've had to walk'. They
complained of men bringing breakfast to work, but they had it comfortably

provided before they left home. While the men clocked in and out, senior managers saw 'their tailor, solicitor, hairdresser and any business they like in the firm's time, with no reduction of salary'.[30] Gertrude listened, and contributed to, the two men's conversations, not as the doting wife, but as an independent-minded critic: 'Although I practically never hear the employees' side I find myself usually able to see what the men feel injured about, although seemingly incomprehensible to the employers.'

Her own response to the industrial relations breakdown in Coventry was informed partly by her involvement in the more deferential social relations of the mining village, and partly by her reading of Peter Drucker's analysis of the appeal of fascism, *The End of Economic Man* (1939), in which the Austrian intellectual—later to become one of the gurus of human-relations management in post-war America—argued the need to re-establish social cohesion on the basis of values transcending the individualistic materialism of contemporary capitalism. Gertrude was all for Joint Production Committees and experiments in industrial democracy, but Sam and George lacked 'the remotest vision of fundamentally different conditions' and 'still go on as if conditions were 1896', hating shop stewards and 'very peeved that men are so "independent"!', prompting Gertrude to exclaim to her diary, 'What are we fighting for?' Her efforts to spread enlightenment among her men folk were unavailing: 'George has never read a book in his life, and Sam [who] has given it up pro tem, has had a try at "*Economic Man*" and can't manage it. Mistake I think, and among the reasons for all his troubles.'[31] During the war, affected by the fashionable Russophilia, Gertrude looked to Soviet Communism for answers—'more freedom there for more people than anywhere else, from what I hear'—though she retained sufficient scepticism to 'wonder if Russia has really solved working man's psychological problem, as is claimed'.[32] As Mathew Thomson has pointed out such psychological understandings of the roots of working-class militancy helped to deflect the challenge it posed to the middle-class culture of character and service which Gertrude inhabited.[33]

Moral Guardian?

However patronizing her approach to rural social leadership, Gertrude was not a woman given to complacent defence of the status quo. She disliked the autocratic style of Coventry's industrial leadership, and yearned for utopian solutions to worker alienation. Her attitude to the position of women, though complex, was similarly inflected with hopes for a radically different future. Gertrude was proud of her suffragette days, and happy to talk about them to local women's groups, but her attitudes to contemporary feminist politics were ambiguous. Now that women had the vote and therefore held their fate in their own hands, there was, she felt, no need to organize around the 'Rights of Women', and she reacted strongly again what she saw as the 'catty bitterness' of feminist militancy.[34] Nothing did more to mobilize feminist protest during the war than the issue of equal compensation for war injuries—regulations decreed that a female limb lost in the blitz was worth less than a male one.[35] Although appointed by the NCW to represent them on an ad hoc committee set up to organize a meeting in Coventry to demand equal compensation, Gertrude clearly did not share the general indignation and was content when the initiative fizzled out in face of difficulties over securing venues and speakers.

At a more personal level Gertrude remained deeply aware of the disadvantages imposed by patriarchal structures. In 1943 she was shocked when Sam's mother, who had brought up eight children, confessed:

'I never wanted one of my children. Not one.' Would stagger her successful sons if they knew. Did me. I asked her why she had them. She said she shouldn't have known how not to. Now she is a typical 'roses round the door' white-haired gentle mother who, men imagine, loved all this motherhood. She hated it, and this hate has stained two generations.[36]

Though convinced that things had improved, and feeling relatively blessed in the behaviour of her own husband, Gertrude believed there was much still to be done to achieve a satisfactory position for women. Involved via the Ministry of Information with a 1941 campaign to recruit married women into the Coventry factories, Gertrude attributed disappointing results to the fact that the husbands refused to take any share in the housework. A long-term supporter of Eleanor Rathbone's campaign for family allowances, she nevertheless opposed equal pay on the grounds that, until and unless housewives were paid an economic rate for their housework, married men with children should be paid higher wages to maintain family income. In an ideal world, however, husband and wife would be financially independent of one another: 'Each partner should receive his or her own salary for work done [including housework], and spend it as he [sic] pleases without penalizing the other.'[37] She was scornful of post-war attempts to reassert the virtues of domesticity, writing in 1947:

All this boosting of home which is going on now is, in my estimation, quite a lot of sentimental slush, and the vast mass of the inert indifferent dough of the population are the produce of too much home.[38]

Having carefully checked the gospels she was confident that there was no biblical authority for the proposition that a woman's place was in the home.

The complex nature of Gertrude's relationship to feminism was not unusual in the post-suffrage middle-class women's movement. Some historians have seen these women, despite their energy, independence, and public presence, as turning away from the more radical aspirations of the struggle for the suffrage, choosing to concentrate their efforts on enhancing the position of the housewife, while putting on a back burner the equal rights feminism which alone could challenge the deep structures of patriarchy.[39] Others have sought to rescue them from the condescension of late twentieth-century feminism, stressing instead their success in raising the status of the housewife, and their readiness to embrace a wider equal-rights agenda when opportunity arose.[40] During the Second World War, while equal-rights issues sent occasional shock waves through the women's movement, the predominant tone was set by leaders like Caroline Haslett who urged her middle-class followers 'to adopt the attitude of assuming our responsibilities rather than asking for our rights'.[41] Most publicly active women in mid-twentieth-century Britain related uneasily to 'feminism', widely seen as a hang-over from a struggle for the vote that had been won. Whatever visions of eventual gender equality they might entertain, they chose to assert themselves less by demanding their rights as women than by embracing their responsibilities as social leaders.

In her public work Gertrude's personal agenda turned not on the ultimate emancipation of women, but on moral questions, particularly those involving the young. She campaigned in the WI county federation for a relaxation of the rules preventing the discussion of religious questions, so that religious education in schools could be discussed. In Coventry she promoted evening opening of the British Restaurant, an initiative originating with the British Women's Total Abstinence Society (which she had joined), to provide young people with an alternative to the pub; and she pursued, at the Ministry of Information committee, the NCW's complaints about unsuitably explicit sexual material shown to audiences

containing children in Coventry cinemas. She also volunteered her own
time and energy to promoting drama among the mobile young women
in the Coventry hostels, in the hope that, like football and cold showers
for the boys, this would divert them from more dangerous pursuits. While
in all this public work Gertrude must have appeared a solidly conservative
guardian of traditional morality, her diaries reveal a much less settled state
of mind.

Answering a series of MO questions about her attitudes to sex, Gertrude
remarked: 'I have never written so much about sex before, always "feeling"
that it was wrong and lowering, and that anyway I am a button short on
it . . . I have had to think long . . . to find anything to say, as my interest in
sex is still negligible . . . '.[42] Despite having spent much of her childhood in
the red-light district of Soho, where she could watch police raids on the
night clubs from her bedroom window, she had been 'raised in the strictest
Victorian hush-hush' and still 'had no idea what prostitutes had for sale'
when she married, aged 26. While insisting that she had tasted the joys of
romance—'a love story which will bear comparison with any'—during
her courtship, she found it deeply depressing that adolescents spent so
much time on flirtation, regretting that her miners' wives would have been
capable of so much more had they not frittered away their youth on boys:

They have only one husband apiece, same as me, and nothing living mentally
or anything else to shew [sic] for the other affairs . . . If those . . . years [14 to 18]
can be rescued from sex, they could be used for mind or art or cultural training
which would be useful when sex is done with . . . I feel passionately that we must
somehow get it through to the youngsters how limited flirtation is in life.[43]

Gertrude had no time for sex, which she saw as a purely animal activity
with no cultural or spiritual meaning, and would dearly like to have seen
it displaced with intellectual and cultural pursuits. Nothing revolted her
more than Aldous Huxley's dystopian vision of limitless promiscuity in
Brave New World. But it was the 'tremendous waste of time sex causes'
which worried her most.[44] Uneasily aware that she herself was 'a button
short' in this department, and had 'never had any leaning towards sex and
therefore no temptation and therefore am in no position to judge those
who have', she insisted that 'right or wrong has nothing to do with it'.
Moral outrage about 'the actual act' itself she saw as disproportionate:
after all, she added, revealingly, it 'doesn't take many minutes and is soon
over and forgotten'.[45] (Gertrude's dismissive attitude to 'the actual act'

may not have been *unusually* sad. As Hera Cook has pointed out, foreplay was largely absent from early twentieth-century sexual activity since most men believed that speedy ejaculation was the essence of spontaneous and 'natural' sex.[46]) When she heard that 'the most efficient secretary of our Girls Club' had spent a night in the air raid shelter in the arms of a boy despite being engaged to a soldier serving abroad, she was baffled. The girl concerned 'is among the highbrows as girls go . . . she has a most responsible and highly paid job, and her father is a higher colliery official'.[47] Incidents like this made her wonder whether 'I and my generation may be quite wrong in our prejudice against promiscuity.'[48] Given the omnipresence of sex in wartime Britain, she wrote in 1944:

I am slowly getting an open mind and wondering just what part this universal obsession should play in civilisation. Not, I'm sure, the insistence of Aldous Huxley, like dogs with other dogs and lampposts. Not, I'm equally sure, the saturating maternity of the Victorians. Not I should say the frigid avoidance altogether of the bitter religious sects. But just what, I don't know.[49]

Issues of sex and social purity had always figured prominently amongst the concerns of the women's movement, and the apparent upsurge of promiscuity in wartime conditions—most strikingly the behaviour of young girls hanging around army camps—put the Coventry NCW on its metal as a guardian of public morality. It has recently been argued that this public discourse around promiscuity can take us to the heart of wartime national identity: images of pleasure-seeking 'good time girls' providing a necessary 'internal other', a foil to the virtues of those 'quintessentially reasonable citizens who willingly and with good humour sacrificed their private and personal interests and desires for the collective good'.[50] The Mass-Observation diaries provide a valuable reality check on the tendency in this kind of analysis to elide stylized public exhortatory discourse with the actual mentalities of real people. To Gertrude and her NCW colleagues the 'good-time girls' appeared not as 'an "internal other" against which the nation was defining itself', but as a deviant part of 'us' who needed to be reclaimed and protected. It is easy to exaggerate the degree to which *anybody*—even those responsible for the propaganda itself—privately bought into official propaganda (or the patriotic mythologies expounded by such iconic figures as J. B. Priestley or Humphrey Jennings) about a country composed of cheerfully unified, self-sacrificing good citizens. Middle-class social leaders like Gertrude were all too aware that the norms of 'good citizenship' to which they personally aspired were likely to remain, for the foreseeable future, restricted to a relatively small proportion of the population: and that the best you could hope for from the remainder was that they would consent to be led by the good citizens. And, however disturbing she found the behaviour of the 'good time girls', Gertrude did not see them as beyond the pale. Indeed, brought up short by the fact that one of her best 'good citizens' in the girls' club was behaving promiscuously, Gertrude was prepared to question the equation of chastity with good citizenship, to wonder whether her own standards of sexual morality were, or indeed ever had been, valid. Far from insisting on an idea of the nation that 'could not incorporate within it pleasure-seeking, fun-loving, and sexually expressive women and girls',[51] Gertrude, confronted with such a women, was forced to query not only her idea of what made a good citizen, but also the adequacy of her own, highly repressed, understanding of sexuality itself. In such ways the public discourses mapped by cultural historians were undermined by private doubts. Notions of collective identity embodied in sexual purity were far more fragile than the moralistic rhetoric might suggest, called into question even by the moral guardians themselves, privately wrestling to make sense of their own contradictory experiences.[52]

Towards the promised land

Behind the moral guardian was something much more interesting: someone who had ranged widely in her search for sustainable sources of selfhood, and who recognized that the best of the young people she encountered in her social work would do the same and, no doubt, come to rather different conclusions. Whatever moral anchorage she had found for herself, she was thoroughly modern in her understanding that each generation had to pioneer its own path. Responding to a 1944 MO directive on attitudes to religion, Gertrude described a life-long quest for a coherent set of beliefs. During childhood she was exposed to a variety of religious influences at successive schools and from parents who combined passionate interest in spiritual truth with an eclectic open-mindedness about where it might be found. Alienated by the excessive religiosity of her teacher training college, she 'chucked it all up . . . and joined the Ethical Society'. Reading Shaw, Wells, William Morris, Edward Bellamy, and the humanist writer Joseph McCabe, she acquired a secular socialist utopianism. But, even as a humanist, her 'intense religious interest' remained and, stimulated no doubt by her mother, who was Secretary of the London Federation of Theosophists during the 1920s, Gertrude turned her attention to comparative religion, gradually working out a position with which she felt comfortable. After a long and complicated voyage, she had:

arrived at the stage were all the pieces of jig-saw I have accumulated from all sorts of sources are fitting in to such an extent that I no longer wonder at an odd shaped gap nor an odd shaped fact which doesn't fit in, but realise that each will find its place in time.[53]

Alongside her civic activities, Gertrude sustained a vigorous religious life. In the privacy of her bedroom she began each day with a psalm and a short service from the 1928 prayer book. This served 'to hitch up my spiritual whatever-it-is to the universal one. I even think that it may be as material as wireless waves, or the communication of moths.'[54] Every night, kneeling at the bedside, prayer brought her 'direct guidance from God';[55] after which she rounded off the day with religious or philosophical reading. At different times the diary mentions St Augustine, Thomas a Kempis, Marcus Aurelius, and Robert Bridges' 1929 philosophical poem, 'Testament of Beauty'. Her Sundays were largely devoted to the church, with early communion, a morning service and Sunday School in the afternoon where, she felt, she failed to communicate to the children her own sense of God's presence:

One has to experience the 'juice' oneself. . . there is something a little embarrassing in public testimony of this hidden power. Nevertheless it is more real than physical life to those who know . . . It is the mainspring of my own life, but can't seem to get its value through to children.[56]

Despite her public adherence to the Anglican church, Gertrude's religious beliefs were far from orthodox. Like many other mid-twentieth-century Christians she embraced an eclectic mixture of beliefs: open-minded about astrology and spiritualism, impressed by Jehovah's Witnesses, and, like Nella, ready to understand contemporary history as an acting out of events foretold in the Old Testament, if not Armageddon itself. In 1942 she felt that the Bible implied that the British would have to be driven out of Egypt before the war could be won, and her view of German brutality towards the Jews was informed by a belief that they had brought it on themselves: as 'God's experimental people' they should have stayed in Jerusalem having visions for the good of mankind, rather than wandering the earth in search of profit: 'What were the Jews doing in Poland anyway?'

These were not views she would have been likely to express publicly: 'I realise how batty all this sounds to people who think in terms of bodies', she wrote: 'Nevertheless I am convinced that bodies hardly come into the picture and that the intangible is the explanation.'[57] She even thought she had discovered a reference to the primary instrument of modern warfare in Ezekiel 1: 'a description of sort of flying creatures with straight wings joined together and wheels underneath—aircraft described by a man who had not the foggiest notion of what he was describing.'[58]

She was also a firm believer in reincarnation. Plagued by migraines and a gastric disorder that had twice led to serious operations and extensive hospitalization, she claimed to have no fear of death, confident of being reborn into a world where 'I shall get treatment from birth and I shall enjoy life quite a lot more'. Over the years she had considered suicide a few times 'solely as an escape from my carcase, but turned it down till such time as I am a bit more useless. I appear at the minute,' she added modestly, 'to fill a niche or two.'[59] Belief in reincarnation was no less comforting in the face of moral weaknesses. The goal she set herself, as her main aim in life, was to achieve 'the character which Christ sets before us'—not as quite as daunting a task as it might appear because: 'as I believe this is evolutionary through many incarnations, I am not unduly worried that in this life I find it difficult and slow.'[60]

Wrestling with the apparent collapse of secular ideas of progress, many mid-twentieth-century intellectuals turned to religion. In some cases the religious turn was also a private turn, cultivating spirituality at the expense of participation in the public affairs of a world gone hopelessly astray.[61] This seems to have been the path taken by Gertrude's son, Austin, who joined the Plymouth Brethren in the 1930s and registered as a conscientious objector during the war.[62] Gertrude, who had belonged to the League of Nations Union and canvassed support for the 1936 Peace Ballot, wanted to follow suit: 'I hauled myself up among the "elect" four or five years ago', she wrote in 1942. But however much she respected Austin's religious quietism she was utterly incapable of embracing it herself:

Now the 'elect' aren't in this war. They just look on. Or so my son . . . told me. However I didn't realise that, and volunteered for everything that came along. Took ARP training in 1938–39, joined WVS, was billeting officer, and owing to being near Coventry yet in the country there were many openings.[63]

Austin's pacifism was the source of some tension in the Glover household. Sam, who threw himself into Home Guard activity and followed the military progress of the war with obsessive enthusiasm, deplored the position taken by his son. Gertrude, though incapable of opting out, viewed the military conduct of the war itself with a mixture of indifference, boredom, horror, and anxiety about her own un-Christian feelings towards the German people. Her husband's enthusiasm for his 'beloved war' she dismissed as very male and rather childish: 'I've felt from beginning that men *like* war, and wouldn't like it to be ruled out altogether.'[64] With an insight anticipating Graham Dawson's more recent discussion of the 'masculine pleasure-culture of war',[65] she remarked:

I am not so unsympathetic as I sound [to Sam's fascination with things military]. My psyche or whatever it is satisfied with drama, discussion and all the lovely mental things I find to do . . . He has no such side to his life, all such things being frowned on by his parents, the stronger of which is still here with him. He is now 62 and will never be free now, so I must appreciate his kindness to me, and understand that war is his legitimate dramatic interest.[66]

Gertrude's inexhaustible commitment to public work was underpinned by a religious sensibility quite distinct from the pacifist quietism of her son or the conventional church-going of her husband (which, to Austin's disgust, Sam happily gave up in order to devote his Sundays to playing soldiers in the Home Guard). She was delighted to discover an exposition of ideas similar to those she had worked out for herself in a book published twenty-five years earlier by, 'of all people!', H. G. Wells.[67] In *God the Invisible King* Wells had detected 'a stirring and a movement' of a new religion across all the world faiths—a religion dismissive of the doctrinaire claims of churches, priests, and theologians, agnostic about the existence of an omniscient and omni-competent Creator, appealing instead to an individual relationship with a personal God within—'that inner light which is the quintessence of the religious experience'—a God striving through the agency of his servants to achieve his kingdom in the here and now on earth:

The kingdom of God on earth is not a metaphor, not a mere spiritual state, not a dream, not an uncertain project; it is the thing before us, it is the close and inevitable destiny of mankind. In a few score years the faith of the true God will be spreading about the world . . . In but a few centuries God will have led us out of the dark forest of these present wars and confusions into the open brotherhood of his rule . . .[68]

It was in this Wellsian vein that, in 1942, Gertrude felt herself to be 'part of the great general surge upwards and outwards'.[69] 'The promised land which existed only in books in my adolescence seems to be spreading itself open to view afar off.' When pessimists of her acquaintance talked 'the old lingo of unemployment, scarcity, misery etc. as if they were natural' she was shocked, realizing that, like her own husband, 'they never will see the visions I see'.[70] Despite being surrounded by Conservative-minded women in the NCW and the county federation of the WI, and despite the *Daily Mail* (delivered daily for Sam, but she rarely read it), she retained the socialist vision learned years earlier from the utopian writings of Morris, Bellamy, 'and I forget how many ... [who] shewed [sic] me the shape of things to come'.[71] The war, she wrote 'has brought to a more vivid reality the "new order" which has been adumbrated in many ways all my life ... All sorts of events, reading, social changes etc. are falling into place. I feel an exhilaration which no amount of bad war news appears to affect.'[72] Though vaguely aware, following the publication of the Beveridge Report in 1942, that there might be a need to mobilize against the attempts of vested interests to water Beveridge down, Gertrude, like many middle-class female activists, had no head for party politics. She claimed to be unable to detect party bias in the views expressed at meetings of the non-partisan NCW, although its president was the wife of the Tory MP for Coventry:

I have always been too hazy about 'politics' to be able to join a party, or to assimilate any party programme. I only seem to see things as straight issues, as nearly as I can from more than one point of view, but ... I don't understand what constitutes a political issue. My opinion of 'politics' for many years has been that they are obfuscations of plain questions. I shall come with an open mind to any election.[73]

Shame at exposing her ignorance, when asked for her views on the wartime electoral truce, was partially assuaged by her understanding that Mass-Observation existed to discover what ordinary people actually thought: 'I feel that I represent the frame of mind of many more voters than does the person who has all the details of either or both parties at his finger-tips.'[74] In the post-war election, unimpressed by Attlee, and shocked to discover, from Churchill's ill-judged election broadcast in which he alleged that a Labour government would need to use 'Gestapo methods' to implement its programme, that the wartime national leader represented 'money, upper class power, royalty, militaristic culture, mastership' and was 'as political as any other Conservative', she voted for a female Common Wealth candidate, an endorsement of a broad Christian Socialist tendency she identified with the late Archbishop Temple and Stafford Cripps, rather than of the Common Wealth Party itself, whose leader Richard Acland she found too self-righteous for her taste. Excited by the election of a Labour government, she anticipated 'the beginning of carrying out all those things described in all the Utopias written during the past few thousands of years and more particularly during the last 50 or 60 years.'[75] Labour's 1945 victory seemed to open the door to a 'New Jerusalem'—a term that in Gertrude's case continued to hold much of its original, millenarian meaning.

Wellsian utopianism aside, such optimism was not unusual among middle-class women in the immediate aftermath of the election, probably because they hoped that the new government would make itself the vehicle for a broad consensus for social reform that transcended party boundaries.[76] Gertrude was unusual, however, in sustaining her enthusiasm for Labour through the difficult years that lay ahead. Attlee, she came to understand, was a product of the same late nineteenth-century socialist thinking that had been her own inspiration and however depressing continuing austerity might be, she agreed with the NCW's assessment of the right-wing Housewife's League as mere 'mischief makers', and approved of the fact that Labour was prepared to 'put the pinch of the shoe onto [middle-class] feet that yelp instead of feet that just endure, as in the past'.[77]

After the war Gertrude continued to play a leading role in the Coventry NCW, taking on the presidency during 1947–8. But her heart was no longer in the work. With a Labour government in power, the middle-class NCW was, she felt, as likely to resist as to push forward social reform. The committee work had become a tedious chore and the discussion meetings so much idle talk. Feeling that her own generation had done its bit towards tackling the 'drawbacks of secular society', her eyes were now firmly fixed on the spiritual health of the next.[78] Alongside her dramatic activities, she preferred to concentrate on her work with the Youth Club and the Sunday School where, she believed, she could still 'get something done that matters'.[79]

In January 1949, in what turned out to be the final instalment of her diary, she drew a sharp contrast between the elderly and middle-aged housewives of the WI and the coming generation. Chairing a meeting of the local WI after an absence of two years, she was reminded just how inarticulate the village women could be, how difficult they found it to organize themselves without leadership from above. Even more depressing was an afternoon as a guest at the Mother's Union Christmas party, where the quiz revealed a quite shocking level of ignorance: 'they hadn't heard of

Robinson Crusoe or Gulliver's Travels . . . Get past how many eyes a cat has, and you're done':

Dear, dear, am I superior or something? But what a boring afternoon! There being heavy and deep slowness and absence of mirth over everything, which I am noticing over all women's meetings. It may always have been there, but my contacts with youth have brought it to my notice . . .[80]

A few days earlier, impressed by the lively, unselfconscious atmosphere at a youth club dance, she had reflected on the young people's capacity for self-organization: 'democracy [has] arrived, with natural leaders arising out of the led. As it should be to my mind . . . '. She fully understood that the society these youngsters would create would be very different from that in which she had grown up; but it would not necessarily be any worse. Just as the promiscuous behaviour of one of the most responsible young women at the girls club had led her to question the equation between good citizenship and traditional sexual mores, so she now accepted that the 'entire absence of that taste and sort of culture which I have hitherto connected with leaders in any movement' was no obstacle to genuinely democratic change. 'The whole atmosphere was [a] breath of hope for [the] future when', she added ominously as the Berlin airlift continued, '[the] next war is over.'[81]

Gertrude's life was not without its disappointments, and one could understand her civic activism as compensation for what would otherwise have been a rather impoverished private life. Her role in the farmhouse, as Sam's wife, homemaker, and carer for his aging mother, provided a useful niche of sorts; but it was not a life that had much to offer to a woman of her creative talents and intellectual curiosity. Although she never explicitly said so in the diary, it seems clear that her experience of motherhood had been more anxiety-making than fulfilling. And she was aware that the sexual side of her nature remained unexplored.

Nevertheless, compared with Nella Last, she held a far more optimistic and upbeat view of the world and of her role in it. It was her Christianity that enabled Gertrude to envisage a process of social reconciliation and reform which would lead eventually, under the guidance of active citizens like herself, to a fairer and more peaceful world. Secure in her self-fashioned religious belief, Gertrude had no need to pursue transcendent meaning through art and culture. While rating herself 'well-educated and cultured above the average', she did not consider herself a 'highbrow'—by which she meant that she was unresponsive to Shakespeare, Bach, and Picasso, but enjoyed novels which 'describe life as it feasibly might be lived': Trollope, George Elliot, Mrs Henry Wood, Arnold Bennett.[82] She loved her creative work, writing and producing playlets, pageants, and mimes, but was well aware that her themes were mundane and had more to do with the social mission of the WI to entertain, educate, and improve the lives of plebeian women than with art for art's sake.

Religion was the driving force of Gertrude's civic activism—'I work entirely by the Spirit', she wrote in 1948, claiming none of her success for herself. But she took care not to shove her religious convictions down other people's throats, remarking of the youth club 'Never mention religion or any sort of pi-jaw down there.'[83] The public religious observance on Sundays no doubt leant some meaning to her life, although she never wrote about it with the intensity or passion that informed her accounts of her private daily encounters with God. It was from these private encounters that she went forward to engage with the world, in the WI, the NCW, the youth club or the Ministry of Information committee, putting her various talents to work to build God's kingdom on earth, or at least in Warwickshire.

Figure 3. Mary Clayton, circa 1937.
Courtesy of the Mass-Observation Archive.

4

Mary Clayton: Bombed out
and keeping going

F or Mary Clayton, who lived alone and ran her own business, personal
autonomy was not a problem. Brought up a Methodist, married and
divorced from a Catholic, she had, reluctantly, given up on religion. But
she retained a powerful spirit of service, manifested in her work as a WVS
leader in working-class Battersea, in her commitment to the Labour Party,
and in her writing for MO, which, more than for any of the other diarists,
was discrete to the point of secretiveness about personal matters. At no point
in the diaries does she give the name of her first husband, or of her business
partner (later her second husband). It took considerable detective work to
establish their identities, and thus, among other things, the name under
which, in 1951, her death was registered. If she needed a room behind
the shop to let her hair down she must have found it with her friends
and perhaps with her partner; but she revealed little of this in the diary.
What Mary Clayton gives us is the *made* self, the product, not the process,
although something of the latter can be inferred from her full and honest
responses to some of the more searching monthly directives.[1] Explaining
her reasons for joining MO in 1937 she struck a characteristic note:

I have never kept a consecutive diary as I found it seemed to lead to overmuch
introspection. Here however was a sensible reason for keeping an eye on oneself,
and for looking outwards to others as well . . . What probably appealed to me most,
was the fact that the originators of the movement didn't promise anything—save a
job of work . . . and the sense of having, in a small way, helped forward something
useful.[2]

Mary Clayton's diary was an exercise in self-possession: the performance of a balanced, rational, responsible persona—sensible, useful, keeping an eye on herself but not self-indulgently introspective. Does this make it any less 'real' than the more intimate diaries? Or does it, on the contrary, come closer to presenting this woman as she appeared, contributed, and functioned in the world than a diary more taken up with the chaos of interior feelings could have done?

First marriage

Mary grew up in a lower-middle class Methodist family in Weymouth where her father had risen in the Post Office from sorting clerk to deputy post master. After winning a scholarship to secondary school her parents supported her through teacher training in London where she started teaching in 1909. Mary, one of the liberated LCC teachers described by Dina Copelman, remarked many years later that 'a teacher in poor neighbourhoods is pretty well bound to be mixed up with Cole, Tawney, etc. in socialist circles.'[3] She also knew and admired the young Herbert Morrison, still a telephone operator, but already formidably efficient as ILP branch secretary in Brixton. It was in this milieu that she met her first husband, Rolf Clayton, 'a dilettante aesthete' from an altogether more elevated social background (his father was editor and part owner of a newspaper, one brother a priest, and uncle Joseph Clayton, an Oxford academic who published extensively on labour-movement history).[4] Rolf, twelve years older than her, was a widower with a 4-year-old son who needed a mother, and Mary, as she later wrote, was 'too young and inexperienced' to resist: 'It was so much taken for granted that I should acquiesce . . . that decisions were announced as if we had both made them.'[5] Rolf ran an antiquarian bookshop in Hampstead, and she was thrilled to meet his friends who included the bookseller and publisher David Garnett, the writer W. H. Davies, and the poet, Edward Thomas. She was both fascinated and repelled by the bohemian world she had married into. Her parents disliked Rolf—'his dark saturnine personality seemed so alien to them'—disapproving of his Catholicism and, still more, his gratuitously offensive attacks on conventional morality. For a time she saw little of her family, and when she did she felt 'torn between standing up for [their] essential good heartedness and excusing [their] narrow-mindedness'.[6] In the end, however, it was the good-heartedness that mattered to her, and she came to see Rolf's world as false and degenerate. Accidentally pregnant—he did not want her to be distracted from the care of his first child—she attributed her subsequent miscarriage to, among other things, her feeling that his was 'a stock which was on the down grade, on the whole better not perpetuated'. Rolf had an unhappy relationship with his son, who escaped to Australia when he was 17. Shortly afterwards, on a health trip to the South of France, Rolf got together with a nurse, 'and that was that', wrote Mary twenty years later with a stoical matter-of-factness that was characteristic of her: 'I have never had any regrets, it was a job I took on, and tried very hard to do.'[7] They were divorced in 1927. After that she reconnected with her family. During the war she spent every Christmas visiting a teacher friend in Dorset and her brother's family nearby. Her brother, a long-term alcoholic, drank himself to death in 1941, leaving a wife and a daughter. She reports all this in the diary or directive replies (retrospectively about the brother because she was not writing at the time of his death), but she does not dwell on her feelings either about her friend, or the loss of her brother which must have been all the more painful since she had lost her only other sibling, another younger brother, in an accident when she was 15.

The business

Despite her subordinate status within her marriage, she had maintained an independent life throughout, teaching at first and then in 1923, perhaps because of the introduction of the marriage bar into London's schools in that year, taking up a post with the National Council for the Prevention of Venereal Disease.[8] She organized their panel of medical and lay lecturers, and did a good deal of public speaking herself. She was also responsible for 'the illustrations side of the campaigns . . . films, lantern lectures, posters, models, exhibitions, etc'.[9] Out of this experience she conceived the project that was to keep her busy for the rest of her life. In 1926 she set up her own business, Visual Information Service, to produce and supply film strips and slides for visual education work, then in its infancy. Working to commission, she handled the finances and researched material for the film strips while her partners, John and Jim Burchett, were responsible for the photography and the supply of episcopes to their clients. By the outbreak of war she was employing five people, one of them a handyman whose wife acted as her cleaner, in addition to the two brothers who she treated as partners in the business although formally she was the sole owner.

Her success in building up the business was achieved despite deteriorating health. The onset of multiple sclerosis in 1929, when she was 40, left her without the use of her left hand and with a gammy leg, putting an end to more active pleasures—playing the piano, dancing, and tennis. For a couple of years before the war she was forced to rely increasingly on her partners to run the business, but by the autumn of 1939, following an operation, and with her illness in remission, she was taking back control. During the first year of the war orders fell off and most of the staff left. Jim rejoined the RAF, leaving Mary and John to cope with reviving demand with the help of one or two part-timers for the rest of the war. Wartime clients included the Ministry of Information, the Czech and Polish embassies, schools, churches, and voluntary organizations in the UK and throughout the empire. Mary was particularly pleased with a schools' order for a series of film strips on American history which kept her busy researching in the London Library for several months. They also made slide sets for individuals, including clergymen seizing the opportunities provided by ready-made audiences in the public air raid shelters—'from what I can see the parsons are having the time of their lives'—and 'a spook-merchant in South London. Should think his pictures of ectoplasm . . . would un-convince the most credulous, but apparently not.' Visual education work expanded during the war and, without being able to take on extra staff, Mary and John found themselves working seven days a week. But she loved the work, as much a hobby as a job and rated herself among 'the luckiest people in the world' for whom work and play were so intermingled that 'I am never quite sure which is which'.[11]

Partner

Her enjoyment of the work was further enhanced by her relationship with John, not only her chief business partner but also her closest friend. After working together all day they spent most evenings in her small modern flat, ten minutes walk away from the studio, on the edge of a middle-class enclave in working-class Battersea. Her flat was on the ground floor of a small block built on the site of two demolished terraced houses in what was then a working-class street behind the big villas overlooking the park. She had a distant view of the park only because the flats were strategically placed opposite a junction with a road running down to the park. Despite her success as a business-woman she did not identify with 'the professional and civil service group' living in the villas.[12] Most of them, she felt, were lacking in human warmth and she was much more comfortable with the large working-class family across the road. In the evenings Mary and John read, listened to the radio, rolled and boxed film, or relaxed with a crossword or a game of cards. At night, John went back to the studio where he had a bunk in the loft. He had been, or perhaps still was, married to a woman never mentioned after Mary's initial autobiographical account for MO in 1937 where she is described as being 'not very strong'.[13] It is not clear what happened to the wife or when Mary came to think of John as her 'partner' in more than a business sense. The closest she came in the diaries to defining the nature of their relationship was in a 1943 aside when describing an unmarried couple, an English woman and a Czech refugee whose former wife was missing, presumed dead: 'in some ways their ménage is a queer parallel of our own.'[14] About her sexual life with John, if it existed, she says nothing. This was private territory, irrelevant to the public persona that she thought it appropriate to anatomize for Mass-Observation.

John was a reclusive man who hated visitors to the studio and appears to have had no social life of his own outside the business, apart from that imposed by his civil defence duties. He often cooked lunch for her at the studio but loathed shopping, even for his own clothes, unable to bear the physical contact with humanity on crowded pavements. Trained as an electro-chemical engineer he loved the work, tinkering and inventing. He read little outside physics—Planck and Rutherford, Mary reported, were his 'light reading'—and she found it hard to interest him in anything 'larger than an electron'.[15] The event that most excited him in the period covered by the diary was Hiroshima, awesome as science and technology, not for its political or metaphysical meanings. Politically, he was a 'hereditary Conservative'.[16] He had fought with distinction in the First World War, held conventional views about the superiority of the British Empire and the innate evil of the German character, and read the *Daily Telegraph* (she borrowed it to supplement her *Daily Herald*, in the interests of balance). One of the very few rows that she mentions was occasioned by their contrary reception of a broadcast by Attlee early in the war which John saw

as an unpatriotic attack on the Empire: 'And I had heard it so differently
and thought it moderate and reasonable. Dear, dear! And we are both
well-meaning people trying to do our best.'[17] The argument, heated on
both sides, upset her. Normally she avoided political argument with John.
A less avoidable source of tension was her introduction of a German refugee
into the office. Mrs O'C, who lived in the flat across the hall from Mary,
was idle, isolated, and willing to work for nothing, so her help was hard to
refuse. She made herself useful, but John hated it, partly because he would
have resented anyone invading his space, but also because he was allergic
to Germans.

Her other source of tension with John was over the extent of her
engagement in voluntary work, which is what had created the need for
Mrs O'C in the first place. In December 1942, ill and overworked, John
'went off the deep end . . . all wild looking and shaking', accusing Mary of
devoting all her energies to the WVS, losing interest in the business and
leaving everything to him.[18] This was quite uncharacteristic of him and she
resolved to go easy for a bit.

Women Voluntary Services

Early in 1940, in better health following an operation the previous summer
and feeling a need 'to be doing something beyond just getting one's bread
and butter', Mary joined the WVS.[19] During the spring and summer of 1940
she took time off from work, where things were slack, to escort groups of
evacuated children and help to settle them in their new homes. When her
diary resumes, after a two-year gap, on her fifty-third birthday in April 1942
she was running a street savings group set up a couple of months earlier. In
July she was approached by the WVS to take on a much larger job as District
Leader responsible for overseeing the work of the twelve local ARP post
organizers in her immediate neighbourhood. For the rest of the war she
devoted all her spare time to this work, confident, despite initial anxieties
about whether she was cut out for the constant socializing involved, that
'usually I can get women to work together without being catty, which is
something'.[20] The job description was vague and had a tendency to expand
as the WVS found new uses for its street-level organization:

I try to know everyone in the area with any willingness to do anything, or time
to do it in; stimulate training courses for housewives; speak at meetings if called

upon; and generally form a sort of connecting link between the wardens, invasion wardens, women Post Leaders, local Home Guard and WVS local Centre.[21]

She was clearly a success in this work, flattered to be cited by a national organizer as a role model for other district leaders. WVS head office also picked up on her professional expertise, using her to demonstrate the potential of visual education methods to national and regional organizers. She worried about the overlap between voluntary work and touting for business, but in the event few orders seem to have been forthcoming. When the blitz returned early in 1944 with buzz bombs, and later V2 rockets, the network of housewives willing to help in an emergency which she had assembled was put to the test and her own work intensified, interrupted only briefly in February by a bomb that demolished much of her own street and made her flat uninhabitable. 'Bombed out and keeping going' was her own summary of the three weeks that followed when she moved in with a friend she had known since her college days, a Labour councillor who was head of the WVS in neighbouring Wandsworth.[22]

Politics

Mary had been a committed Labour supporter throughout her adult life—a socialist 'by membership and conviction'—and had once, in 1934, come close to being elected as a Labour councillor in Wandsworth.[23] She canvassed in the Battersea by-election in April 1940 and delivered leaflets in 1945. In the later 1930s her illness had made public work impossible, and when her strength returned she decided to put her energies into voluntary work rather than Labour politics, seeing WVS 'as the most direct way of helping my country and those around. The impulse was the same but war conditions altered the method for a time.'[24]

The Battersea WVS was a very different organization, socially and politically, from Nella Last's middle-class Tory enclave in Barrow. Three of Mary's twelve post leaders were Labour councillors, and the others 'were always consulting their [overwhelmingly Labour] councillors about anything which troubled them'.[25] Even fellow members of the Labour Party, however, 'strenuously avoided any politics' when they met on WVS business.[26] Through WVS, Mary felt she could serve the cause of 'social betterment' in practical ways: dealing with evacuation, post-blitz services, care of the elderly, etc. 'All these', she noted, 'are, or may become acute political questions, [but] now we meet them in the raw, as it were, and do the best we can under present circumstances.'[27] 'Service', which she wrote with a capital S, had always been at the core of her socialism, and it was the same philanthropic urge to help her working-class neighbours that underpinned her wartime work with WVS:

I have plenty of opportunity now to try and put right anything immediately around me that seems to be wrong, and I can help guide people's desire to be helpful into useful channels. I cannot help guide great affairs, nor those more remote, so had best concentrate on what is near at hand.[28]

She approved of the wartime suspension of partisan politics, and was dismissive of political attacks on the government, feeling that 'it might be better if the energy expended were directed into present service'.[29] While the war lasted she thought it pointless to try to argue about top-level decisions, whether on the home front or the conduct of the war:

I don't think anyone has the right to criticise unless they are doing everything they possibly can . . . to bring about victory. The idea of casting blame on this or that was natural enough esp. in the earlier stages, but all happenings have combined to emphasise personal responsibility, and sympathy for those who direct and control. Co-operation rather than criticism must be the line.[30]

She noted the care with which the WVS women, head-office Tories as much as neighbourhood socialists, avoided potentially disruptive topics: 'there is a kind of veneer over their general behaviour and conversation, something of discipline which has by now I think got into speech and even thought. A carefulness not to talk too much or to sow discouragement . . .'.[31] She was confident that service would bring its own reward, and that 'whatever their party may be, those who do most for their fellows in the present juncture, will have greatest influence in shaping the conditions after the war.'[32] While she expected the two-party system to return and, in line with most 'informed' opinion, anticipated a Conservative post-war election victory, she did not see this as necessarily meaning the triumph of 'property and power' over social betterment. The war, she believed, had fostered a public opinion which 'would force progressive action on any government in power'.[33] She was impressed by a series of lectures provided by the WVS designed to educate the membership 'on good impartial lines, to focus the attention of this large body of non-party more or less intelligent women on post-war problems, in which their influence may be widely felt'.[34]

Mary Clayton's optimism about future social progress was not dissimilar to Gertrude Glover's. Both women had been influenced in their youth by socialist thinking, and they both now saw themselves as belonging to a broad social-reformist current extending well beyond the Labour Party. It was in this milieu, sharing an undoctrinaire spirit of service, that Mary felt at home. Despite her membership of the Labour Party, she felt little affinity with the trade union core of Labour politics. She read her *Daily Herald* dutifully, approved of its 'balanced and sensible' leaders, but found that industrial matters left her cold. Union conferences always seemed to 'make the most important thing uninteresting', inducing 'a dullness, dryness, staleness . . . which I can only liken to co-op propaganda and co-op pre-war cake'.[35] This was not so different from Gertrude Glover's demeaning attitude to the Keresley miners, incapable of effective revolt without leaders from the outside. Like many middle-class socialists, Mary saw trade-union power as a blunt, dull, and unimaginative instrument, however necessary it might be to the achievement of political power by the socialist leaders of whom she approved—men like Attlee and Herbert Morrison.

Religion

One thing Mary did not share with Gertrude Glover was a religious basis to her social optimism. Both women had encountered a variety of religious standpoints, but while this had encouraged Gertrude, after flirting with agnosticism, to work out her own relationship with a personal God, the upshot of Mary's exposure to the conflict between the provincial Methodism she was born into and the metropolitan Catholicism of her first marriage was a rejection of religion altogether, although she occasionally attended church in connection with her WVS duties:

To what I think might be called an adult mind, no inducements, sentiment, aestheticism nor benefit hereafter are felt necessary to produce right living. I have given up all but purely conventional observance myself, having come to an agnostic-ethical-stoical position.[36]

Nevertheless, she regretted her loss of faith, and would have welcomed a religion that could justify itself 'in a way that didn't outrage the very faculty which one supposes is most "godlike"'.[37] In 1940 she was still searching, reading Christian apologetics: but one writer treated incarnation and resurrection as established facts, claiming that modern physics could explain them, while another, selected because he was 'a Methodist parson who has gone RC', rested his case on nothing more than 'authority and revelation'.[38]

Her cultural life was sparse, and she found no substitute for her religious yearnings in art. She hardly ever went to concerts, theatre, cinema, or art galleries, and she spent her evenings with thrillers, the radio and work-related reading. Although she read widely, researching her film strips, she saw the work in a strictly utilitarian way: not creative, just assembling information which might serve to educate and inspire others to creativity. Despite the very real satisfaction she drew from her voluntary work, and her humanist belief that 'right living' required no supernatural sanction, she continued to hanker for something more, confessing that elements of her old beliefs still lingered, powerless, disembodied, tenuous 'like a forgotten language'.[39] With an uncharacteristic lack of precision she described moments when she found herself praying:

Prayer [she insisted], not petition, not praise, but a memory and consideration of those things and happenings in which I have experienced something something something [sic] finer and higher than ordinary day by day living. Some sympathy, beauty, or unexpected strength. Some small divine spark.[40]

For all her rationality and agnostic stoicism, Mary Clayton remained deeply marked by her Christian upbringing, unwilling to let go altogether the possibility that a higher power could dignify and lend meaning to her life.

In 1944, faced with worrying symptoms suggesting a resumption of her multiple sclerosis, she rejected medical advice to give up her voluntary work, remarking with characteristic realism: 'surely best to do things while I can, even if it means a sooner ending'. Her final years were unlikely to be 'so rosy as to make one want to lengthen it out'.[41] In 1939, aged 50, she had not expected to live more than five or ten years, fifteen at the outside. She died in 1951, her death registered by John Burchett who she had finally married two years earlier.

Despite her ill-heath and her reticence about the private dimensions of her life, a picture of a satisfying and fulfilling life emerges from Mary Clayton's diaries. Self-directed and independent, even when bounced into an exploitative and temporary marriage to an older man, the twin touchstones of Mary's sense of self were reason and service. In her professional life she saw herself not as a creative artist but as a purveyor of facts; and it was her investment in rationality as the key to human dignity that made it impossible for her to accept religious doctrines that defied reason. Her participation in public life, whether through the Labour Party or WVS, was driven by an ethic of service which required no supra-human underwriting. Her socialism, like her film strips, was, above all, sensible, moderate, and reasonable: Herbert Morrison and Clement Attlee were the men who spoke to her, not the romantic effusions of a Nye Bevan or the utopian rhetoric of the Common Wealth Party which attracted the much less politically sophisticated Gertrude Glover. For all this, however, there was a lingering doubt. Perhaps there was more to life than reason and service alone could supply. She did not find it in cultural life; and whatever sustenance she drew from her intimate relationship with John it does not seem to have been sufficient to close down entirely her unfulfilled yearning for 'something, something, something finer and higher than ordinary day by day living'. Mary Clayton may not have been able to answer the question that she posed, but her ability to pose it, and so clearly, testifies to the openness and honesty with which she addressed the puzzling incompleteness of the lights by which she lived.

Nella, Gertrude, and Mary had a good deal in common. All in their fifties, they belonged to a generation of middle-class women for whom 'service' to the community through voluntary work was an important source of self-respect and personal fulfilment. Marriage dealt differently with each of them. The nature of Mary's partnership with John, and Gertrude's accommodating husband, left both women free to pursue their voluntary work largely uninhibited by the demands of private life—although, in Mary's case, the competition between WVS and her business did cause some tension with John. Nella, on the other hand, was engaged in a continuous battle for personal autonomy. To the extent that she succeeded this was a product, not only of the wartime legitimation of her voluntary work, but of also of the basis laid by her pre-war engagements in the public sphere and by her self-directed project of motherhood. Though none of them claimed great originality or creativity, they were all women who thought for themselves about life's deeper mysteries, arriving at a sense of the meaning of life that they had thought out for themselves rather than simply imbibed uncritically from their surroundings—and in this way they were agents of cultural change. Gertrude and Mary had both been exposed early on in life to the cross-currents of metropolitan radicalism—Gertrude to theosophy, both of them to humanism and socialism: and, while they drew very different conclusions about both religion and politics, the exposure helped shape a progressive cast of mind. Nella, in her Northern fastness, had less cultural capital to work with, dependent as she was on the maxims of her Quaker grandmother, and trapped in a social milieu that provided none of the intellectual stimulation that Gertrude found in the women's movement, or Mary in researching her film strips. Nevertheless, like Gertrude, Nella was a good deal more open to the ideas of the coming generation than most of the women in her circle. Perhaps the most striking difference between these three women and the two younger women to whom we now turn was in their relation to their own sexuality. Mary thought of herself as 'undersexed'; Gertrude admitted to having always been 'a button short' in this department; and there is nothing in Nella's writing to suggest that sexual feelings had ever played a significant part in her life.[42] For both the younger women, by contrast, awareness of their sexual attractiveness to men played an important role in the strategies of personal autonomy that they chose to pursue.

Figure 4. Eleanor Humphries, 1939.
Courtesy of the Mass-Observation Archive.

5

Eleanor Humphries: Serving genius

Women have served all these centuries as looking-glasses possessing the magic and delicious power of reflecting the figure of man at twice its natural size.

(Virginia Woolf, *A Room of One's Own* (Harmondsworth, 1972), 70)

The face Eleanor Humphries presents to the world in the photograph she sent to Mass-Observation is that of a well turned-out housewife, looking younger than her forty years, proudly framed in the doorway of her modern semi-detached house. This was how she wanted to be perceived. But her voluminous diaries, covering the first four years of the war, tell a very different story. Behind the house-proud image lay a woman whose self-development had been crippled by the most patriarchal of marriages. She used her diaries to monitor every fluctuation in the state of her personal relationships, with husband, parents, servants, friends, and colleagues. Her characterizations of others were vivid. She had a novelist's eye for the quirks of individual appearance, behaviour, emotional state, and social caste, and a particular sensitivity to the play of eroticism in everyday life. But the diaries also reveal an emotional life beset by jealousy, suspicion, and insecurity. 'How difficult are human relationships,' she wrote on one occasion, 'they hang on such a fine balance and one has to be so constantly on the alert with those one loves . . .'.[1] Living only through interpersonal relationships, her selfhood was held hostage to the moods of others: she lacked composure.

As a voluntary worker she participated in the public sphere, but she was not able to use her social work, as Nella Last did, to redress the balance of power within her marriage. The public sphere, for Eleanor, was simply an extension of the private, another arena for the interplay of personalities. In contrast to the three women we have considered so far, a sense of obligation to serve the public good played little part in Eleanor's make up. Despite her social work, and her commitment as a mass observer, her world was essentially private and personal. Abstract ideas about rights, duty, citizenship, ethics, or the meaning of life meant little to her, and where other diarists wrote about their intellectual lives, or their moments of transcendence in communion with nature, music, art, literature, or God, Eleanor remained silent. She lacked the ideological resources with which to resist the patriarchal structure of her marriage: if everything came back to the personal, then the personal could not be politicized. There were moments, especially during the bombing, when she felt that her own life—as against the life of the man whose genius she serviced—took on a larger meaning, a meaning in relation to wider public purposes. But they were rare, and her normal state was that of a woman trapped in patriarchal structures, lacking self-sufficiency, restlessly seeking affirmation. The photograph projects a composure that could exist only in the gaze of others.

Marriage

The 'life story' that Eleanor wrote when she joined Mass-Observation in 1939 tells a tale of unfulfilled potential. Born in Chicago, her American parents brought her to Blackheath when she was 2 years old, but she spent much of her childhood being moved around continental Europe: France, Belgium, Austria, and Berlin where her father's employer, the telephone engineering company Siemens, had its headquarters. Her childhood disrupted by frequent illness and her father's travels, she never went to school, but 'wore out a series of governesses . . . [and] grew up poorly instructed in all the usual subjects'. After a late start, she became an omnivorous reader, learned the violin, wrote poetry, aspired to a career as a singer, and bullied her parents into sending her to art school (at Goldsmiths'

College) when she was 14. There she made her first girl friend: 'life was marvellous. We edited a magazine, she too wrote sentimental tosh and verses so did not think me queer. Puffed up by her praise I . . . began a novel.'[2] A couple of poems found their way into print, and the novel was later rejected by Bodley Head, where her friend Allen Lane was starting his career in publishing (in the 1930s he founded Penguin Books).[3] But these 'wild aspirations' of adolescence quickly succumbed to patriarchal control. Her father, unimpressed by 'precocity in all the wrong directions', insisted on a secretarial training, and then put her to work in a small company he had set up on the side to manufacture one of his inventions, where she learned bookkeeping on the job.

This phase of her life ended abruptly with her marriage, aged 21, to an Australian telephone engineer who she met shortly after he came to England to work at Siemens as a promising young protégé of her father's. Horace, five years her senior, was 'an expert at anything he ever takes up' and he had no time for his wife's amateurish pursuits. Dazzled by her good fortune, the young wife 'most cheerfully dropped all my former occupations', abandoned most of her former friends, threw herself into entertaining, domesticity, and voluntary work, and awaited the joys of motherhood. They never came. Six years into her marriage her first pregnancy ended in stillbirth leaving her unable to conceive (although she was still hoping for a miracle during the war every time her period was late): 'It was a terrific mental jolt and completely changed my outlook. That year I had my hair cut short and also suppressed the last lingering desires to write fiction. Started a large correspondence.'[4] The letters she wrote, many of them to her husband's Australian relatives, became a lifeline for her repressed creative talents. When, ten years later, she started writing for Mass-Observation, her diaries were often carbon copies (literally) of her correspondence.

'There seems to be no point in marriage if parenthood is not the ultimate goal', Eleanor wrote in response to an MO directive at the end of 1943.[5] She was no longer keeping her diary by then so we cannot know what exactly it was that provoked such negativity, but the strains of wartime had certainly taken their toll. Before the war she had had no difficulty in specifying the point of her marriage:

My husband is my first and foremost interest and the most important factor in my life. Everything is subordinated to his requirements. His interests govern my engagements and leisure as his work does his, so his work controls the household.[6]

Up at six, she took the dog for a walk and fetched the newspaper, laid out his clothes (he did not know where to find them) while he shaved and bathed, sat down with him over a cooked breakfast while he read the newspaper from cover to cover. Once he was off to work she got down to the housework. 'A home', she wrote, 'is a sort of beloved vampire that needs constant attention.' Her standards of cleanliness were high, and she often spent the whole day over it.[7] Celia Fremlin, a Mass-Observation full timer who had been a participant observer in domestic service before the war, believed that women like Eleanor with easily maintained homes, no children, and a woman to do the rough work, took pride in 'having no time', cultivating their self-imposed burdens in a desperate attempt to hide from themselves the futility of their existence.[8] It is true that contemporary advice literature advocated high standards, but Eleanor herself was aware that many of her neighbours managed the housework with far more time to spare than she achieved.[9] When the house was hit by a blast from a landmine in October 1940 she took it in her stride, but the struggle to keep things clean intensified as badly damaged ceilings shed plaster dust until, two years later, Horace finally agreed to have them repaired. With less regular help after her daily maid left to work in Woolwich Arsenal in November 1941 the housework became still more onerous, squeezing the time available for shopping, visiting friends, social work or writing. Trying to fit in more than she could manage she ran out of time, and was occasionally caught out 'all grubby... unwashed and unchanged' when Horace came home from work.[10]

As Horace gained responsibility at work—he was put in charge of all the telecommunications departments from the summer of 1942—her subordination intensified. Home from work tired and irritable, 'prowling around... emanating waves of annoyance and disapproval', he demanded to be waited upon while offering little companionship in return.[11] They never went out together in the evenings, except to visit her parents (when she looked after her mother and the two men talked shop), or to play darts with friends across the street. When Horace listened to music she had to keep quiet and sit still; if she got up and tiptoed out of the room to answer her mother on the phone it destroyed his pleasure. Always a workaholic, he now went in to the office most weekends and brought work home regularly in the evenings, often typing half the night. But 'he loves company, someone to wait on him, when working', and she accepted that it was his right to have her on call to make him a cup of tea or read a draft.[12] She herself was seldom able to write when Horace was around. The Mass-Observation diary was a secret and could only be done when he was at work, but even her letter writing, though mostly to his own relatives in Australia, was a major source of irritation. He was, she believed, unconsciously jealous of her 'attention being wholly absorbed in something not to do with himself or his comfort'.[13] 'It would be so nice [if I] could sit down too of an evening while he's working', she wrote, wistfully.[14] But any assertion of her right to write was perceived as a direct challenge to his authority: 'I much too independent of recent years and it must stop . . . if we are to continue happily', he proclaimed, accusing her of sacrificing housework to her writing.[15] Though fully aware that her writing constituted her 'final bid for autonomy', she responded by attempting to resist its allure:

I did ache to write some letters today but there was so much else to do. H. has been so very sweet since I've desisted—but I don't know how long I can last. I'm getting bored and fed up with my work—it all seems to no purpose if I can't tell anyone of my daily doings.[16]

A year later, requested to read over a letter she had written to his parents, Horace gave full vent to his irritation about his wife's compulsive need to 'tell [her] daily doings':

He dissatisfied, said he could make no sense of my letters, they are just one breathless jumble. Too journalese. Why do I have to write such a long letter . . . Why can't I write a letter like a normal person. I'm not a Gertrude Stein. I apologised. Sat up till midnight, wrote them a prim little bread and butter letter full of 'I do hopes' and 'we are pleased to say' sort of thing. Seemed to me like so much cotton wool in one's mouth but H pronounced it an excellent letter, and why can't I always write like that . . . I gave up and went to bed.[17]

Bathed in his contempt, she lay awake a long time thinking things over:

I had to agree with H that I almost illiterate . . . I'm so anxious to grasp at every experience that passes & to know something of everything, I just skim the top & never become proficient in a thing. Can I alter myself now at 40? I doubt it. I couldn't even stick up for my own point of view tonight—if I had done so we would have had a first class row. I apologised, as I always do. Blast.[18]

The young girl who had cheerfully abandoned pursuits deemed frivolous by her husband became a middle-aged woman vaguely aware of her unfulfilled potential: 'I suppose I've been a fool all these years being rather the woman H wanted me to be rather than being myself—so much of me is not what he and Parents like.'[19] Despite this she remained in thrall to him, desperate for his approval and affection, pathetically grateful when she got it: 'I love him so when he gives me a chance and does not rage.'[20] Complimented on her clothes on one of the rare occasions when he took her out for the evening she remarked, wistfully: 'If only he realised how it enslaves me when he says a few kind words and means them.'[21] But he was also frequently *un*kind.

It was the strain of the blitz that was responsible for the worst of their rows. After a land mine blew in their windows and removed two thirds of the roof tiles in October 1940, Horace became increasingly anxious about Eleanor's relatively relaxed attitude to taking shelter during air raids. Unable to talk this through, their differences spilled over into bitter accusations:

> I foolishly said I did not care if I get bombed. H. perfectly furious replied, 'what about him then' and I unkindly cut back, 'then he'd have no one to wait on him', or words to that effect. After that I was told I could do what I liked, he'd stick it till after the war but from now onwards I'd get no affection or consideration from him . . . He knows how to get me every time. I begged pardon most humbly and H stormed out into the barrage . . . I so distraught and unhappy. More so than I can ever remember, for H. also said I was losing all sense of love making and losing intuition about it too.[22]

Hostilities thawed and their sex life recovered. She knew how to seduce him when she felt like it, and, though the diary contains no very intimate details, she had read Havelock Ellis and Van de Velde's sex manual and probably knew a lot more about sexual technique than did most of her contemporaries. Her mother told her the facts of life as she grew up, and she never had the frights and alarms that, she gathered, other girls had. But mother told her not to expect to enjoy sex when she married: it was what men did and she must be 'accessible' and 'put up with it' to have children: 'it was also a way of paying for her keep . . . Marriage proved a great surprise to me but I was lucky in having a husband with great understanding. It has been a perpetual surprise ever since. I have tried to explain it to my Mother on several occasions but she thinks me unduly sensual.'[23] Although occasionally subject to Horace's unwanted attentions she also had to be careful not to overtax him, since lovemaking generally left him feeling rotten the next day.

The worst of all their rows occurred during renewed bombing in July 1941, revealing a selfishness and brutality in Horace's treatment of his wife that she found it difficult to come to terms with. Running for the shelter in the middle of the night she fell over a gate he had just erected on the garden path to keep her dog out of his vegetable patch: 'H. came down cursing and flashed torch onto my face. He dropped it and buried his face in his hands saying I'd lost three teeth. Instead of he comforting me, I had to cheer him. The irony of it amused me and I laughed hysterically.' He cursed the dog; she retaliated by complaining that he put his garden before everything else, and immediately regretted her words:

I do say the most awful things. H. bounced out into the raid and wept, but with rage that time...The shock came down on me then, so I hugged one of the shelter bottles and took sips of water, meantime feeling so perfectly unhappy and the future hopelessly hopeless. Later H came back and I apologised. [!]

Although he eventually calmed down enough to make her a cup of tea, she remained in disgrace, and he went on about the spoiled dog, her unkindness to him, his pain at the loss of her prominent front teeth—'about my one good asset [she believed] on the appearance sheet'. Horace's reaction fed her own misery and guilt, which she compared to her blackest-ever moment, years before, 'when I came out of the chloroform and guessed my baby was dead'.[24] Horace, she implies elsewhere in the diary, had behaved with similar selfishness on that occasion. She was deeply hurt. The dentist did a good job on restoring her teeth, but seven months later she still felt unable to respond fully in their lovemaking:

He doesn't rouse me at all...Some things died inside me...when we had that awful scene the night I bust my teeth last summer. For weeks after that I couldn't bear him near me. That's alright now, and I'm still fond of him. He's my life. I don't particularly, no, I definitively don't want anyone else. Passion has to die some time or other, I had a long innings in my affection for him. I can't complain.[25]

Such resignation was the hallmark of her marriage: 'Someone has to serve genius,' she wrote in March 1941, 'and you must be of the door-mat type to be able to do it. I'd not change, but,' she added wistfully, 'I do wish I sometimes got more consideration.'[26]

Class identity

Beyond the marital relationship, Eleanor certainly did not think of herself as a door mat. She had a clear sense of her status in the wider society. At the head of each instalment of the diary she sent to Mass-Observation, she described herself as a 'middle-class housewife' living in Blackheath, a part of Kentish London whose 'decaying gentility', she wrote snobbishly, made it 'quite equal to the older parts of Hampstead'.[27] There was, however, nothing decaying about Eleanor's gentility. They lived in a modern semi in a suburban street two miles up the hill from the Siemens works. As Horace's career advanced some of their friends were surprised that they did not move to the more up-market, Victorian district of Blackheath where Eleanor's parents lived. But she was comfortable in her suburb, where she could feel superior to most of the neighbours—'fussy little middle (working) class housewives', she described them, rather vaguely.[28] Her own class identity owed much to the mobility and dynamism of the international Anglophone bourgeoisie to which her menfolk belonged. Her grandfathers had both been successful businessmen in the USA, and Horace's father, who had migrated to Australia in the 1880s, was the adventurous younger son from an upper-middle-class English family, 'county folk who hunt and do all the right things, sending their children to Winchester, Eton and Marlborough'. Horace's English relatives rather looked down on Eleanor as their nephew's 'American wife', disliking particularly what she described as her 'unpleasant speaking voice with an indefinable accent' (reflecting, perhaps, the peripatetic childhood).[29] She responded to such condescension with the pride of a technocratic middle-class, confident that her husband's work was contributing to 'progress' while his gentry relatives, for all their distinction in public life, would leave nothing of value behind them. She was much more comfortable with the Australian branch of the family with whom she kept up a vigorous correspondence. Her friendship network, apart from two or three long-standing women friends with whom she kept in contact, consisted largely of other businessmen and their wives, including several of Horace's subordinates at Siemens as well as the people she saw most of, the neighbours across the road, Woodie (manager of a sack-making factory) and his wife Madge. Among these friends she distinguished, slightly shamefacedly ('Damn it all. I am a snob'), between those, like Woodie, 'whose polish is but a veneer' (he had risen from humble origins) and those, like herself and Horace, who had 'breeding'.[30]

Like others of her class it was domestic service that gave Eleanor her most intimate contact with working-class people. Kathleen, her daily maid, had started with her in 1934, aged 20, working seven days a week (including Christmas Day) with an afternoon off and occasional holidays. Eleanor came to see the younger woman as a friend, visiting her home and inviting her mother to lunch, glimpsing aspects of working-class life (an interest in Labour politics, stoicism in the face of bombing) which she compared favourably with the more empty-headed of her middle-class acquaintances. The two women shared confidences about their respective love lives, Eleanor encouraging Kathleen to make the best of an affair with a married man, Kathleen providing moral support when she overheard Eleanor's arguments with her husband. But they were still mistress and maid, and Eleanor, annoyed at Kathleen's sulks when required to adapt shared routines of housework to her mistress' convenience, confided to her diary that Kathleen 'has rather overstepped the line between employer and employed'; 'I spoil her and now am paying for it.'[31] In August 1941, dismayed by Kathleen's decision to desert her for war work, Eleanor's first reaction was 'to sack her on the spot, [but] realized that that would merely spite myself. So I just said that if that was the case I did not feel inclined to give her any further holiday . . . I would get as much service out of her as possible.'[32] Despite this petulance, Eleanor was pleased that Kathleen kept in touch after she left, interested in her tales of shell filling in Woolwich Arsenal.

Personal cleanliness was, for Eleanor, an important marker of social status: 'My peace of mind . . . depends on my appearance. I must always be clean . . . neat and well-groomed . . . The amount of care expended . . . on one's toilet is a definite index to character.'[33] The live-in maid employed by Woodie and Madge, who never took a bath, was a constant source of complaint, as was one of her mother's maids who 'has only changed her undies once in five weeks'.[34] But it was not only working-class girls who served as foils to Eleanor's powerful sense of the well-turned out female body as an icon of respectability. She was equally disturbed by the persistently dirty face of one middle-class acquaintance, and mocked the traditionalist resistance of Horace's posh relatives to modern norms of female cleanliness: 'Among my husband's family one has to be as nature made one, it is not considered nice to improve on it.' So the women did not shave their legs and, since 'ladies do not perspire . . . deodorants are not necessary'.[35] Eleanor belonged to a _modern_ middle class which took care not to smell.

Friendship

Friendship was a large part of Eleanor's life. One long-standing women friend, Gretchen, who she had known since childhood, died slowly from cancer during the first nine months of the war. Another, Gladys, an art teacher and book illustrator who had been with Eleanor at Goldsmiths, lived out of London, and when she came to stay the two women talked long into the night. The friend she saw most frequently was her neighbour Madge. They popped in and out of each other's houses, drank tea, had lunch together, gossiped about the neighbours, servants, friends, relatives, husbands. Eleanor took a close interest in Madge's two boys, Royden (born 1930) and particularly Ken (born 1936) who she adored, looking after him when Madge's voluntary hospital work kept her away from home during the day. The ups and downs of her relationship with Madge occupy many pages of the diary, complicated—as in most of her friendships with married women—by Eleanor's flirtation with her husband.

In her 1939 'life story' Eleanor reported that she had two men friends. One of these, Bill Boswell, was a tall, ruggedly handsome Australian scientist (after the war he was to become a leading figure in the politics of Australian science) who had been in England for sixteen months from the autumn of October 1936 attached to Siemens.[36] During this time, some of which coincided with a long absence of Horace on a trip to Australia, Bill had become her closest friend and confident: 'nothing was ever secret between us'.[37] Subsequently she wrote him long letters, unfailingly noted the anniversary of his departure from England in her diary, sorely missed their uninhibited conversations, and continued to 'instinctively turn to him for comment' when thinking over her doings of the day.[38] Visiting his old landlady she found it 'soothing to sit in that neat little breakfast room where Bill used to eat'; made excuses to go upstairs to sneak a nostalgic peep at the room he had slept in; and left feeling 'so happy...all clean and comfortable inside', delighted at the landlady's confirmation of Bill's devotion to her.[39] She had struggled not to fall in love with him, and their physical relationship does not seem to have gone beyond the occasional 'very brotherly' kiss.[40] Nevertheless the memory of Bill was, she wrote in 1943, 'the only stable thing in my world'; stable, perhaps, precisely because he was now on the other side of the world and happily married.[41]

After Bill left she tried to replace him with Madge's husband, Woodie (short for his surname, Woodford). In the early months of the war, with less opportunity for private chats with Woodie, she feared that they were 'drifting apart'.[42] Despite this he felt free in the summer of 1940 to unburden himself about not having been in Madge's bed for six weeks: 'She does the love-making in that family and he has to wait for a sign.' Although Eleanor 'felt a bit inclined to have a grumble myself' she decided, without apparently noticing the double standard involved, that this would be unfair to Horace since the two men were as much good friends with each other as were Eleanor and Madge.[43] They did however talk about Horace's refusal to take her out anywhere and Woodie, like Bill before him, ticked her off for being such a doormat.

In September 1940, as the blitz intensified, Madge and Ken were evacuated to Buckinghamshire (the older son was already lodged in Tunbridge Wells where he was at school), leaving Woodie alone in the house with Rose, the attractive (if smelly) young live-in maid. Horace, who seems to have had no inkling of Eleanor's interest in Woodie, immediately decided, on the thinnest of evidence, that Woodie and Rose must be sleeping together. What followed was a comedy of unconsummated passions: Eleanor and Rose jealous of one another, Madge jealous of Rose and Eleanor in turn, and Woodie, who had the good fortune to be liked by everyone, illicitly enjoying the attentions of both his maid and his neighbour's wife, while doing his best to reassure Madge, whom he loved unreservedly.

Eleanor, unsympathetically critical of Madge's decision to run away from the blitz, felt that if Woodie, who had seemed 'very sprightly' since his wife left, was indeed having an affair it would serve Madge right for deserting him.[44] But she was horrified at the thought that the affair was with Rose. On the night that landmines wrecked the street, Eleanor's main concern, emerging from her shelter, was not the damage to her own house, but Woodie's safety. When he emerged, praising Rose for coming upstairs in her bare feet over broken glass and plaster to see if he was alright, Eleanor found herself paying 'more attention to him than to what had happened all around and . . . really jealous of Rose'. These feelings surprised her, since 'jealousy is one of the things I really despise and here I was indulging in it myself. Middle aged madness.'[45] Age was certainly in play, but so was class. The really horrifying thought was that Eleanor's imagined rival was a mere servant girl, and a smelly one at that. The fact that Woodie didn't appear to mind the smell seemed to Eleanor all of a piece with his lack of 'breeding', a penchant for working-class girls going hand in hand apparently with his board school accent, unrefined table manners, and taste for crude sexual innuendo. That she herself could enjoy his rougher side only made her jealousy of Rose all the more humiliating. But it was all in her imagination. Though Woodie admitted he found Rose attractive, and Rose certainly fancied him sufficiently to flounce out of the room when he was visited by 'that old mother Humphries', he was in fact irritated by the maid's advances.[46]

Over the next few months the intimacy between Eleanor and Woodie increased, with long chats over lunch or on roundabout car journeys when he gave her a lift. They talked about their marriages, accusing each other of letting their respective partners push them around. She dismissed, perhaps a little too vehemently, his worries that Horace might be jealous of their friendship: 'Could not be anything in W's absurd idea,' she reassured herself in the diary: 'I know H. well enough to detect the slightest variation in mood.'[47] With Madge away, Eleanor played the role of wife, waving Woodie off to work as his car passed her house every morning. Once they laughed at the discovery that each had simultaneously resisted an impulse to phone and meet for lunch. Another time they went to the pub while Horace worked late: 'I rather sleepy and tottery when we left but he perceptibly more cheerful.'[48] He gave her a romantic novel, which she found significant. In June 1941 he took her away for the weekend. Although the purpose of the trip was to visit Madge and Ken, the drive out to Buckinghamshire sounded more like a lovers' tryst. They stopped for drinks three times on the way: 'I quite merry by then . . . I felt young and gay. We bought biscuits and both ate steadily through the packet to sober down.' They talked about Madge's jealousy of Rose, but Madge's barbed comment on her son's delight in seeing Eleanor may have been more to the point: 'all my men folk seem to go for you'.[49]

Shortly before this trip, Woodie had finally succumbed to Madge's demand that Rose—who had behaved offensively on a weekend visit, dressed to kill and bragging to Madge's landlady about her power over Woodie—should be sacked, but he refused Eleanor's offers to enable him to stay in the house alone by providing meals on the grounds that Horace would resent the intrusion. After Rose left, Woodie discouraged Eleanor from visiting him at home because 'he did not want the neighbours talking . . . At times the darling is quite archaic.'[50] But it was more than that. By the autumn Eleanor felt that a 'wall [had] grown between us', Woodie was often aloof and distant, and with Madge's return home imminent in the new year he responded to Eleanor's birthday present (a pair of braces) by coldly insisting that 'from now private things must cease between us'.[51] Hurt and puzzled she wondered whether it was the loss of her front teeth that had made the difference, but gradually the truth dawned: 'Evidently I nearly made a fool of myself over the man . . . It's queer how one can hold a man's attention as long as you're only mildly interested—directly you begin to care they cool.'[52] Woodie backed off because he feared the flirtation was becoming too serious and he didn't want to jeopardize his marriage. But the hurt lingered. When, at Christmas 1942, Woodie, for the first time in the ten years they had known each other, declined the opportunity to kiss her under the mistletoe, she cursed her susceptibility: 'I doubt if I've ever felt so hurt in my whole life . . . so ridiculous and yet so out of proportionately serious to me . . . At my age, to behave like a jilted kid.'[53]

Despite the self-disparaging remarks about her appearance at the time of her accident, Eleanor had a positive sense of her own sexual attractiveness. She was not above deliberately flashing a shapely leg at bystanders when getting out of Woodie's car; she enjoyed sending out sexual vibes to younger men—a stranger on a bus; an Australian friend of Bill's in the RAF who visited a few times. She had conducted long-standing flirtations with two of Horace's married colleagues. Pat, who had been sweet on her before either of them were married, contrived the odd kiss and hand-holding when Horace wasn't looking. But Pat was an ambitious man and she suspected that his keenness to visit reflected the politics of advancement at work: 'I fear that at the moment I am only attractive in connection with the future H. appears to be arriving at.'[54] Of Ernie's devotion, on the other hand, she had no doubts—'he . . . loves me more than anyone had ever done'—but this left her feeling 'mean at not being able to get thrilled over him' herself.[55] Nevertheless she appreciated his attentions, especially when promotion to a more responsible position increased his self-confidence: 'Always rather pretty he is now definitely good looking and really manly. First time his kisses ever felt masculine . . . Gave me quite a man hug.'[56] When Pat and Eddie called at the same time, she had fun manipulating their competition for her affections. Relatively powerless with the men she really cared for—Horace, Woodie—she much enjoyed her capacity to 'wangle and manage . . . men I don't care two hoots over'.[57] With Pat and Ernie she behaved, as Bill had put it in terms she was happy to accept, like 'a bit of a bitch'.[58]

Consoling the wife of another of Horace's colleagues, who was misbehaving himself with his 'malodorous little secretary' (body odour, again) Eleanor 'tried to explain to her that most men wandered physically at times. I remember my first awakening to H's interest in pretty faces, I created a scene and wept. But H. has never made a fool of himself. Bless his heart—at least I've never found out about any extensive philanderings.'[59] Horace, most of the time, was similarly relaxed, and she could play her little sexual games without fear of serious consequences:

Pat called lunch time for coffee. I am always very amused, I believe H is secretly jealous. Pat always tries to wangle me on my own, H never leaves us alone for more than a minute. All done so nicely no one could say anything. My conduct is more than correct so H dare not mention it to me.[60]

When, however, Horace in one of their rows accused her of neglecting him while 'being very nice to all the other men who came around here', she turned a cold shoulder to a dismayed and uncomprehending Eddie, unlucky enough to call a few days later.[61]

On one of the rare occasions when she reflected more generally on her flirtatiousness, Eleanor wondered whether it could be explained by the fact that she had no children to occupy her attention. She felt no guilt, insisting that she always tried 'to play fair to' Horace, by which she meant, presumably, that she did not sleep with her various conquests. 'I'm not immoral,' she wrote, 'only unmoral in outlook.'[62] Whatever she meant by this distinction, it testifies to a more general refusal on her part to engage with ethical or any other abstractions. She lived a life of concrete, immediate, personal relationships, and had neither the wish nor the ability to stand back and judge herself, or indeed others, by abstract standards of behaviour. This is what prevented her from seeing her own subordination to Horace in anything but personal terms. And if she lacked a politics of private life, she was equally reluctant, or unable, to engage with the impersonality of the public sphere.

Voluntary work

Eleanor was a conventionally a-political Conservative. Apart from paying dues to the local party and voting Tory she had never been politically

active and held no very clear political views. Among her women friends
and colleagues politics were little discussed. She listened to her husband
and his friends complain about state interference in business life and
indiscipline among the workers, but, partly under the influence of her
Labour-supporting maid, thought that a post-war Labour government
might be a good thing, providing a fair deal to the workers. Due to paper
shortages, they could not get their *Daily Telegraph* every week and took
the *Herald* in its place. Horace and Woodie considered it a rag, but she
rather liked seeing the other side. She had a vague sympathy for egalitarian
ideas, reading Acland's *Unser Kampf*—admirable but 'so childish'—and
moved by Priestley's 1940 Postscripts.[63] A few days after her street was
blitzed, chatting with the neighbours, she caused offence by suggesting
that it was better the bombs fell on their own district than on the more
densely populated working-class areas of Greenwich and Woolwich:

A very strained and huffy silence, and I was told that middle class people had more
to lose than the poor, whose homes would be rebuilt for them but around here
folk had sunk their last savings into buying these little houses.[64]

But she was not above the politics of naked self-interest herself, believing
that Bevin should be 'absolutely ruthless' with trade union resistance
to the conscription of labour, while fiercely defending, in the face of
Kathleen's scorn, the right of women like herself to claim exemption
from conscription for their maids (and of course themselves) so that they
could continue to contribute to the war effort through the relatively
undemanding routines of voluntary work.[65] The nearest that Eleanor came
to a deeply felt politics was in her bitterness about the way the war had
exacerbated the servant problem. After Kathleen left domestic standards
dropped: 'We have breakfast and lunch in the kitchen ... on Sundays ... I
tremble lest someone call but so far we have escaped detection.'[66] Although
she found alternative domestic help she did not dare to employ 'more
than casual assistance' for fear that this would lead to her being conscripted
into full-time work. The result, as she complained in the last thing she
ever wrote for Mass-Observation, a directive reply in November 1944,
was that everything she did at home or in her social work was rushed and
scamped, and that she was left with no time of her own to read, write,
go to the theatre, cinema, visit or entertain friends: 'If time for such is
ever snatched it takes months to retrieve the work neglected.'[67] It is hard,
reading this, to remember that she was a childless housewife in a modern

labour-saving house. Self-imposed the burdens might have been, but they were genuinely felt.

Although Horace ran the fire-watching rota in their street, Eleanor declined to take on the parallel role of 'street leader' for the WVS, preferring to fulfil her social responsibilities away from home. Since 1925 she had been involved in friendly visiting for the Invalid Children's Aid Association (ICAA) in Deptford, and during the war she did her rounds at least once a week, collecting contributions from working-class housewives towards the upkeep of children convalescing in homes run by the Association.[68] With her regulars she established the kind of relationship—a carefully gauged mixture of sympathy, respect, condescension, and discipline—that had been the staple of female philanthropy since Victorian times.[69] 'Poor dear Mrs Stevens', for example, 'gives a welcoming smile when she sees who it is' despite knowing that 'I've come to get as much out of her as possible.' The two women exchange gifts, a tomato for Mrs Humphries, Bournvita and tinned milk for Mrs Stevens; but it was clear who was in charge. 'She looks so hopefully in her greasy little purse—always seems surprised when there is not much there. I hate taking her few pennies but she must learn to pay her debts, so I do.'[70] With Mrs Skivington, who was less obliging—'slammed the gate in my face when I asked had she anything for me'—Eleanor felt entitled to use deception in her efforts to instil financial discipline, collecting money that was not (yet) owed:

How wild she would be if she knew the assessment was dropped and she has already paid in full for the repair [of her invalid son's jacket]. It was my idea to try to collect the rest of the pound, they are always such poor payers, it would be a help to have something in hand for next time Alfie's jacket comes adrift.[71]

Though the visiting was sometimes an unwelcome chore, it clearly helped to affirm Eleanor's superior place in the scheme of things, while at the same enabling her to pull rank over friends and relatives who knew little of the lives of the poor.

On the outbreak of war she offered to spend one afternoon a week doing secretarial work for the newly established Citizen's Advice Bureau (CAB). Because of her previous experience with the ICAA the other volunteers looked to her for advice, but Eleanor resisted pressure to take on a more responsible role: 'I'd rather work than run things.'[72] She preferred not to interact with the clients, happy to stay in the background copying and tidying up the accounts. After two years of this work, in November 1941, she quit, unwilling to spare the time from her housework now that Kathleen was leaving.

Meanwhile, in March 1941, she had become more active in the ICAA, rejoining the committee (of which she had been a founder member in 1925) and giving another afternoon a week for secretarial work in the office. Here, as well, she resisted responsibility, refusing to chair meetings, and choosing to make the tea even though that meant missing a good deal of the committee business. In the spring of 1942, due to register at the Labour Exchange and worried that her ICAA commitments might be insufficient to earn exemption from conscription into war work, she resumed her afternoon with the Citizen's Advice Bureau, only to give it up again nine months later when (anticipating Bevin's insistence that childless wives must work) she seized the opportunity presented by the departure of the ICAA's secretarial assistant to take on the job, working four afternoons a week. Treasured by the full-timer, she was able to fit the work flexibly around her household tasks. Both at the CAB and with the ICAA what she valued most was the quiet, backstage secretarial work, a soothing counterpoint to the emotional roller coaster of her difficult marriage.

In taking on this voluntary work Eleanor was driven at least as much by the threat of conscription, as by her desire to serve the community. Where other middle-aged women—notably Nella Last—seized the opportunity provided by the wartime demand for voluntary workers to legitimate their adventures into active citizenship beyond the housewife role, Eleanor had no inclination to follow the call of the WVS leader, Lady Reading, to put 'nation before husband':

I'm frankly angling [she wrote in the summer of 1942] to have just enough outside work to keep me free from being directed to a part-time job if I'm ever interviewed. Told H. about it later, it is a job to get him to listen to any of my affairs but he quite interested this time and hopes it comes off. I wonder if he is secretly dreading in case I do have to go out to work.[73]

Horace remained throughout her first priority, and her voluntary work was designed more as a defence against the state taking her away from wifely duties than as a means of asserting herself against his authority.

The work itself was undemanding, but social relations in the voluntary sector were a minefield of jealousies, misunderstandings, class resentments, and personal rivalries. Unlike Nella Last she did not see herself as a significant player in these power struggles, and was content to observe, fascinated by the personalities involved. Some of the conflicts which she recorded involved significant differences over policy—for example the CAB's move away from the interrogating aura of charity with which its first full-timer, true to the traditions of the Charity Organization Society (the local CAB's parent organization), had infused its work.[74] This, however, was not what interested Eleanor, who skipped lightly over the issues of principle, treating them as mere background to her real subject, personality.

An example of Eleanor's observational style is the long account she gave of an emergency ICAA committee meeting in March 1942, called to reconsider an earlier decision to sack a typist because she had declared herself to be a conscientious objector. Head office objected, their policy being that personal convictions could not be grounds for dismissal. Somewhat reluctantly, Mr Sherwood, a 'perky little cockney' who chaired the local hospital board and had recently taken over as chair of the ICAA committee, thought they would have to bow to higher authority, but the long-serving president and his wife, an upper-class couple with a large house and estate in Chislehurst, argued furiously for the committee's right to do as it pleased, even offering to fund legal action if necessary. 'We could not employ a "gel" who held such views,' protested Mrs Wheen. Some months previously this lady had distinguished herself, discussing the case of a working-class client who claimed that her housekeeping money was insufficient to pay her debts to the association, by remarking: 'I can't see that at all ... there is so little in the shops to buy these days ... I spend less and less on housekeeping as the months go by ...'. During the awkward silence that followed the chairman had caught Eleanor's eye and winked: 'Seeing I was facing Mrs Wheen', she wrote, 'I do hope my face was as blank as I tried to make it.' Feelings ran high during the emergency meeting, and Mr Sherwood, 'evidently very class conscious', 'glared', 'barked', and 'snarled' at the Wheens, while Eleanor, worrying that the ICAA might lose their patronage, found herself transfixed by the 'the veins in Mr W's face and neck pulsing harder and harder'. At the end of her detailed blow-by-blow account Eleanor felt she had not done justice to the occasion, adding apologetically that she 'ought to have taken notes, it was all so quick and [I] could not take in every rise and fall of emotion'. But she had found the time 'at intervals during the afternoon ... to analyse what it was [that] made class distinctions'. Surprisingly, given that she voted with the majority against them, and given her critical attitude to her husband's upper-class relatives, she found that her social sympathies lay more with the Wheens than with their 'cockney' persecutor: 'The Wheens . . . came in all county. (I'm not being sarcastic there). Nice voices, everything just right about them.' It was a question of dress sense as much as of accent: 'the others were as nicely dressed, one or two very wrongly but expensively clothed', and they, in their ignorance, probably thought that the Wheens, and Eleanor herself who did not dress up for meetings, were shabby. But, 'I felt we looked "right". I'm as snobby as anyone else, very humiliating.' What really interested her was 'the rise and fall of emotions', and her own complicated feelings about class, not the merits or demerits of sacking conscientious objectors.[75]

The flirtatious eroticism that played such an important part in Eleanor's private life did not desert her even in the female community of the office. A mutual fascination grew up between herself and Miss B., the full-time secretary at the ICAA, an unhappy, overworked young woman with a stern Christian sense of duty:

She is always asking me odd questions, with great interest, about myself . . . I forget about her being there, look up suddenly to find her watching me with great intentness. Instinctively I begin to harden my face and feel the makings of a blush spreading, in that way natural to the sexes when caught unaware by one of the opposite. Sometimes the air almost tingles.[76]

If this was a sexual overture, it was one that Eleanor had enjoyed fostering over the previous year recording small intimacies in her diary with reflections such as: 'I do believe the woman likes me. Strangely gratifying.'[77] When Miss B. remarked in her 'meditative sort of way' how much she enjoyed her company, Eleanor always had 'a feeling that at any moment she may start making love to me', however 'preposterous' this might seem given the other woman's strict religious views. Not altogether displeased at the prospect, Eleanor compared her feelings for Miss B. to her feelings for Ernie, the colleague of her husband's whose devotion she never doubted: 'I do wish she was not quite so mannish. At times she is disconcertingly like Ernie . . . the masculine is as predominant in her as the feminine is in Ernie. In lots of ways they are very much alike.'[78] Whatever she was discussing, Eleanor always came back to the personal. In the office as much as in her private life what intrigued her were the dynamics of personal relationships, issues of social status, and the play of eroticism in everyday life.

'My secret vice'

Although she prided herself on the sophistication of her musical and literary tastes, high culture did not play a very significant part in Eleanor's sense of herself. Unlike the neighbours she and Horace enjoyed listening to classical music—above all Sibelius whose music she wanted played at her funeral—and they had treated themselves to a very superior radio for this purpose. She read light fiction and some books about current affairs, but only scanned the newspapers and weeklies (unlike Horace who read them from cover to cover over his meals). Despite living within easy reach of central London she made no use of its cultural resources. It was the cinema, which she visited occasionally with Madge on what they ironically called their 'chars night out', which did most to stir her emotions. The film of 'How Green Was My Valley' brought her closest to an epiphanic moment:

> I can't describe my reaction to it. I hate undue emotionalism, seldom cry over tragedy but that did get me down. Not that I really wept, the tears just welled up and over . . . so much emotion had produced a state of ecstasy.

This was not something she expected to be able to share with Horace. But ecstasy turned to dismay, that evening, when, to her surprise, 'he wanted me to go to his bed'. Lovemaking was 'the very last thing' she had on her mind and it seemed, in the circumstances, almost sacrilegious, 'like coming from dark dawn communion service (when church meant something to one) and going to a brothel. I think it was the very first time he has just had my body.'[79] Afterwards, back in her own bed, she found herself, for the first time in many years, saying her prayers. Brought up in the Church of England, religion had gradually faded out of her life. Horace, reacting against a strict and pious Baptist upbringing, had no time for it, and Eleanor took her cue from him. By the late 1930s his indifference had weaned her away from any 'active and outward observances'. Tempted to go to church at Easter, she desisted since 'H would have thought me mad'.[80] Earlier in her marriage her loss of faith had worried her, but now she accepted the 'fuddled' and 'confused' nature of her own beliefs, 'content to be passive in thought at the moment'.[81] Her resort to prayer, on the night of 'How Green as my Valley', reflected deep and confused emotions, but not a return to religious faith: 'I must be on the verge of a breakdown,' was her conclusion.[82]

What kept her sane was her writing. Eleanor's daily life—the endless housework, the ups and downs of her relationships with husband, servants, neighbours, colleagues, friends—seemed to her largely without meaning or purpose unless she could find the time to write about it. Given Horace's attitude to her letter-writing it is hardly surprising that she felt the need to hide from him the fact that she was also typing thousands of words every week for Mass-Observation. He knew about her interest in the organization—they listened together to radio talks by MO's director, Tom Harrisson; he read and discussed with her at least one MO publication; and she was quite open in distributing copies of the in-house newsletter, *US*, to his parents and various friends. Given that he supplied the typewriter ribbons (for which relief he deserves the gratitude of the eye-strained historian poring over microfilm of faintly typed text) he must have known she was doing a great deal of writing. Probably he just lazily assumed it was her eternal, wordy letters. Absorbed in his work he really wasn't interested in what she did when he was not around, so long as his domestic comforts were sustained. They never seem to have talked, for example, about her charity work, although she listened dutifully to every twist and turn of his problems at the factory. Horace was one of those middle-class husbands, identified in 1941 by the co-founder of the Marriage Guidance Council, as being 'quite uninterested in their wives' lives' and what they termed—confusing insensitivity with level-headedness—'women's rubbish'.[83]

Finding time to write was Eleanor's constant preoccupation. Unlike Nella Last, the only diarist to rival her in quantity, she was unable to write every day. So long as she had daily domestic help she was able to put aside Kathleen's afternoon off for typing the diary, but this was seldom enough and she squeezed in bits of typing whenever opportunity arose—when Horace was late back from work, during her fire-watching, and when he slept. During daylight raids she wrote by hand in the shelter. She often fell behind, and was frequently writing up the diary a week or more after the event, sometimes from brief notes take at the time, but more often from memory. Although she occasionally apologized to MO for the scrappy and unrevised character of her diary, she was not really interested in the quality of the writing. Very occasionally there are signs of an attempt at literary shaping, but it is clear that what mattered to Eleanor was simply to get the information down on paper.

Why did she do it? Partly because she identified with, and was pleased to serve, the goals of Mass-Observation as she understood them. She was a conscientious observer, recording everyday events, conversations, and overheard remarks; she answered the monthly directives when she could find the time; her 'day surveys', running to as many as four or five closely typed pages, are among the most exhaustive supplied by any of the mass observers; and during the blitz she made time after Horace left for work each morning to supplement her own personal diary accounts with detailed reports on the effects of bombing in the neighbourhood. She was proud that, unlike Madge, she had not run away from the blitz, and her conscientious reporting of its effects was perhaps the closest that she came to a disinterested embrace of the obligations of citizenship. On the night her own house was wrecked she surprised Horace with her insouciance:

Don't worry, dear, it doesn't really matter, we are alright and you know I've expected this to happen from the start...I felt strangely elated...I was already mentally writing down all that had happened.[84]

Although she declared herself 'intensely interested' in the project of doc-umenting wartime life for the benefit of posterity, most of the time the public objectives of Mass-Observation were marginal to her motivation. Naturally enough she was gratified when MO thanked her for her con-tributions and when once—*only* once in all these millions of words—she found herself quoted in a MO publication. But the pleasure she got from the writing—'my secret relaxation'—was not dependent on feedback from her readers.[85]

What the diary provided for Eleanor was a technology of the self that took her momentarily out of the flux and flow of a life overwhelmingly dominated by personal relationships. She used it to analyse her feelings, rehearse her grumbles, stand back and reflect on her life (usually a rather dismal story of disappointments). But mostly it was simply the act of recording itself that she found so pleasurable. 'Before I start,' she wrote, 'I have to sit blank for a second or two and delve back and re-live the days.'[86] This was her 'secret vice', this is what she so often 'ached' to do, whether in the diary or in her letters: to suspend the flow of life for a moment in order to become 'actively conscious of being alive', to savour in memory the fleeting happenings of a day, and, by writing them down, have done with them: 'I find that once I have gone over a backday's happenings and written it down that it is difficult to relive that day at a later time...'.[87] She thought of the diary less as a duty, a contribution to the public good, than as a therapy, a source of private calm and composure: 'writing always rests me.'[88] However stretched she felt by the demands of housework, she had to make time for the diary: 'I'll not give up doing it. Often feel I ought to, when I have to leave so much else undone, [it] seems selfish to secretly have such relaxation.'[89] But without it, she feared, she would be overwhelmed by the rush and jumble of day-to-day living.

Eleanor's problem was not just that she was trapped in a patriarchal marriage: it was that she could not understand this as anything other than a function of the personal dynamics between herself and her husband. Nella Last also blamed herself—her 'weak streak'—for the oppressive nature of her marriage, but alongside this she could analyse her situation in wider cultural and historical terms: her husband's 'Victorian-Edwardian attitudes', her own intermediate position 'between Victorian submission and the today's career girls'.[90] And she was able to devise and pursue strategies, via motherhood and via her WVS activity, to enhance her sense of self-worth and her personal autonomy. Eleanor had no such proto-feminist understanding of her situation. The only time she showed any awareness of the wider cultural determinants of wifely subordination was in response to an MO directive in the summer of 1939, when she wrote that:

My Godmother, my husband's aunts and two of my friends who are about 10 years older than myself look on men as childlike gods. Beings to be deceived if you have done anything wrong, to be placated if anything has gone amiss in the house and to be petted and teased if you want anything.[91]

To the reader of her wartime diaries what is surprising about this remark is how close it is to the reality of her own marriage. That she did not see her relationship with Horace in this description testifies, not to the companionate nature of her marriage, but to her own very low expectations. Her main complaint against Horace was not that he expected her to devote herself to serving his needs, but that he showed so little appreciation of her efforts to do so. Being childless she was unable to use motherhood, as Nella did so successfully, to shift the centre of gravity within her household from the needs of the patriarch to the needs of the children. Far from the demands of motherhood serving to enhance her oppression, Nella's relationship with her children helped her to resist her husband's claims on her attention: and the children, as they grew up, lent valuable support to her struggle against her own 'weak streak'. But childlessness could, of course, have worked to Eleanor's advantage, making it easier for her to develop an independent life outside the home. Despite her longstanding involvement in voluntary work, however, she seems to have been unable to draw from this any feelings of self-worth capable of counterbalancing her sense of herself as Horace's ever-willing domestic slave.

Lacking any political analysis of her position, unable to view Horace's demands on her as anything other than the service due to genius, Eleanor conducted her quest for an independent selfhood in a fog of secretive devices and half-articulated desires. She lived in a private and personal world, with no abstract or higher principles to lend broader meanings to her life, no engagement with religion, politics or culture. She had a powerful sense of duty, but one that was narrowly focused on her duties as a wife. Her voluntary social work, substantial though it was, did nothing to refocus her sense of duty on the impersonal demands of the public world. It was in her secret writing for Mass-Observation that she felt most at home with herself, deploying all her skills as an observer of emotional life and personal relationships, and giving us a rare voice from the depths of patriarchy. It was through her flirtations that she came closest to achieving a sense of power or agency. But it would not have occurred to Eleanor—as it did to the very different woman discussed in the next chapter—to articulate a *politics* of flirtation, to claim a *right* to deploy erotic appeal as a means of enhancing personal autonomy.

6

Lillian Rogers: Birmingham flaneuse

To be modern is to find ourselves in an environment that promises us adventure, power, joy, growth, transformation of ourselves and the world—and, at the same time, that threatens to destroy everything we have, everything we know, everything we are.

(Marshall Berman, *All That Is Solid Melts Into Air: The experience of modernity* (London, 1983), 15)

L illian Rogers, wife of a garage mechanic, was the most plebeian of the nine diarists; she was also, in most understandings of the term, the most 'modern'.[1] Like Nella Last, she often complained of her husband's lack of ambition, and considered herself misplaced in the working-class district of Birmingham where they lived. Although she found satisfactions in her commitments as housewife and mother, she looked, like Nella, for a richer and fuller life. There, however, the similarity ended. Where Nella was driven by an ethic of service, and reconciled to life's disappointments by a fatalistic religion, Lillian was altogether less dutiful and more adventurous. The same age as Eleanor Humphries, she was equally convinced of her own erotic appeal; but she deployed it not, like Eleanor, as a pleasingly safe enhancement to an otherwise conventional suburban existence, but in flamboyantly role-breaking behaviour in the city streets and dance halls of central Birmingham. Although she was the least well-educated of the diarists and read comparatively little, she had an unquenchable thirst for knowledge—'my everlasting question mark look on my face', she called it—which she pursued by joining discussion groups with other active citizens and searchers after truth. Her work as a mass observer lent legitimacy to these various adventures—all undertaken in the interests of research, she claimed, more or less playfully—while at the same time helping her to establish some coherent sense of self amongst emotional and intellectual upheavals which would have surely driven a lesser woman over the edge. 'A diary', she wrote to Mass-Observation's director in July 1940, 'helps to keep one sane. Instead of my being thanked, I should thank you Mr Tom Harrisson for giving me a channel into which to pour my feelings.'

Lillian's diaries take us beyond the Victorian virtues of the older women we have considered, beyond the repression and timidity that held Eleanor Humphries in thrall, into the open horizons of a late modernity of which, for all her unique peculiarities, she can stand as an exemplary pioneer. By paying attention to the links between her conventional class and gender identity, her unconventional sexual behaviour, and the untutored intellectual curiosity that led her to delve deep into herself and her world, we can glimpse the instabilities of modern selfhood and the sources of the more complicated relationship between self and multiple identities that were to explode into cultural revolution in the 1960s and beyond.

Marriage, motherhood, milieu

Not being working-class was a central plank of Lillian's identity. Her father was a fervent Christian sectarian who had preferred preaching the gospel to earning a living in his trade as a French polisher, leaving her mother, a tailoress, to supplement the family income. When she was born in 1901, the family lived in a quiet lower middle-class street in suburban Yardley: neighbours included a teacher, several clerks, and an accountant.[2] As the fifth of nine children, Lillian was relied upon by her mother for help with the younger boys. While various siblings went off and made careers for themselves (one brother became an architect; another, a chartered accountant), Lillian seems to have been taken out of school at 14, trapped as mother's helper. This 'ruined my future and caused me to . . . grow bitter and incensed at the injustice of life. I gave up a career for my Mother . . .'.[3] She was left with an abiding sense of unfulfilled potential, further increased by chronic discomfort and fatigue which her doctors diagnosed as 'visceroptosis' (the dropping of the internal organs), a catch-all explanation fashionable in early twentieth-century medicine for symptoms which some contemporary medical opinion believed to be psychological in origin.[4] In 1928, aged 27, she married Stan, a workaholic garage mechanic who turned out to be insufficiently pushy to secure the staff position that Lillian was sure he deserved. When he was unemployed during the depths of the depression she went out to work again as a shop assistant. In 1933, when their only child, a daughter, was born the couple moved to Tyseley, a working-class neighbourhood of factories, railway lines, and council housing, where they could afford to pay the mortgage on a terraced house.

Life for Lillian had been a struggle against downward social mobility. She had no time for 'the slutty type of women' from the council estate across the road who lived in their aprons and curlers, never took a bath and spent their time gossiping on street corners, avoiding their company by shopping, not at the local Co-op, but in Acocks Green village three-quarters of a mile away, where 'the class of [shopper] is totally different. They come in from the residential areas.'[5] Watching the ebb and flow of 'the teeming masses', hundreds of workers passing her window on their daily journeys between the council estate and the local factories, she did occasionally fantasize about her capacity to interpret and speak for the needs of the working class.[6] But despite occasional moments of social optimism, she was sceptical about the possibility of educating the poor 'out of their pig-sty existence', and her distaste for the local women bordered on racism—greasy and 'dirty skinned'.[7] Skin colour mattered a lot to Lillian. She confessed to 'an innate dislike . . . I loathe coloured men', and the very sight of 'Hindus and most blacks', she told a Mass-Observation enquiry about 'your prejudices', gave her a feeling of physical disgust akin to looking at someone covered in open sores.[8] She approved of her husband's participation in a threat to down tools if 'a nigger' was taken on at his workplace, and, as for the Jews—'parasites who live on mugs like us'—she hoped that their Birmingham neighbourhood would be wiped out by Hitler's bombs.[9]

Even with the immediate neighbours, homeowners like herself, she felt she had little in common. Occasionally she exchanged books with the engine driver next door, but she found him 'not terribly intelligent' and dismissed his wife as a dull housewife with a 'small . . . country bumpkin mind'.[10] But the neighbourhood was not a total social desert. Although

Lillian's search for the civilized middle-class company to which she aspired was to lead her well beyond Tyseley, her closest female friend, Esther Empson, lived in a larger house in the next street. The Empsons were local social leaders. They ran the air raid wardens, had a car, a phone, and bookshelves for Lillian to raid. The two women chatted about everything from astral travel—'she believes we travel from planet to planet according to our endeavours' to the absurdities of male sexual behaviour: 'what a difference', wrote Lillian, 'from the nasty . . . minds of the women who are too small to think'.[11] Esther was the only person with whom she could talk freely about Mass-Observation, understanding that it was work of social importance not just a rather peculiar hobby.

One thing she shared with Esther were the concerns of motherhood. They first got to know each other just before the war, meeting their daughters at the school gates. Lillian, who had had her fill of childcare looking after younger siblings, had not wanted children of her own, but when Rachel arrived, five years into her marriage, she was determined not to treat the girl as she had been treated by her own mother. Years later, when a teacher told her that, remarkably for an only child, Rachel was the best behaved girl in the school, Lillian explained that she had endeavoured to bring her up 'on psychological lines', and never smacked her.[12] She had been impressed by Ethel Mannin's, *Common Sense and the Child*, feeling that the anarchist novelist understood 'the undercurrents and working of the human body and brain'.[13] Although confident that 6-year-old Rachel was 'self-reliant, can converse well, and isn't easily frightened', Lillian decided against evacuating her when war broke out, fearing that no one else would be able to cope with her frail health and dietary needs.[14] In the summer of 1940 she agonized over sending the child to live with her husband's cousin in New York, but decided against. Following the blitz in November—comparable in intensity to the Coventry raid a few days earlier[15]—Lillian was eventually persuaded to let her daughter go to a small country town in the East Midlands where her school was evacuated. Rachel was badly treated in her first billet, and Lillian fetched her home after a few weeks. It was not until March 1941 that she was finally settled with an acceptable family. Eighteen months later she returned home for good and, to Lillian's delight, started to do very well at school, passing the Grammar School exam at the end of 1943, and restored, Lillian wrote proudly, from 'a poor nervous little mite to a tall healthy, composed girl'.[16] By the time the diary ends four years later Rachel, aged 14, was excelling in English, biology and art, and her mother felt 'a mantle of warmth descend . . . upon me and I felt at last that my sacrifice when I was young and showed promise, had not been in vain . . .'.[17] What she meant, presumably, was that she had avoided burdening Rachel with the kind of complicated relationship she had with her own mother—a 'mother complex which caused me untold suffering'.[18] Until her late thirties, Lillian had allowed her mother to remain 'the mainspring of my life . . . risking my married happiness . . . com[ing] before my husband in my thoughts'.[19]

Being a good wife was important to Lillian. She looked after Stan, who was dogged by bronchial problems, intervening with employers and doctors to 'drag him from the grave' on at least two occasions during the war.[20] She was also instrumental in helping him negotiate terms in a succession of jobs setting up and managing repair and maintenance shops for small haulage firms and pushing him to secure a staff position, 'out of overalls'.[21] This was a doubtful blessing for Stan, who seems to have been happier as a mechanic than as a manager, but a triumph for Lillian who confided to her diary at the beginning of 1941: 'For me [Stan's new job] opens up a new future if we live to enjoy it. I pray so: a new social life for I shall leave Tyseley after the war and mix again with my equals. Oh Goody.'[22] Much of the time she thought of her marriage as one of 'harmony and friendship',[23] and even when, nerves jangled by the onset of the blitz in 1940, he disgusted her by blundering in late at night, 'coarsened with drink and bad companionship', she was anxious to explain to Mass-Observation that 'my young man', as she affectionately referred to him in the diary, was far from being the lout that this behaviour suggested: 'He is studious, terribly sensitive, his deafness has caused him to be retiring, he has a poker face to anyone meeting him, he is polite and well mannered . . . he has the . . . inborn instincts of a gentleman . . .'.[24]

Nowhere were these instincts more valued than in their sex life. Lillian had been traumatized, aged 15, by an attempted rape. She ascribed her feelings of racial disgust to an incident six years after this event, when she was panicked by an insensitive examination by a dark-skinned doctor investigating her 'visceroptosis', and as late as 1942 a consultant diagnosed a sudden loss of power in her left arm as a result of the attempted rape twenty-five years earlier. She was deeply grateful to Stan for the 'sympathy and understanding' he had shown about her 'inhibitions regarding sex'. He was, she wrote, 'an artist at lovemaking'. In the autumn of 1942 they were studying sex 'scientifically' with the aid of a borrowed copy of Norman

Haire's *Encyclopaedia of Sex* whose enlightened discussion of the female orgasm no doubt further improved Stan's artistry.[25] 'I couldn't imagine anyone else being as interesting to me,' she confided after a long winter evening on the cushions in front of the living room fire, 'for they haven't studied technique in love making as Stan has.' 'But you can't do that it isn't nice, not in the room you live in', said a shocked woman friend, confirming Lillian's belief that she and Stan were sexually 'far more advanced than others I mix with'.[26]

Lillian wrote about sexual matters with a matter-of-fact frankness that would certainly have been unusual in her milieu. Responding to a 1944 MO directive on contraception she relayed a story about the Queen meeting a woman nursing her thirteenth baby during a visit to a Liverpool maternity ward. Impressed, the Queen promised to ask the King to send her a letter: 'Thank you Mam', replied the exhausted mother, 'I 'ope it's a better one than the kind my old man gets.' Though keen on the promotion of sex education, Lillian was critical of what she saw as the anti-erotic implications of much standard contraceptive advice. 'We have had a go at making our own [contraceptives] years ago and they were quite successful, quinine and coconut butter', she explained in 1944. 'At the moment we have acquired a technique that requires nothing.'[27] Given the unpleasantness of most pre-pill methods of contraception, the withdrawal method was widely practiced in mid-twentieth-century Britain, despite being seen as psychologically damaging by much medical opinion.[28]

Stan's artistry in bed, however—or on the living room floor—was never sufficient compensation for his other deficiencies. Lillian wanted more from life than good sex. Early in 1941, with Rachel evacuated, Lillian was free to look for a role for herself in the war effort. Earlier, when she had toyed with the idea of a paid job with Esther's lady wardens, Stan wouldn't hear of her exposing herself to the danger. Recommended by Esther to the WVS, who were looking for a local organizer, she felt out of place amongst the 'charming' bourgeois ladies who 'looked at me with pity' when she dared to disagree with their plans for mobilizing the Tyseley housewives.[29] ('That WVS', said Stan dismissively, 'is for women to play at [who] have nothing to do but sit in their cars and look pretty. I know because I have a lot of their cars to do.'[30]) She offered to work voluntarily in the YMCA canteen, but they already had more helpers than they could use, and Stan went ballistic when she suggested taking a munitions worker into the house as a lodger. Briefly, she looked for paid work, but with her limited schooling and no previous work experience apart from serving as a shop assistant her applications for clerical jobs were unsuccessful, and she drew back from part-time factory work fearing it would undermine her health. In the event her war work was restricted to the informal economy. One useful skill she had acquired from her mother was tailoring and dressmaking, and she regularly took in sewing for family, friends, and an impoverished local family on whom she took pity. In the summer of 1941 she started doing domestic work for the Empsons, freeing Esther for her role as head of the lady wardens, pleased to be able to contribute in this way to the war effort. When an accident put paid to Esther's ARP activities, Lillian continued to help her out with the housework during various family crises. None of this, however, was sufficient to overcome her feeling that life was passing her by.

Sexual adventures

In the spring of 1941, feeling 'bored stiff... wasted and unwanted', Lillian raged at Stan for blocking every attempt to find herself a useful role in the war effort.[31] He protested that he was thinking only of her health, and that she had no cause to unload on him her bitterness about her own wasted youth, or for the vacuum in her life caused by Rachel's evacuation. But he was no help in filling it, falling asleep every evening if not out in the pub with his friends. Above all she resented his killjoy refusal to take her out dancing—the major pleasure of her youth when she had visited dance halls four or five times a week—or, indeed, anywhere else. Confronted with tears and suicidal thoughts, Stan made an effort, helping her to buy new clothes, joining her on visits to old friends, and even agreeing to take her to the local ARP social on Saturday night.

    She threw herself into the social life of the ARP post. Stan was not happy when he discovered that one of the wardens, a married engineering worker known as Clev, was in the habit of dropping in for 'a cup of tea and a chat' on his way home from work:

Why did I need men calling on me when I'd got him. I said I'd always liked men, I liked the mental stimulus they afforded me, Stan said, I'm not enough for you then, I remarked that he hadn't been but he was improving... He asked me what was between Clev and I said nothing except that we were mutually attracted to each other. That's where the danger lies he said.[32]

By the spring of 1942, under pressure from Stan to give up her ARP
friends, fighting off a suffocating 'bitterness of spirit', she was fantasizing
about leaving him to live with her sister in London and work as a volunteer
in the MO office.[33] A few days later she changed tack. Positive about
their sex life, grateful for his generosity with the housekeeping money,
she pressed him again 'on the one thing that could make our marriage
100%... why couldn't he be more of a companion to me'. Up against the
wall, perhaps reassured, Stan capitulated: 'You can go out where you like
so long as you don't want me to take you.'

'So that's that,' she told MO, 'and I'm taking him at his word.' Or,
rather, more than his word. Given the green light to go out and enjoy
herself she quickly decided 'that I've got to get artful if I'm ever going to
have a bit of fun'.[34] Eighteen months before, when her sister-in-law, who
was looking after Rachel for a few days, urged her to go out and 'fly her
kite', Lillian had been shocked at the thought: 'when one hasn't had free
nights for seven years one doesn't know what to do with them.'[35] No such
hesitations held her back now. Contacting Clev she arranged to meet him
on his warden's round, in the blackout. 'I walked slowly up the road to our
tryst quite like 20 years ago... (and) he immediately put his arm around
my waist as though it belonged there.'[36] There and no further. The deal
she offered Clev was to go out and have fun, but sleeping together was not
on the agenda—the most he would ever get was a kiss. The first of many
men to be offered this deal by Lillian, Clev was understandably confused
since, at the same time, she did her best to keep him sexually aroused and
on tenterhooks. On one occasion, entertaining him at home wearing only
her underwear—'because it was a warm day'—she found the poor man
'starting to make love to me'. 'I intrigue him,' she had written earlier, 'I
tease him, I tantalise him, he gets worked up to fever pitch and then I
tell him it's time he went.' 'I cannot understand men getting so het up,'
she wrote disingenuously, 'I still keep cool and that makes them worse.'[37]
When, after several months of this torment, Clev started to avoid her she
threatened to revenge herself by befriending his wife so that 'he'll find me
in his home when he gets in at night'.[38] Meeting him in the street five
months after the end of their 'affair' she told him that all the details were in
her MO diary and would one day be published: 'I was only hotting things
up to make him lose a bit of his self-complacency... I haven't finished
with his peace of mind yet. I've a nasty mind.'[39] There is little in the diary
to suggest that she ever actually liked Clev, or had much in common with

him. The whole adventure seems to be about nothing but the deployment of sexuality in the service of power. Not content with laughing with Esther at the absurdities of male sexual behaviour, she was taking direct action to tease, provoke, and humiliate. Was this, perhaps, her revenge for the attempted rape twenty-five years earlier?

Lillian's pursuit of 'fun' was not confined to the Tyseley wardens. In the spring of 1941, shopping in the city centre, she had stopped for tea in a couple of dance halls, enviously watching the floor, and reflecting how much the style had changed since her pre-marital dancing days in the 1920s. On one of these visits she met a couple of regular daytime dancers, two married women who 'did the round of the dance halls, but they didn't tell their husbands'.[40] Within weeks of restarting her relationship with Clev, Lillian decided to follow suit, 'flying her kite' once a week at the Casino dance hall and 'flattered that so many men took an interest in me. I was not evidently quite a back number.'[41] When her partners made it clear, as most of them did, that they had more than dancing on their minds, she explained the ground rules—no sex: but, as with Clev, her delivery of the message was often ambiguous. Pursued by a Polish soldier who 'saw me to the bus and kissed my hand, my cheeks and my lips'—'and it doesn't mean a thing, how funny men are'—she nevertheless promised to meet him the next Monday, forgetting that it was a bank holiday and that Stan would be at home.[42] Her diary relates with relish her solution to this problem, a high wire act involving the seduction of Stan into breaking the habit of a lifetime and taking her to the Casino, and, once there, manoeuvring to dance with the Pole without Stan guessing that she had met him before. Stan, she noted shortly after this incident was 'improving marvellously again. He is much nicer, he has got over his nastiness [over] my friendships with other men', although, she added with obvious pleasure, savouring the tension, he was 'like a cat sitting on a wall, waiting to pounce'.[43] But these were dangerous games. Pining for a Canadian solider, whose invitation to a hotel room she had refused, she tracked the man down at his base and invited him to visit her at her home next time he was in Birmingham. She knew at the time that this was a hostage to fortune and may not have been altogether distressed when the Canadian's intended visit coincided with Stan's annual holiday, forcing her to abandon her deceptions and confess all: 'I had to put my cards on the table. That brought my pet warden episode up and the outshot [sic] of it all was that I had deceived him and that he wasn't going to trust me anymore.' In that case, she retorted, she might as well 'go the whole hog'. After two nights of arguing into the small hours a compromise was reached. She convinced him that all she really wanted was the dancing, and he consented on condition that she didn't see her partners outside the Casino or bring them home. 'I had gained my point', she reported to Mass-Observation:

after nearly fourteen years of married life I am at last free to take myself to an afternoon dance...Dear, dear, what a job it is to modernise some men, he is as early Victorian as his dad and it's a fine thing when one has to appear fast and loose to gain one's end.[44]

When the Canadian arrived, worse for drink and pleading with her to go with him to his hotel, he was marched off unceremoniously to the bus stop by Stan. An understanding had been reached.

Intellectual life

Lillian's search for life beyond the housewife identity was not confined to dancing and flirtation. Her intellectual life had taken off in 1937 when she enrolled in an evening class in psychology, the beginning, she later recalled, of her 'emancipation'.[45] Lillian was strongly influenced by the 'practical psychology' of the interwar years, which, as Mathew Thomson has shown, popularized something quite distinct from either the individualism of Freudian psychoanalysis or the disciplinary power exercised by the experts of institutionalized psychology.[46] She read popular psychology magazines and made use of new technologies of the self like the 'psychology chart' that she drew up on one occasion in an effort to understand her difficulties in one of her dance-hall flirtations.[47] While this latter exercise was effective in helping her to understand quite how selfish she had been, it did nothing to change the way she behaved in subsequent flirtations. Her interest in the psychological may have done little to mould her behaviour, but it marked the beginning of an intellectual voyage which, as Thomson has suggested of popular psychology more generally, opened out into wider ethical, social, and spiritual concerns rather than drawing its followers inward into a merely solipsistic fascination with their own interiority.

She missed the psychology classes when they were closed down on the outbreak of war, but she found consolation in Mass-Observation which enabled her to 'rise above' wartime worries and 'take an intelligent interest in everything and everyone'.[48] She responded to most of the monthly directives, and sent in diary entries from the outbreak of war until the end of 1947, although for a period of fifteen months, between the beginning of 1944 and April 1945, these have not survived. Seeing herself quoted in MO's weekly magazine *US* produced a 'glow of pleasure . . . It made me realise that although so tiny a unit, I count . . . [I] belong to something that matters.'[49] She wrote in detail about the experience of being bombed, in the hope that these accounts would be published so that future generations would understand what horrors their parents had lived through—a hope partly fulfilled in 1976 when Tom Harrisson quoted from her diary in *Living Through the Blitz*.[50] At moments of political excitement she sought out crowds or indoor meetings to report for Mass-Observation, although objectivity was frequently overwhelmed by the delights of participation. During the May 1941 King's Norton by-election, for example, her outrage against the pacifist candidate, Stuart Morris, spilled over into a noisy altercation with one of his supporters, and she had to be shut up by other members of the audience. Her account of the local VE Day celebrations in 1945 paints a vivid picture of drunken revelry, including—despite her earlier resolve to avoid censorious neighbourhood gossip by refusing to 'be drawn into anything'—her own boisterous flirtation with the head warden cross-dressed in his wife's clothes.[51] In March 1941, when her efforts to find war work, paid or unpaid, were getting nowhere, she thanked MO for helping to sustain 'faith in myself' by lending meaning and purpose to her life. 'Moving amongst and mixing with humanity' in her work for MO, she wrote in 1944, 'has been the moving force [of my life] in this last five years.'[52] When, in July 1942, MO wrote to say that they would no longer be able to send individual acknowledgements to the diarists, she replied that although she was 'going to miss my personal letters from you as much as anything I have been deprived of since war started', she was convinced that MO 'has a future in the new order of things to come and to that end I shall consistently serve'.[53]

   It was a service which allowed her to combine duty with pleasure. Leaving a note for Stan on one occasion she explained that she had gone to a dance organized for workers at the Town Hall because she was 'doing [it] for MO', adding in the diary: 'I wanted a legitimate excuse for giving it the once over'.[54] Mass-Observation, she knew, was interested in popular leisure, and her diaries contain extensive reportage of social life in the dance halls. Resuming her liaison with Clev in the spring of 1942 she noted that MO directives had several times asked 'what is sex-life like in your area ... I am now about to work in a good cause, and shortly I shall know quite a lot of what goes on underneath.'[55] And as for her multiple flirtations at the dance hall she remarked: 'Considering I go to the Casino to meet fresh men and to find out what sex problems go on right under our noses for the benefit of MO I feel I have [to accommodate] even these silly blighters ...'.[56] In role as a mass observer Lillian, it seems, could justify to herself almost anything, short of actual adultery.[57]

In September 1942, in the immediate aftermath of her daytime dancing compact with Stan, she found a new way of broadening her mind. Responding to an advertisement in the *Birmingham Mail* she discovered Wilfred Burden, a 'well upholstered, comfortable' builders' merchant and 'a seeker after knowledge [who] wanted a few to get together to discuss things ... as he felt that the future would sadly need clear thinkers'.[58] Burden lived in the same street as the Rogers and was delighted when Lillian turned up—not only the sole person from the locality to show an interest but also the only woman. Lillian recruited the Empsons, two of their lady wardens (whose membership was short-lived), and Frank Easton a 38-year-old railwayman, a local warden from whom Lillian had borrowed the *Encyclopaedia of Sex* (she had to steer him away from the topic for fear he would wreck the group with his advanced ideas). Among the other founding members were John Brown, a young man employed by Burden, who, by the end of the war, was intending to take holy orders; and Mr Doughty, 'the brainiest and best informed of all of us', who was a shunter on the railways and keen on women's rights.[59] Later, a number of other women participated, including one who took on the secretarial role which Lillian had declined. Attendance fluctuated between five and eleven people, which may be why the group eventually renamed itself as 'The Eleven Study Group'.

Initially the fortnightly meetings were organized around a short talk by one of the members followed by discussion, with a second hour devoted to items culled from the week's newspapers. Burden kicked off with a talk on Federal Union and others brought their own hobby horses—Russia, proportional representation, or, from Lillian, Mass-Observation (a disappointing session, poorly attended). Early in 1943 they decided to operate as a reading group and, after consulting the local librarian, chose Lowes Dickenson's, *Causes of International War*, working their way through a chapter at a time. By the end of the year the group had reached consensus around the principles of Federal Union—Burden's passion from the outset—and was discussing issuing some kind of public statement on the issue. Lillian's diary is missing between then and the end of the war, but shortly before the 1945 election the group received a visit from the local Labour candidate, Henry Usborne, who came to discuss a pamphlet they had published dealing with war and its causes.[60] Though critical of some details, he was in broad agreement with their conclusions, thanking them for having 'made a noble contribution to humanity' and urging them get involved in the political parties in order to proselytize their views.[61]

In March 1944 Burden was instrumental is establishing the Birmingham Ethical Society, also meeting fortnightly on the evening after the study group.[62] This met in the centre of Birmingham, or sometimes at the University where Dr Baier, a lecturer in German and son of a leading member of the Church of Humanity in Liverpool, was an influential member.[63] Lillian was a regular attender, and by May 1945 had become a member of the inner group which drew up a constitution for the society and a few months later plotted the exclusion of a particularly difficult man who felt that his forty years' membership of the Mecca of humanism, the South Place Ethical Society in London, entitled him to 'take the floor on every conceivable occasion'.[64]

Lillian drew enormous satisfaction from her involvement in this world of intellectual discussion: 'I am happiest', she wrote in 1945, 'in the company of my mental superiors.'[65] By mixing with those 'mentally superior to myself', she felt that she was gaining 'a better knowledge of the world, the civic duties, the rights of man, politics, the future and the hereafter'.[66] Not a modest package! Painfully aware of her own educational deficiencies, she often struggled to keep afloat. But fortunately she was a good listener and 'therein lies the fact that I can be amongst and about the things I long to know and they talk to me and think I know more than I do because I say little, only yes and no in the right places'.[67] When she did assert herself it was usually to bring to bear ideas she had picked up at her pre-war psychology classes—war as a product of the 'herd instinct' of the masses, Hitler's 'thwarted childhood'.[68]

Political reasoning was rather less to her taste. Her own political evolution mirrored the wartime disintegration of the Chamberlain dynasty's hold on popular politics in Birmingham. Already in March 1940 Douglas Reed's best selling right-wing, anti-Semitic denunciation of appeasement, *Disgrace Abounding*, had shattered the unthinking Unionism she had inherited from her parents. What this unleashed in Lillian is indicated by a remarkable dream she recounted at the time when France was crumbling in June 1940, a time of invasion fears and heightened emotion when everyone, perhaps, was just a little crazy. Before dropping off to sleep she had been reflecting that Hitler and Mussolini had risen to positions of power despite the fact that 'neither [was] educated even as much as myself'. In the dream she sees 'millions of upturned faces—the men in the street' clamouring for the imprisonment of the royal family:

we needed something different but [they] didn't know what. I came up at the back of a large raised platform and on it were a few men speakers and some loud speakers. But the crowd was pretty restive, they needed a leader and they were offered the usual platitudes. Just as a roar started to break out I pushed my way to the front, I shouted 'let me handle them I know what they want.' I raised my hands, I felt impelled then by sheer personality because I had their welfare at heart. 'I am the voice of the British Working Man', I said, 'Listen to me. You are asking for annihilation of people who have done you no wrong...'

Having told them to allow royalty to retire quietly into private life, she continued:

'From among those here the people themselves shall choose six leaders, men of initiative, common sense, justice and humanity. We shall collect all the brains and pool them, the man in the street shall be put first... [with opportunity for the cleverest] to forge ahead unhampered... The "capitalist system" as we know it today shall be wiped out, politics be a thing of the past. We all work for each other, but above all we work for Christ... reborn in the simplicity and purity of Christ... Every week I will stand before you and give you news of our work, our progress and our reborn happiness...'

'Oh God what a dream.' Quite carried away she added: 'and why couldn't it come true same as Hitler & Musso making pacts with the Devil... I too feel that I have a terrific power in me—but to do good, to at last blend the forces of the earth for our united good.'[69]

Lillian's belief in the capacity of an alliance of popular democracy and enlightened expertise to deliver social justice reflected a widespread response to the crisis of Britain's political system in the early years of the war.[70] Her contempt for 'the thin bloodied top notchers... educated sissies and old school tie morons', who had led Britain to disaster, knew no bounds.[71] Shortly after D-Day in June 1944 she declared that she had shifted from being 'a non-thinking Conservatist' [sic] to 'a much thinking... [supporter of whichever party] is going to be the strongest opposition to the ruling classes'.[72] Although her husband, Stan, was a socialist, like many others radicalized by the events of 1940 she resisted partisan affiliation, and in the run-up to the 1945 election was more inclined to support the Liberals or the Common Wealth Party—both of which had advocates inside her discussion group—than to throw in her lot with the Labour alternative to Conservative rule. It was to 'our lower middle class', the stratum with which she identified, that she looked to provide the 'new blood, outlook, brains and vigour' that Britain needed: 'a far finer man and womanhood than either the upper middle class or the governing classes'.[73]

When, in June 1940, Lillian dreamed of implementing a new social order, she chose to describe it in the language of apocalyptic Christianity: 'reborn in the simplicity and purity of Christ'. This was no mere figure of speech. As a child of ten she had been 'immersed' when her father, believing himself to be 'the chosen of the Lord' had marched his unwilling family out of the Church of England into an (unidentified) non-conformist sect.[74] Although Lillian had abandoned the chapel at 16, and hardly attended any church since, the coming of war stirred a latent millenarian sensibility. Assured by a neighbour, a member of a revivalist sect, that the war had been foretold in the bible, she resolved to look it up for herself; and she was equally receptive to the apocalyptical prophecies of the American Jehovah's Witness, Judge Rutherford, one of whose books, lent by her mother following a fierce argument over religion, 'has at last struck open the darkness I have been moping in'.[75] Her father, whose views had been ridiculed by the children once they were old enough to stand up for themselves, was listened to with a new respect when he prophesied that his offspring, being among the chosen, would not perish in the Armageddon to come. 'Not even the fittest will survive this time,' she wrote in June 1940, trumping Darwin with St John, 'only those who have their names written down will survive, if it is only a handful, they will be the chosen ones.'[76] And two months later when the bombing started: 'If our lives are to be reserved [sic] it is already written . . . I only trust I will be spared to see through to the other side, to see what really happens and the rebuilding of the new world.'[77] In April 1941, following Birmingham's second major blitz, she wrote:

this question of religion, Christ and the coming world is on nearly everyone's lips . . . If only I could live to see the Armageddon if that is the future of this troubled world, if only I could see in reality what I feel in the spirit now, to be

able to walk across open spaces with Christ beside me, to have the harmony in life
that I have always craved for.[78]

Religion had provided no comfort to Lillian during the years of 'visceroptosis' that blighted her twenties. Following Rachel's birth, however, when
continuing pain and post-natal depression prompted thoughts of suicide,
she believed she had been restrained from walking deliberately into the
path of a speeding train by an unseen hand closing over hers. In 1941
she confided to Mass-Observation that this experience had made 'a deep
influence on my life ... today I can feel the touch of that hand, that Christ
walks beside us. One never talks of these deepest things. I have never told
my husband [Stan dismissed religion in the name of science], nor have I
put it on paper until today.'[79] Walking with Christ did not involve church
attendance, but, like Nella Last, she observed the daily ritual of prayer
when Big Ben struck nine o'clock, sending, through God, a message of
'comfort and courage for the poor souls in the concentration camps and
occupied countries'. 'Sitting quietly in the coming night', she wrote of
these evening prayers 'one seems to become apart ... I'll never know who
gets my messages but they give me comfort ... Life goes on. How small
we are.'[80]

In the end, however, it was not religion that brought Lillian the harmony
she craved. Two years of enlightenment in the discussion group all but
dissolved her religious beliefs. The Bible, she discovered, was 'too much a
matter of contradiction and blind faith'.[81] Despite earlier fantasies of Christ
descending to earth down the beam of a searchlight, by the spring of 1944
she was ready to dismiss his much-discussed miraculous appearance over
Norwich as an atmospheric illusion. 'Science and Ethics have a terrific
pull to the thinking person', she remarked on this occasion, but added
uneasily:

I am not truly Ethical for I still feel that Christ is a person instead of a symbol ... I
have already arrived at the conclusion that there is no Hell, then why cannot I
accept the fact that there is no Heaven. You see I don't want to, because if I have
to accept the fact that when we die, we die, there is no afterwards, then to me that
seems a waste of living and striving.[82]

If the 'heroism of unbelief', acceptance of the meaninglessness of the universe, remained too much for her, she nevertheless found in the company
of the humanists in the Ethical Society a community of 'pleasure and
learning' more meaningful than anything offered by church or chapel—'a

finer living more Christian set of people I never wish to meet'.[83] There was nothing particularly paradoxical in this formulation. Although Burden had insisted at the inaugural meeting that members should affirm that they did not hold any 'supernatural religious beliefs', one of Lillian's companions in the Ethical Society was a clergyman in training, and, more generally, the ethicalists' 'religion of human fellowship' sought a basis for the ethical life 'independent of belief as to the ultimate nature of things' and felt no need to impose atheist beliefs on its followers.[84] Lillian's proudest moment came in August 1945 when the national secretary of the Ethical Society, H. J. Blackham, came to speak and she was able to reveal her own part in the Mass-Observation survey Blackham had commissioned into contemporary ethical and religious belief, later published as *Puzzled People*.[85]

By 1944−5 Lillian was a very much happier person than she had been earlier in the war.

> I have read and heard of emancipation [she wrote in September 1944] but I have never experienced it myself until these war years. I am a totally different person now to the person I was in 39 . . . Instead of being excitable or just up and down, I am today steadily happy for I run my own ship. My outlook is broader on every topic. I can talk intelligently on a lot of things. I am definitely younger in looks and mind through my mixing and dancing. I feel now that I have poise and personality instead of frustration.[86]

Asked by Mass-Observation for her views on the development of sexual morality during the war she distinguished sharply between the dissolute pleasure-seekers she came across in the dance hall, who 'use the war as a cover for their looseness', and 'decent living and hardworking people similar to ourselves . . . thinking people . . . [who] have uplifted themselves and others, instead of loosening their morals and having only the sexual side of life before their eyes, they are more inclined to the spiritual side of life'.[87] The sources of Lillian's contentment, however, were not confined to the spiritual and intellectual dimensions of her life. Equally important was the right to an autonomous social life that she had extracted from Stan: 'I am happier and more at peace with myself and the world', she wrote in August 1945:

> I have my private life, my private thoughts, my friends, my freedom to a great extent and a husband who obviously trusts me or he wouldn't say: 'You have more freedom than the average woman, I don't ask who you go with, nor where you go or what you do when you are with them.'[88]

More sexual adventures

After the September 1942 compact with Stan, reviewing her summer
of liaisons at the Casino, Lillian had concluded: 'Then the fall of the
curtain...So that's evolution. I am more interested in our study group
now.'[89] But she still went out dancing, and finding a partner who was
not interested in her sexually proved difficult. Over the next year her
diaries relate countless encounters with dancers good and bad, all of
whom propositioned her, all without success. With her most regular
dancing partner, an unhappily married man called Ernest, she also went out
regularly to the pictures and for country walks. Inevitably he fell for her,
which, she wrote, was a pity 'because I had hopes of a dancing partner for
some time yet'.[90] When he told her that he loved her because she was so
'good' she translated this for the diary as 'in plain English...he only wants
me because he sees he cannot have me...Aren't men damn fools.'[91] For
some months she strung him along, acting 'selfishly I'll admit, I've expected
him to give in to me on every occasion'.[92] When, late back to prepare
Stan's evening meal, she found herself inventing excuses, she resolved to
put an end to the affair: 'intrigue and lies don't suit me so I'll pack up
Ernest'.[93] Ten days later Ernest called on her at home (which she had been
letting him do for some time, breaking the rules of her pact with Stan).
Stan was there, ill in bed and already 'working things out' having come
across a lighter that Ernest had given Lillian as a memento of their affair,
so she had to confess. To Stan's complaint that she was 'unnatural' in not
having more women friends and constantly surrounding herself with men
she responded:

> I don't go after them, they [seek] me out and so long as they keep sex out of it I like
> their company...I said I get on extremely well with women if I don't have too
> much to do with them, I hate their mental outlook and I don't suffer them gladly.[94]

Refusing to take her out himself, Stan had no choice but to accept her
liaisons with dancing partners, and he trusted her not to fall in love with
them and to resist their sexual advances. So the compact held.

But it was not only dancing partners. In the course of 1943 she had
sexually charged encounters with, among others, the postman (unhappily

married to a melancholic wife), an insurance salesman (an unacceptably 'quick worker' who, after getting the sharp end of her tongue, 'seemed really sincere and subdued and . . . said: "in all my 41 years you are the only woman who has ever told me where I get off and I must say I admire you for it"'), and a local air-raid warden with whom she played truant from an ARP social—'the dear boy' bought her a drink and was rewarded with 'two kisses'—returning to scandalized greetings from one of the local women, 'a lispy and coy piece with a gossiping nasty mind and tongue: "Ttt-Ttts, she said, your child's really broken hearted over being left, such goings on." I had to laugh.'[95] Ten-year-old Rachel had been given presents by Ernest and, Lillian believed, shared her mother's fondness for male company.

Apart from the sexual titillation, what she really enjoyed about these encounters was the opportunity they offered for playful switching between her various identities. Exchanging repartee with the fast crowd—thoroughly immoral, into group sex—on the balcony of the Casino, she reflected on the contrasts in her life: 'Whatever sense of values these people have, they are the other extreme from my Ethical friends. They live for today, they think on nothing deeply, they cannot converse on anything, and yet in their ignorance they live intensely.'[96] Intrigued by their thoughtless hedonism, she was also assertive of her own moral standards and gratified at being seen in this company as something of an intellectual—introduced with the remark: 'She's smart you know, you ought to talk to her'—an image she played up to from time to time by sitting alone on the balcony reading serious books.[97] On one occasion, ostensibly monitoring public reactions to D-Day for Mass-Observation, she found herself advising an unhappy young man, within ten minutes of meeting him, how best to improve his marriage:

I have acquired a technique [she wrote] in finding out secrets and ways of life of almost any man after I have been with him a short time. Firstly they become attracted to me and get conversational, then they realise that I don't talk like the average woman. They wish to make an appointment, though teasing, tantalising, scoring [sic: the word cannot yet have acquired its modern sexual meaning], holding out hope, etc. I get out of them their ideas, methods and hopes. I usually strike them as unusual because I can talk of things that the average woman would blush at . . .[98]

These conversations were not solely about sex. A year later, she picked up a man in the town centre crowd waiting to hear Churchill speak in the run-up to the 1945 election:

LR: Have you found yourself?

AM: (who is carrying a copy of *Monthly Psychology*) No, unfortunately that's my trouble. I have tried everything...Are you a student of psychology?

LR: Yes I am. Why do you ask?

AM: From the way you've been talking. I'd like to have a talk with you.

[It quickly becomes clear to Lillian that the man, married for twenty-five years to a wife who relentlessly exploited his good humour and kindliness to exercise power over him, was on edge of a nervous breakdown.]

AM: I have been to three psychiatrists but none of them spoke so plainly or made me see what I am up against as you have done this afternoon.

LR: I am only a student and anything I can say will only be from a very human point of view. Frankly from my studies and reading of learned books I think you have married a vampire and she lives upon you and it is only the power she holds over you that keeps her alive.

AM: I dare not leave her for fear she will end in an asylum. Though the doctors already say she will anyway.

LR: You are at a crossroads in your life and endurance. Are you prepared to go ahead and find your manhood and individuality?

AM: Yes, but how to start?

LR: You have no appropriate friends to help. What you need is a night out a week mixing with intellectuals as you are intellectually starved, to get a fresh outlook...I am stewardess at the Birmingham Ethical Society. I can introduce you to thinking men who will help you, will you come, you can sit and never say a word but it will be a beginning.[99]

She left him with her address for when he felt ready to try the ethical life.

Nor, at 'the Ethical' (as she called it), did she leave her sexual self behind. Reluctantly in the chair at one meeting, she teased the main speaker, John Brown, the budding vicar, about having to hold old ladies hands when he took up the Ministry, to which he responded, to much merriment: 'I'd much rather hold yours.'[100] As in fact he did, furtively in the back of the Burden's car on their way to the meetings, earnestly 'trying to fathom how was it I could have men friends and remain Ethical...The trouble...is he's dying to have a mild flirtation and his conscience will get in the way.'[101] In 1945 she organized a Christmas party in her own house for the Ethical Society, with organized games (including postman's knock, 'by request') and mistletoe strategically placed to ease any delicate consciences. Dr Baier, the academic, came with his family, which did not prevent him from joining in the fun although, Lillian commented wryly, 'he could really have done with a lesson or two from me, these learned men are not efficient in the art of kissing'.[102] She had even invited her imagined reader, the acting director of Mass-Observation, Bob Willcock, promising that if he came 'I will let you do it for MO'.[103] The *double-entendre* was, surely, intentional.

But her deepest source of contentment was Ronnie, who had replaced Ernest as her steady boyfriend. Ronnie, who drove a newspaper van part-time for a living, was in his mid-twenties, lived with a mother who neglected him, and doted on Lillian while making no sexual demands upon her: 'since we are both on the cool side we suit each other admirably . . . He little knows how rare he is, giving in friendship and adoration what other men only give until they find out it is a waste of time.'[104] Shy, depressed and badly dressed when she first met him in August 1944 she smartened him up, encouraged him to get a full-time job, and 'brought a colour and warmth into his life it certainly lacked'.[105] He didn't dance and he resisted her attempts to interest him in the study group, the Ethical Society or writing for Mass-Observation, so they spent their time together at the pictures or on country walks. Sometimes she'd join him on his rounds in the van. She liked to pretend that he was her charitable project, that she was grooming him to get a girl his own age who he could marry. But, after two years, the prospect of eventually losing him left her feeling bleak, and she reassured herself with the thought that she'd given him a taste for older women 'and I'm too perfect to match'.[106]

Post-war

Such contentment could not last. Her involvement with the Ethical Society petered out early in 1946 after Dr Baier, who had been its 'leading spirit', departed to run the German department at Hull University.[107] Meanwhile Doughty and other luminaries of the Eleven Study Group had been heavily involved in the establishment of a local community centre. Although initially excited by the informing ideas of participatory citizenship, Lillian declined to join the project committee and, when in the autumn of 1946 the study group (which had fizzled out after the war) was successfully revived, meeting in the community centre, she decided not to attend: 'I cannot find the interest now.'[108] A year later she was equally resistant to Burden's attempts to involve her in a new local campaign, organized in concert with the MP, Harry Usborne, to promote the study group's ideas on World Federation: 'The trouble is I am not so enthusiastic, I still agree wholeheartedly with the idea and the endeavour and I expect I shall help but I wish to heaven I didn't feel so tired all the while.'[109]

Her tiredness was partly a product of post-war austerity and inadequate nutrition, about which she complained bitterly, especially on behalf of Stan whose health was deteriorating rapidly. During 1946, with much of her time taken up caring for sick relatives, Lillian became depressed. In September, hearing that a diabetic brother had died (she believed from malnutrition), Lillian broke down in tears, something she very rarely did. Thirteen-year-old Rachel, clearly an astute observer of her parents' difficult relationship, was taken aback by the gentleness with which Stan comforted her mother, remarking: 'Me dad was different, I've never seen him like that before.' When Lillian explained that her crying upset Stan as much as it did her daughter, Rachel responded, after due thought: 'Why don't you try crying more often?'[110] But things had got beyond the reach of tears. Feeling at the end of her tether, with pains presaging the return of her 'visceroptosis', Lillian moved out of her sick husband's bedroom in October 1946. Persuaded by a female doctor that Stan's pleasure was being undermined by the need to 'ensure that I ran no risks' she had a Dutch cap fitted—'my last one try to make a success of married life'—but this did nothing to revive their flagging sex life and she continued to sleep on the divan in Rachel's room.[111] Stan's sexual artistry now left her cold: 'he little realises', she wrote after a romantic moment on Christmas Day, 'how small and little he seems to me, how cold his lips are. He would be very amazed to know that he chills me instead of warming me. I know it is due to his illness . . . and he cannot help it but I can very easily do without it.'[112] By the summer of 1947, after writing him a four page letter explaining why she had married him and how he had disappointed her, she confessed bleakly to the diary: 'I have lost all that striving to please him . . . I don't like him.' Defiantly she wrote:

Well I'd passed another milestone in my life if he fails me this time I'm going out to find a man who loves me more than himself, a man who adores me for what I am, a man who can give me a love that creates a love in me instead of barriers. I wonder if my fool of a husband will ever realize what he's missed.[113]

Of course she already had such a man. Stan knew nothing about Ronnie, who continued to bring 'a warmth into my life that marriage has never done'.[114] But, when the diary finishes, her future with Ronnie remained 'in the lap of the Gods, does he go ahead and get a wife, does he develop his friendship and love for me?' She found it hard to imagine life without Ronnie, but also worried that she was ruining his future. Would she be big enough to 'step down' when he found a girl of his own age: 'maybe I'll be wise to persevere with Stan and our misunderstandings, I may one day be glad of his shoulder to weep on when R. has vanished from my life. Even husbands have their uses at times.'[115]

Shortly after moving out of Stan's bedroom, Lillian suffered a further blow when she accused Esther's daughter Molly of stealing money from her purse, leading to the irretrievable breakdown of her closest female friendship. This may help to explain why she did not rejoin the study group, in which the Empsons were fully engaged. In its place, however, she had found a new outlet for her intellectual energies. As an adolescent she had kept a diary and harboured the ambition to 'have it made into a book . . . called "The Diary of Lil" '. When, in 1941, Bob Willcock wrote from Mass-Observation thanking her for her contribution she reflected that although her diary would never become a book, 'I shall at least have small portions in a book'.[116] Three more years of regular diary writing improved her skills, and by 1944 she was considering making use of her quasi-erotic adventures by writing 'a comprehensive study of people and sex . . . a history of persons and their reactions to life and their partners and sex'.[117] Mindful as ever of her educational deficiencies she enrolled in an evening course on English grammar over the winter of 1945–6, taking the Higher Matriculation exam in the spring. During the autumn of 1946, responding to an advertisement in the local paper, she joined a writers' group which, she wrote in the final instalment of her MO diary a year later, 'fills my need for social mixing. A very nice group of people who are so interested in making a go of writing they have no time for idle gossip or scandal.'[118] The group turned out to be run by the only other mass observer Lillian had ever come across. Iris Forrest, who had sent in a few diaries and directive replies between 1942 and 1944, had given up a good job in a Lombard Street bank before the war to live in a village close to her husband's work, hoping to earn a living by writing fiction.[119] In many ways this turn from the political and philosophical concerns of the study group and the Ethical Society to issues of literary technique, human interest, and psychological understanding suited Lillian's cast of mind. But she was not entirely comfortable, noting early on that 'my weighing up of people and things is very different from [the] others'.[120] The writers' group movement catered primarily for people who wanted to earn money by selling short stories to mass-market periodicals, something that Iris Forrest clearly knew how to do: 'she writes light work and seems to have quite a decent market'. By contrast, Lillian aspired 'to write about real people of real worth in a restrained style'. When, in August 1947 she received her first rejection slip, for a 3,000-word short story, Mrs Forrest advised her to lighten her tone, saying 'I shall have to get only a little truth well covered with fiction'. Lillian was not convinced: 'I can never see myself writing twaddle.'[121] Lillian was too adventurous a searcher to be satisfied for long with the light-weight pleasures of romantic fiction.[122]

In her dancing; her flirtations; her relationship with Ronnie; and her political, ethical, and theological discussion, Lillian found sources of self-hood that marriage, motherhood, and female friendship alone could not provide. Writing for Mass-Observation enabled her to chart, and to legit-imate, her restless questing beyond the normal expectations of her role, playing reflexively with the possibilities of different identities. Lillian was, of course, unique; but her ways of living belonged to a structure of feeling, a regime of identity, in which essentializing categories of self-hood—housewife, mother—existed in tension with a quest for personal identity that pushed beyond the limitations of conventional role models. We do not know whether the tension between these various selves even-tually blew apart her core normative identity as a respectable middle-class wife and mother, but for several years, between 1942 and 1946, she was able to hold it all together and feel a sense of individual growth and contentment which did not rest on the closure of alternative possible selves.* More than any of the other diarists, Lillian's restless exploration of multiple identities pointed the way towards a modern reflexive selfhood.

Mathew Thomson has argued that the popular impact of psychological modes of thinking during the first half of the twentieth century did less to encourage the narcissistic individualism familiar in our own times than to 'foster the imagining of social dimensions of the self', in ways that were compatible with, may even have helped to shore up, older ideas of

---

*By June 1953, however, when she responded to a Mass Observation directive about the coronation, Stan had died and Lillian, now working as a clerk, had not remarried. TC 69/7/F

duty, character, and service.[123] That the Victorian synthesis was alive and well in mid-twentieth-century Britain is apparent in the writing of our older diarists, Nella Last, Gertrude Glover, and Mary Clayton. But Lillian, the diarist most directly influenced by popular psychology, displays an altogether more individualistic outlook. While her search for the ethical life bore witness to the continuing power of Victorianism, her forays into the erotically charged delights of dance hall and city streets, belonged to a quite different construction of the self. Contrasting her life with the unrelenting domestic toil that her mother had endured—bringing up a large family, never going anywhere for months on end—she remarked in 1939: 'Our present generation are not so unselfish we look on ourselves as individuals. We do our duty by our dependents but keep our personalities.'[124] In thus contrasting 'personality' to the fulfilment of duty, Lillian was breaking away from the altruistic language of character and service, towards an altogether more individualistic understanding of the self, one that embodied the modern tension between 'our desire for clear and solid values to live by, and our desire to embrace the limitless possibilities of modern life and experience that obliterate all values'.[125]

She was not, however, inventing an entirely new way of being. Rather, she was acting out a different nineteenth-century script from that embraced by the older women, the avant-garde script of the urban *flaneur* for whom the city streets provided 'a theatre of operations for the self'.[126] Tramping the city streets at moments of political excitement, picking up men in dance-hall encounters, Lillian was using Mass-Observation, not inappropriately, to give her the prerogatives of the urban *flaneur*: the right to observe in anonymity the excitements of the city, the casual meetings and the unlikely juxtapositions, the exploration of urban space as an arena of adventure and self-creation. In her erotically charged adventures in the city, she was not doing anything that had not been done before, *except* that she was lower middle-class not bourgeois; female not male; and in Birmingham not Paris, London, or New York; and in all these ways she was a pioneer of modernity in her own social milieu.

Figure 5. Ernest van Someren, 1946.
© Laurie van Someren.

7

Ernest van Someren:
The good life

Friday, November 8th, 1940

Went to town instead of to the works, for the first time since August
[when the London blitz had started]...I walked to Piccadilly, bought
some coffee and French mustard at Fortnum & Masons. There was a
warning. I went to the Chemical Society and worked in the library
there...Then I went to a music shop and bought a recorder...I was
rather depressed by the mess around Oxford Street. Went home on the
5.10 train which was very full. I sat on a ledge in the guards van and
played the recorder most of the way, after asking the guard if there was
any regulation against it.

The diary of Ernest van Someren betrays no hint of a struggle for
personal autonomy. He had, as we know from a memoir left by
his mother, suffered agonies as a child and a young man achieving an
independent sense of self, but these were long since buried by the time he
took up writing for Mass-Observation. Scientist, family man, civic activist,
Quaker, pacifist, socialist, he enjoyed a rich intellectual and cultural life in
concert with wife and friends in an affluent Home Counties suburb. In
some ways his life was exemplary of the mutualism espoused by Edward
Carpenter or the Christian socialist philosopher, John Macmurray, both
of whom he read and admired. Perhaps there is nothing of less historical
importance than a truly happy man, which is how Ernest presents himself

throughout his Mass-Observation diary. Discontent is history's driver, not the capacity to play the recorder (regulations permitting) in the guard's van of an unlit train rumbling through the blitz.

But even while he lived the 'new life' Ernest had his devils to confront, if only because his lifestyle depended on a successful career as a research chemist in war industry. The Quaker Meeting was Ernest's preferred technology of the self, not the self-reflective diary. Nevertheless, reading between the lines, and with the help of his responses to MO's monthly directives, one can glimpse the ways in which his civic activism helped to assuage the contradiction he was living between his pacifist beliefs and the satisfactions he derived from his work in war industry and the privileged lifestyle that it paid for.

The good life

Thirty-six years old when the war broke out, Ernest had spent his early childhood in Venice where his father, an English doctor, practised medicine in the ex-patriot community. His mother, Ivy, was the step-daughter of Horace Fletcher, a wealthy American who was to become famous as the inventor of 'Fletcherism', the doctrine that saliva was essential to digestion so that all food must be chewed until it became liquid: 'Nature', he warned, 'will castigate those who don't masticate.' Ernest's father was Fletcher's first convert, overseeing experiments which helped to gain scientific credibility for his views.[1] Ernest grew up something of a prodigy, reading easily in two languages when he was three, and speaking English with his parents, German with his nurse, and Italian with the domestic servants. His mother, a much-travelled, much-courted but rather over-protected young woman who, since the age of 9, had never spent a night apart from her mother, revelled in the social life of upper-class Venetian society, and played muse to various artistic talents including 'Baron Corvo', an eccentric bohemian Catholic novelist with a well-deserved reputation for ingratitude towards his patrons who moved in and lived off the English doctor for nine months.[2] A few years into the marriage, however, this happy life began to disintegrate; not so much because she had four children to take care of, of whom Ernest was the eldest, but because her husband, urged on by an evangelical sister, turned his back on their life of parties, good food, dancing, and the arts and took to a literal interpretation of scripture, proselytizing on the bridges of Venice and giving whatever money came to hand to the poor. Many of his patients deserted the practice, alienated by his religious extremism. In a memoir that she wrote for the family in the 1950s,[3] Ivy remarked that 'it was difficult to live with a saint'—a kinder version of Corvo's ungrateful description of him as a religious maniac who served 'crank food sauced with the most unctuous of rancid piety'.[4] But worse was to follow. Her husband, who was diabetic, died suddenly in January 1913, leaving the family destitute.

Family legend has it that Ernest, 9 years old when his father died, told her, 'don't worry mama, I will take care of you'.[5] In reality the boy was immediately taken under the wing of a wealthy, but childless, family of Scottish landowners, Plymouth Brethren friends of his father's, who whisked him away to their Highland estate before sending him to a preparatory school for the sons of missionaries in south London. Meanwhile his mother, supported by family and friends, came to London where she set about reinventing herself as a journalist, with help from Ralph Blumenfeld, editor of the *Daily Express*, who she had got to know in London many years earlier when travelling with her parents. Aware that her son was miserable at school, where his previous education in the German school in Venice made him an obvious target for the other boys after the outbreak war, Ivy, who had never shared her husband's religious convictions and wanted to free him from the clutches of the Brethren, put him in for a scholarship to Clifton, which Ernest duly won in summer of 1915. His benefactors were convinced that Clifton was a den of iniquity and Ivy, partly in deference to what she imagined would have been her dead husband's wishes, gave way to their insistence that he should go as a day boy and live with a family of Brethren in Bristol. As a result he was, according to Ivy's memoir, ostracized at school: 'he was too "pi", went to religious meetings three times on Sundays, was not allowed to ride his bicycle or read anything but the Bible or religious books on the Sabbath'. Far from resenting his indoctrination, Ernest embraced his benefactor's faith and was baptized into the Brethren. Troubled by what he perceived as the spiritual jeopardy in which his mother stood—she was making her way successfully in the secular world of metropolitan journalism—the young man 'implored me with tears to be "saved" and have the faith he had been taught. It was a painful scene.'

After Clifton, Ernest won a scholarship to University College London where he graduated in chemistry and finally broke with the fundamentalism

of the Plymouth Brethren. After five years working with ICI in Birmingham, and some time spent in Scandinavia, he held various short-term
industrial research jobs before settling down in 1938 with a firm specializing
in welding processes in Waltham Cross, on the northern fringe of London,
where he was to remain for the next twenty years.[6] He worked 'on the
borderline between chemistry and physics', developing techniques for the
spectrochemical analysis of welds.[7] The job was satisfying and intellectually
exciting, particularly after 1942 when the firm bought him the apparatus
needed to return to the line of analytical research on which he had worked
in the 1930s and on which he edited several collections of abstracts.[8] He
enjoyed conferring with his peers at the Institute of Metals, the Rheology
Club (rheology is the science of deformation and flow of matter), or the
Association for Scientific Photography (in 1942 the Royal Photographic
Society gave him a prize for an article on the photography of welds). The
work also appealed to his skills as a handyman, the 'practical inventiveness'
which enabled him to recycle an old shaver or a gramophone needle when
improvising apparatus needed for his experimental work: 'I have a good
head for gadgets.'[9]

Ernest married in 1936. He had first met Kay in his Birmingham days,
when she was working as a secretary. He says very little about her in the
diary, but the description he provided in response to an MO directive
about the foundations of a successful marriage can probably be taken as a
descriptive own marriage, at least as he perceived it:

[mutual] enthusiasm and tolerance . . . an agreed community of interest, especially
in religion, art, some sort of recreation, and parenthood. On religion, education,
discipline and diet there must be more agreement than tolerance, this also applies
to the physical manifestations of sex, over which divergent attitudes are bound to
cause trouble. Hobbies need not be shared, and each partner should have a field in
which their superiority is undisputed, and preferably unclaimed.[10]

They had two children, both unplanned: Laurie, born in 1938 and Julia
three years later. Ernest was much involved in the childcare, giving his
baby son his first feed in the mornings and potting him before Kay got
up. Later he read bedtime stories, took Laurie out to watch the trains or
to bathe in the river in a neighbour's garden. A good deal of the diary is
devoted to documenting Laurie's development, his first step, his first word,
his first sentence, the first window he broke, his disobedience and his
clever technique (aged four) for evading deadlock with parental authority:
'he says "shut your eyes" and then does what he has previously refused

to do, without loss of face'.[11] Nothing pleased Ernest more than the boy's affection: 'To be greeted with a shout when coming home seems to me the crowning feature of being a father.'[12] Ernest also pulled his weight in house and garden, applying his skills to household repairs, vegetable growing, egg production, and an impressively precise system of domestic account-keeping which provided the basis for an article on family wartime expenditure published by the journal *Housewife* in 1942.[13]

They lived in a well-appointed Victorian house in Broxbourne, sixteen miles north of central London, one of a street of houses built close to the station for affluent commuters when the railway arrived in the 1840s.[14] From here he could cycle the five miles to work, or take the train one station down the line when the weather was bad. The cultural resources of London were close at hand and, once the worst of the blitz was over, Kay and Ernest took time out for concerts, art galleries, theatre, movies, and visits to friends in town. Although their most immediate neighbours were 'elderly people of whom I know nothing', Broxbourne, and the nearby town of Hoddeston, far from being anonymous suburbs, provided the van Somerens with a dense network of sociability, mainly with professional people like themselves.[15] Friends living locally included doctors, journalists, architects, lawyers, scientists, social workers, and a radiographer. Many had young children and they helped each other out with childcare. In the evenings and at weekends cultural and intellectual pursuits proliferated. This was a district where the proprietor of a local sweet shop, threatened by wartime austerity, could salvage his business by selling Penguin paperbacks.

The van Someren household itself was a hive of sociability. Friends dropped in for a chat, to arrange meetings or attend them, to watch films of their children shot by Ernest, who had a cine camera and access to sophisticated photographic equipment at work. Now and then they had parties with organized games, or more frequently less-planned gatherings where, he noted on one such occasion, 'we talked about children and astrology and mountains and houses and semi-superstitious cults'.[16] Friends living further afield often visited for the weekend. At the outbreak of war they took in evacuees, two young girls for the first six months, and bombed-out neighbours in the autumn of 1940. Subsequently a succession of friends came to stay when wartime job changes or bombing forced them to leave their own homes. By the autumn of 1942 Ernest counted fifteen people who had lived with them, some for a few days, some for several months, since the outbreak of war, and others came later. Some of these were friends or friends of friends, whose company enriched Kay's and Ernest's lives. Others, bombed-out local working-class people who the vicar persuaded them to take in, were less satisfactory guests and they were glad to see the back of them.

  Music was, central to Ernest's life, arousing some of his deepest feelings: 'joyful peace' (Mozart's oboe quartet); 'a deep satisfaction, an inner tranquillity' (Elgar's Enigma Variations and Sibelius); and even, he observed with characteristic scientific precision, 'physical symptoms of emotion in the spine and eyes' (the Last Post at a military funeral).[17] The closest he ever came to expressing a patriotic sentiment was in his response to Chopin played at a National Gallery lunchtime concert: 'for once I felt really conscious of the existence and continuity of this nation.'[18] (One can grasp something of what this evoked from Humphrey Jennings' use of a Myra Hess lunchtime concert at the climax of his poetic celebration of wartime unity, the film 'Listen to Britain'.) Evenings at home usually included time spent listening to broadcast concerts or gramophone records, and he sometimes attended a gramophone club in Hoddeston. Live concerts were rare in the locality before 1944 when Ernest was instrumental in establishing a Music Club which put on professional and amateur performances and, in cooperation with the local education authority, ran orchestral and choral evening classes. Kay and Ernest both played the recorder, and were delighted when in October 1939 they got to know the Holmes, new neighbours—he an Australian food scientist, she an English music graduate—with whom they could play informally. Mrs Holmes ran a music course for the WEA, which Ernest attended, and from May 1940 a music listening group met in their house, shifting to the van Somerens when the Holmes left the area a year later. Other close neighbours included a fellow scientist and Quaker pacifist activist, John Strange, who, with his wife, had been a member of the national folk-dancing team. In the summer months of 1943 and 1944 Ernest spent many hours happily practising sword-dancing on their lawn, reviving an interest which had been dormant since the mid-1930s.[19]

  These cultural delights were enhanced by the proximity of nature. What could be more lovely, he wrote in (of all times) June 1940, than 'listening to the Beethoven Eroica symphony with friends on . . . a fine evening with a ripple of birdsong in the . . . garden making a background to it'.[20] Broxbourne, on the River Lea, provided endless opportunities for swimming and boating, picnics and days out cycling to country pubs.

After one musical afternoon at the Holmes', they went walking in the woods with a younger couple and 'carried on an intermittent discussion on D. H. Lawrence and cosmology and the future of mankind'.[21] Like Lawrence, Ernest was attracted by Edward Carpenter's vision of companionate marriage, friendship, and community.[22] Ernest cited Carpenter as one of the writers who had most influenced his thinking, alongside the Christian Socialist, John Macmurray whose belief that 'human nature expresses itself most concretely and completely in friendship' he shared.[23] The highest form of self-realization, Macmurray wrote, was to be found through participation in 'the personal and cultural life of the community'.[24] One reason for paying attention to this happy man is that his existence was in many ways exemplary of the 'pure relationship', that non-instrumental pursuit of intimacy which Anthony Giddens argues has become central to the making of the modern self:

In conditions of high modernity...the pure relationship...comes to be of elementary importance for the reflexive project of the self... The pure relationship is above all dyadic, but its implications and influence are not limited to two-person settings. A given individual is likely to be involved in several forms of social relation which tend toward the pure type: and pure relationships are typically interconnected, forming specific milieus of intimacy.[25]

Carpenter, Macmurray, Giddens all reverberate in W. H. Auden's 1937 sketch of a good life not too far removed from Ernest's happy existence:

The walks by the lake, the weeks of perfect communion;
    Tomorrow the bicycle races
Through the suburbs on summer evenings.

But Auden's 'tomorrow' was no more than a 'perhaps', the gleam of a future made possible only by facing up to the dark time, 'the conscious acceptance of guilt in the necessary murder'.[26] What the poet had not imagined was the capacity of the bourgeois scientist, turning his back on the 'necessary murder' (in which his work inescapably implicated him), to enjoy the good life even while the bombers prowled overhead.

Civic activism and religion

There was more to Ernest's life than work, family, friendship, and the pursuit of happiness. Throughout the war he was secretary of the local

WEA, which ran two or three lecture courses most winters covering literature or the arts, current affairs, and psychology, with a combined membership of about fifty people. Much of Ernest's spare time was spent organizing tutors and venues, entertaining speakers, attending committee meetings, or sampling lectures. Many of his friends were also involved and the drudgery of organization and committee work was relieved by parties and socials as well as the intellectual stimulation provided by some of the courses, particularly those on psychology—the most popular and his own favourite. As a spin-off from the WEA, Ernest also found himself organizing, and participating in, Brains Trusts put on for a variety of organizations including—remarkably given his pacifist views—the British Legion and the Army Bureau of Current Affairs. His mother sometimes joined him on the platform, well-informed after her years dealing with foreign affairs for the *Daily Express*.[27] Although no longer anxious to save her soul, Ernest argued fiercely with his mother about politics and pacifism where their disagreements were fundamental 'and somewhat bitter'.[28] Ernest enrolled as a BBC 'local correspondent': 'rather like MO's work, they send out a little newsletter and a questionnaire for the month . . . You see,' he told Mass-Observation, 'I am a chronic informer.'[29] But two attempts to get up a BBC listening group failed. He took responsibility as 'street captain' for the organization of the fire-watching rota, and from 1943 he was a member of the local Youth Advisory Committee. Sometimes he felt he was taking on too much, but, as he had explained to MO when he signed up with them in 1937, 'I am the sort of person who joins movements'.[30]

Ernest's civic activism was underpinned by religious faith. After he broke with the Plymouth Brethren, he subscribed to no church, although from his student days until the mid-1930s he was active in the socially progressive Christian Auxiliary Movement which according to an early account:

provided a home for the 'self-excommunicated', the large number who fail to find in the particular place of worship to which they have been traditionally attached a religious ideal set forth which they can feel to be large enough to express what Christianity means to them . . .[31]

At the same time, reacting against the dogmatism of the Brethren, he was drawn to the Quaker rejection of scriptural authority and formal creeds in favour of what he described as 'the continual and diverse revelation of God by Himself to man in Religion, Art and Science'; a trinity which, significantly for Ernest, gave religion no higher claim to truth than the sense of meaning and order that he found in music or in his scientific research.[32] His agnostic attitude to central tenets of Christian doctrine were nicely revealed when, responding to detailed questions in a MO Directive in 1944, he said of the Virgin Birth that 'artistically it seems to me a fine story. Genetically it seems unlikely, but Jesus was so far from being a normal Jew that there may well have been something unlikely about his genes'; and of the Creation: 'I don't know ... it seems *a priori* unlikely to have occurred, but still more unlikely not to have occurred.' Above all, he insisted, it really did not matter what he thought, because beliefs about such questions were unlikely to have any practical effect on his behaviour. Like the philosopher John Macmurray, one of the men he most admired, he believed 'that only the opinions which affect my conduct are worth calling beliefs'.[33]

For many years he had attended occasional Quaker meetings, but put off joining the Society of Friends, feeling that he had not yet understood 'their difficult technique of worship'—waiting in expectant silence for the spirit to move. As with marriage, where pre-marital sex (not promiscuity) seemed to him a sensible practice among responsible people, membership of the Friends should 'be the recognition of a developing condition rather than an initiation'.[34] Although he later denied that the war had had any significant effect on his attitude to life, it seems to have been the catastrophic events of May–June 1940 that triggered his decision to apply for membership, a process which took nine months to complete and involved searching discussion with two members appointed by the local meeting. One of them was Stephen Hobhouse, jailed as a conscientious objector in the First World War and now a writer of mystical theology, who lived a few doors away.[35] Thereafter Ernest attended the meeting on most Sundays and was often moved to speak, although he was not entirely comfortable in a group which included 'a wealthy stockbroker and his large family who try to manage everybody else'.[36] The stockbroker did not share the pacifist beliefs normal among Quakers, and his presence prevented the meeting from taking a public position on the war.

Pacifism

For Ernest it was not possible for Quakers to abstain from political life: 'if not active we are in fact supporting the existing order'.[37] In 1942 he was much impressed by a talk given by David Davies, an opponent of

Christian Socialism, who explained why after more than twenty-five years of left-wing political activism he had finally concluded that the social gospel was the illusion of the epoch and that the only reason for Christians to involve themselves in politics was to help humanity to understand the impossibility of building God's kingdom on earth.[38] Although Ernest rejected this other-worldly position and sought out meetings on Christian political responsibility, he approached political life more as an intellectual than as an activist. As a member of the Fabian Society he attended several weekend schools, but did not involve himself with the local Labour Party. He sampled with relish WEA lecturers on political topics—Margaret Cole on the USSR, Norbert Elias (making his living as a WEA lecturer after being released from internment as an enemy alien) on the 'Future of Europe' (excellent, but thinly attended), or (at the Peace Group) a scholarly lecture on Marxism by an elderly local publisher and music-lover, E. C. Fairchild, who had led the opposition to Bolshevik affiliation in the pre-1918 British Socialist Party.[39] Ernest took a particular interest in education and, informed by meetings arranged by the Council for Educational Advance, gave several talks on the subject to the local WEA. Although as WEA secretary he saw it as part of his job 'to stimulate other people's interest in their political responsibilities', his own direct involvement in political activity was confined to a brief spell in the winter of 1944–5 when he helped to establish a short-lived branch of Common Wealth, a popular home for middle-class socialists during the later years of the war, and found himself sharing platforms with the local Communist Party in protest meetings about British suppression of the left-wing resistance movement in Greece.[40]

But it was pacifism that was at the centre of his politics. Many of his closest friends belonged to the local Peace Group which met regularly throughout the war, although attendance slipped from around twenty-five in 1939 to less than ten in the later war years. Their stance was quietist and constructive, not militant. In May 1940 someone aroused the ire of the British Legion by picketing the local recruitment centre, but the Peace Group had no idea who had done this and, as noted above, Ernest was later to organize Brains Trusts on behalf of the Legion. The main focus of the group's activity was discussion and education, much like the WEA. Indeed there was a large overlap of membership between the Peace Group and the WEA—for a time the chair of the latter was also secretary of the former—and occasionally they held joint meetings. Beyond this, the group organized support for two German refugee schoolgirls, and, in 1945, set up and staffed a Café Club for local youth in an under-used sixteenth-century house belonging to Toc H.[41] The Club was Ernest's initiative. As a member of the local Youth Advisory Committee he had been trying unsuccessfully for months to get the local authority to establish a club. Here was a constructive project for the group, something more worthwhile than discussion meetings which, increasingly, he found 'incoherent', 'rambling', or 'footling'.[42]

As early as January 1940 he had been 're-considering the political practicability of Pacifism', and eighteen months later he was arguing against the 'cheerful disregard of the impossible' characteristic of those members of the Peace Group who wanted to press for a negotiated peace.[43] Sooner or later, however, he believed the time would come for negotiations. He had a realistic grasp of the difficulties of invasion and thought it improbable that the war would be ended either by a German conquest of Britain or, later, by an allied invasion of the continent. (Paradoxically, his own research on the technology of welds contributed to the success of the allied invasion.[44]) Until 1944, the most likely outcome seemed to him stalemate and a compromise peace. Although he deplored British bombardment of German cities and the denial of self-determination to India, he did not believe in the moral equivalence of the two sides. When victory finally came he joined in VE-day celebrations, and saw the exposure of the concentration camps as irrefutable evidence that victory over Nazi Germany had been preferable to defeat. While the war lasted, however, he neither supported nor opposed it. It was a question of watch and wait, meanwhile accepting the war as 'abnormal but humanly inevitable'.[45] The oddity of the phrasing, so unlike the usual precision of his writing, betrays an unease of which he was well aware. Recording his September 1941 argument against those fellow pacifists who 'cheerfully disregarded the impossible' in their advocacy of a negotiated peace, he felt compelled to acknowledge in the privacy of the diary that such a 'free use of the word "impossible" often amounts to a denial of the omnipotence of God', meaning, presumably, that he was not entirely comfortable with the realist position he had adopted against the impossibilist idealism of his comrades.[46] With God, after all, all things were possible.

Conscientious objectors had a much easier time than in the First World War and, partly for this reason, there were far more of them. Most objected to killing on religious grounds and were not concerned to evangelize.

Nor, apart from members of sects like the Plymouth Brethren whose Christian fundamentalism Ernest had experienced and rejected as a young man, were they inclined to chop logic about the ethics of serving the war effort indirectly in non-combatant roles. Indeed, concerned to avoid the negativity of mere refusal, they were anxious to serve as a positive way of bearing witness to their values and beliefs.[47] It made every sense for the state to avoid persecution of such constructive and un-subversive people. Establishing the right to conscientious objection necessarily involved the authorities in opening windows into men's souls, but objectors and tribunals often conspired not to probe too deeply. One of Ernest's friends—Stuart Morris, the secretary of the Peace Pledge Union whose candidature in the 1941 King's Norton by-election had so outraged Lillian Rogers—refused any such fudging and went to jail. Other friends were more of Ernest's mind. Lew Chanter, a political journalist on the *Daily Telegraph*, was initially refused exemption on the grounds that his readiness to work for a pro-war paper contradicted his profession of pacifism. He won on appeal, arguing that he had no control over the editorial policy of the paper. Another friend, who worked in a bank, was exempted from military service but required to work full time in civil defence. Despite his status as a CO, the bank agreed to treat him like any other conscripted employee and to supplement his pay to normal salary. 'This is a Good Thing',[48] Ernest wrote in his diary, and such benign fudges served to allay his earlier fears that the warfare state would be ruthless in its suppression of dissent:

Three years ago (he wrote in September 1942), I would have betted (only I don't bet) 10 to 1 in fivers that I would be in prison within two years . . . The government has proved less efficient and more tolerant than I expected, and I am still at large and at work.[49]

In April 1941 Ernest had registered as a conscientious objector. As a willing employee of a firm working on military contracts, the rationale for his objection to military service might easily have been challenged. But when he finally came before a tribunal two years later they acknowledged, after questioning him 'patiently and at length on my not quite logical position', that while he was eligible for military service in a non-combatant role, his employers would be able to secure his exemption because his work was essential to the war effort.[50]

Ernest's central dilemma was that his firm was producing more or less exclusively for the war effort. He could find himself offering expert advice on improvements to naval gun mountings in the morning and then, after work, discussing the ethics of war resistance at the Peace Group meeting. At the outbreak of war he had considered resigning his job, following the example of a colleague and friend who left to do voluntary work with the Friends Ambulance Unit while his wife took a secretarial post to become the bread winner. By 1944, when this couple are again mentioned in the diary, the friend was in the Lebanon re-training as a pharmacist while his wife, in London, learned midwifery. In the end Ernest, with a child to support and passionately engaged with his research work, was not prepared to sacrifice career, family cohesion, and comfort on a matter of principle. But, it is clear that he thought seriously about doing so. A characteristically laconic diary entry in October 1939 records an evening with Kay when, instead of reading as planned, they had 'started a discussion ... and finally talked the whole evening about all sorts of things, from pacifism to marriage'.[51] That is all he chose to say, leaving his reader none the wiser about who said what to whom, or how the dynamics of their marriage affected the way in which he handled the implications of his pacifism. More than twenty years later, however, Kay was to confide to her son, on the eve of his own marriage, how deeply shocked she had been by her husband's declaration that, if it ever came to choosing between her and the children and sticking to his principles, he would choose the latter.[52] Ernest, it seems, kept his options open; and Kay, who would have been told by her mother-in-law about the religious convictions which had led Ernest's father to bankrupt the family during his final years in Venice, had every reason to fear that her husband might one day decide to follow in his father's footsteps. In 1939, after talking things over with his wife, he had decided to stay in his job. But three years later he remained uneasy about 'the hypocrisy of ... continuing to do "Essential Work" when I feel as I do about the war' and to salve his conscience he resolved that after the war he would try to find work through the Society of Friends towards relief or reconciliation in Europe:

I want to remain sufficiently footloose to go and do such work if something turns out which I am fit to do. If I get through the war without any large change in work or family position I don't expect to do the same much longer. I haven't been sacrificing much in wartime, and may have the courage to do better in reconstruction time.[53]

Shortly before D-Day, after another talk with Kay, he wrote that he had 'decided to change my job after the war, and get out of purely industrial work'.[54] These vague and implausible plans—why would he be any more courageous after the war when there would no longer be reason of conscience to press him?—were sufficient to still his conscience.[55] He loved his work, and while he regretted that the factory was largely devoted to military work this was, he wrote in 1943, 'inevitable . . . and I like the work so much that I am practically reconciled to its purpose'.[56] Once again, the word 'inevitable' was used to push to one side issues of conscience that he chose to leave unresolved.

The disjunction between his ideals and his way of life was perfectly apparent to Ernest. In 1942, when salving his conscience with the prospect of deferred post-war self-sacrifice, he defined his ultimate goal as being the achievement of:

a sense of being in tune with the general direction of the Universe, of being in tune with God, or in harmony with order. As I have begun to reach this sort of security, I feel that whatever happens to me I am being used as part of an ordered movement, or perhaps I am being swept aside as part of the resistance to a disorderly movement; in any case I am on the side which will ultimately win, though only on a very long view. I may be destroyed in the process, but it would not matter very much.

This was as close as Ernest came to embracing the asceticism advocated by the leading intellectual of 1930s pacifism, Aldous Huxley:

The ideal man is the non-attached man. Non-attached to his bodily sensations and lusts. Non-attached to his craving for power and possessions. Non-attached to the objects of these various desires. Non-attached to anger and hatred; non-attached to his exclusive loves. Non-attached to wealth, fame, social position. Non-attached even to science, art, speculation, philosophy.[57]

But Ernest was the first to admit that he had not yet reached the degree of 'non-attachment' necessary to place himself 'in tune with the general direction of the Universe': 'My personal relationships with my family are still to me as much part of ultimate reality as is God.'[58] If it was an uncharacteristic sense of 'impending doom hanging over me' which had finally persuaded him to apply for membership of the Quakers in June 1940, already by that autumn, speaking at a Quaker meeting, he was 'giving thanks that the past year had given me a deeper capacity for enjoyment' of the ordinary pleasures of life, 'in particular home life and my neighbours and music'.[59] But the more he attached value to these things, the less capable he would become of the 'non-attachment' necessary to that ultimate security of 'desiring only what cannot be taken from you'.[60] Even the happiest and most honest of men, it is reassuring to know, have to live with bad faith and insoluble dilemmas.

No Eden is without its serpent, but Ernest, living a fulfilling and happy life, does not appear to be a man wracked by existential angst. This impression may, of course, be an artifice produced by the diary itself. Unlike most of the women diarists, he made very little use of his diary to explore his emotional life, behaving towards his readers at Mass-Observation with all the restraint to be expected of a public-school educated English gentleman. In 1943 his sister, who had been working as personal assistant to Gracie Fields in Hollywood was found dead, shot through the head by man who may or may not have been her ex-lover. Ernest, who learned the news on his fortieth birthday and had to break it to his mother, recounted the events of the next few days in unusual detail. But there is not a word about how he felt; nothing, either then or later, about his grief; no reflection on his relationship with his sister or, for that matter, on the impact of these events on his feelings about reaching middle age. He is similarly silent about his relationship with Kay. While reporting, in response to a directive, that his wife's mood was crucial to his 'day to day feelings', there is nothing in the diary entries to illustrate this.[61] And, as we have seen, discussions of the utmost importance to both of their lives are passed over in silence, or reported in bland one-liners.

Why did he keep a diary? Early on in his relationship with MO he had shrewdly observed that the original objectives of the organization were too confused to sustain any 'corporate purpose', explaining that he wrote because he enjoyed it, despite the fact that no one really knew what MO was for.[62] There is nothing to indicate that he ever revised this view, even though he continued to write until 1952. Perhaps the diary—typed up neatly once a week from brief handwritten notes—met a need for order, for a routine of observation and record keeping as precise and scientific as his work in the lab, or the budgets he compiled of domestic expenditure. It is to Mass-Observation's credit that its intrusive regime of monthly questionnaires extracted from this emotionally reserved man rather more than he bargained for: most of the discussion of his inner life derives from material elicited by the directives, rather than from the diary itself. Without the directives, Ernest might have appeared to be a man without feelings—except for his delight in his children—his enjoyment of life just too unproblematic to warrant the attention of the historian. Even with them large areas of his emotional life remain beyond reach.

Gender played a large part in Ernest's self-possession. Mary Clayton was the only person among the female diarists to approach his degree of personal autonomy, in her case rooted in job satisfaction. But she achieved her contentment at the expense of—or at least in the absence of—anything resembling the rich domestic, social, and cultural life enjoyed by Ernest van Someren. Despite his work, and the context of war, Ernest's pacifism did not seriously interfere with the manner in which he chose to live. Denis Argent, the subject of the next chapter, was also a conscientious objector. But being younger, and not employed in war industry, his pacifism had very different consequences for his personal life.

Figure 6. Denis Argent, circa 1941.
Courtesy Alison Hancock.

8

Denis Argent: Between the acts

> ...somehow they felt—how could one put it—a little not quite here or there. As if the play had jerked the ball out of the cup; as if what I call myself was still floating unattached, and didn't settle.
>
> (Virginia Woolf, *Between the Acts* (London, 2000), 93)

War interrupted lives. Evacuation split up families. Young 'mobile women' were conscripted into the auxiliary services, the Land Army, or munitions factories often in areas remote from their homes. And millions of young and not-so-young men were called-up into the armed forces, most of them spending years being moved around the country from camp to camp, billet to billet, before being sent overseas. Between 1939 and 1945 there were 60 million changes of address in England and Wales, in a population of about 38 million.[1] This extreme geographical mobility created upheaval in countless individual lives, especially among the younger age groups. Whatever plans individuals had made for the future in peacetime—developing a career, settling down to marriage and a family—had to be put on hold. Conscripted and directed by the state, they had, for the duration, lost control of their lives. Or so it might seem.

The determinants of young people's life plans were many and various—parental and peer pressure, education, social convention, etc. Within a stable social order the shape of a life could seem predetermined. Wartime conditions weakened many of these conditioning factors. Paradoxically the

blind and arbitrary intervention of the state could serve to liberate people
from the social networks which constrained them. Compulsion opened up
a space of freedom, of self-determination. Some parents—Nella Last, for
example—feared that their young ones would be crushed into uniformed
conformity. But, beneath the veneer of military discipline, life in the
forces offered promiscuous social mixing and unanticipated opportunities
for experimentation and growth, as MO noted in respect of young women
in the auxiliary services, especially middle-class girls made restless by their
time away from the steadying influence of home and reluctant to return to
conventional roles.[2]

Mass observers tended to dry up when they were conscripted. One of
the most extensive forces diaries was written by Denis Argent, a young
journalist, aged 22 when war broke out.[3] Registered as a conscientious
objector, he was conscripted into the Non-Combatant Corps (NCC). The
notion that the Second World War army acted as a democratizing agent of
social mixing can be exaggerated.[4] But, ineligible for officers' training as a
member of the NCC, Denis cultivated a staunchly 'other ranks' attitude,
and his friendships spanned what was often a gulf separating middle-class
from working-class pacifists. Unlike most accounts of Second World War
conscientious objection, written by convinced pacifists, Argent's diaries
describe the breakdown of pacifist convictions in the face of the Nazi
threat. Conscription disrupted both his career plans and his love life, and he
experienced the war as a time 'between the acts', as he put it borrowing the
title from Virginia Woolf's last novel: 'as if what I call myself was still floating
unattached, and didn't settle'. But the experience was not unwelcome.
Although he was intensely interested in left-wing politics, a stance of
detachment suited his professional identity as a journalist, and he relished the
freedom that the army gave him from the vexatious pressures of civilian life,
particularly the demands of women—mother, elder sister, girlfriend—that
he should 'settle down'. Secure in the masculine comradeship of barrack
and billet, enjoying the opportunities army life afforded for reading and
political discussion, Denis was happy to postpone growing up.

Phoney War

Born in 1917 during the First World War, Denis grew up anticipating the Second. At 14 he acquired a boyish fascination with military

aircraft which remained with him for years, undimmed by his conversion to pacifism a year later. His father, a commercial traveller, had died in 1924, leaving the family in straitened circumstances, although the Freemasons paid for the boy's secondary education as a boarder at the Royal Masonic School in Hertfordshire. He left school in 1934, aged 17, to take up a job as a reporter on the local paper in Tonbridge, in cycling distance from Tunbridge Wells where he lived with his mother. In April 1938, after a short spell of unemployment, he got a job on a weekly paper in Chelmsford (Essex), where he found lodgings with an aunt of a school friend. Between August 1939, when the diary began, and his call-up in March 1940, his life was divided between work in Chelmsford; London where most of his friends lived; and his girlfriend back home in Tunbridge Wells.

As a journalist Denis prided himself on his objectivity, his 'detached reporter's outlook',[5] and he brought the same spirit to bear on his work for Mass-Observation. His diaries during the first six months of the war contain much reporting on what he heard and saw around him—in the newspaper office, among the print workers who he made a point of visiting to get a working-class point of view, on his frequent train journeys. When more subjective material intruded, about his personal life, feelings, or political views, he often apologized, reflecting his belief that 'MO ... exists to record talk and opinions of that vast inarticulate class known as "the masses"', not to document the lives of educated, articulate people like himself and his friends.[6] Fortunately, he quickly discovered his mistake, realizing that MO was interested in his subjective reactions and that he was not obliged to write only in his role as the 'extrovert reporter'.

For many young men who had imbibed pacifist ideas in the 1930s the outbreak of war demanded a searching reappraisal of belief. Denis had been an active member of the Peace Pledge Union (PPU) in Tunbridge Wells, but he was also attracted by the apparent realism of Communist politics, so different from the 'pallid wishful thinking' characteristic of much Christian pacifism, the 'tract-bandying' of the religious sectarians, or the 'fussy, cranky atmosphere' of the PPU's journal *Peace News*. Christian belief lay at the basis of Denis' own pacifism, but his Jesus was a revolutionary leader and the Christianity he admired was a 'potential rallying point of world revolution'.[7] While clear that he could 'never be a devout Marxist because Communism sanctioned violence', he read the *Daily Worker* and did his best to keep abreast of the twists and turns of the party line during the opening weeks of the war.[8] Although he chuckled over the fate of

young Communists who 'joined up to smash Fascism in accordance with
the party line, only to be left high and dry a week or two later . . . fighting
in an Imperialist War!', and was dismayed by the Soviet attack on Finland,
his respect for the Party was dented only temporarily.[9] After all, everyone
he knew had been thrown into confusion by the peace movement's failure
to prevent war. Several friends abandoned their pacifism altogether, and he
listened with sympathy to the anxieties of his most intimate friend, Stuart,
whose pacifist commitment was deeply compromised by the fact that his
uncle had wangled him a career civilian post in the Air Ministry, which
he would lose if he sought to avoid combatant service by registering as a
conscientious objector.

Denis' own position was, for the time being, relatively coherent. From
the start he accepted that 'it is too late now for pacifism as such', and rejected
absolutist non-cooperation.[10] In the absence of a local branch of the Peace
Pledge Union in Chelmsford he attended meetings of the Fellowship of
Reconciliation, which he found humane, sensible, and mercifully free
from the 'crankiness which has been the worst enemy of the pacifist
movement'.[11] Alongside intelligent discussion of the pacifist dilemma, the
Fellowship organized first-aid classes and mock tribunal hearings to help
non-absolutist young men prepare their applications for ambulance work
or other non-combatant status in the armed services. By the time that he
was required to register, in December 1939, Denis was well prepared and
he faced his tribunal in January in a calm and confident spirit.

While he waited for the war to take control of his life, Denis sought
to maximize his enjoyment of what he described as 'my private worlds
of music, poetry, art . . . and love'.[12] He used weekends in London to
make the best of 'a world which this war is going to destroy: a world of
decency, orderliness, culture, good citizenship, independence of thought,
democracy-in-action'.[13] He visited Collets' bookshop—'a left-intellectual
Woolworths'—and Zwemmers further up the Charing Cross Road to
ogle art books he could not afford to buy; he went to exhibitions of Ben
Nicholson and Stanley Spencer at the City Literary Institute, 'a cultural
oasis', and to classical concerts at the Queens Hall; he made regular trips to
Levy's, a specialist jazz record shop in Whitechapel—he had been a moving
spirit in setting up the Tunbridge Wells Rhythm Club in 1935.[14] Most
of all, he valued the company of his London friends, particularly Stuart
(who he had known since school) and Stuart's girlfriend Rosie, infant
schoolteacher and part-time Unity Theatre actress. Together they dined

and wined in Soho, spent evenings watching French or Soviet movies, Unity Theatre productions, or just lying around listening to Beethoven on the gramophone and talking about culture, politics, and the meaning of life. 'It's at times like that,' he wrote after a weekend spent with Stuart and Rosie shortly before his call-up arrived, 'that life seems good: a moment when we can shake our fists at the war and curl up in our cosy private world.'[15]

He had a second, quite separate, private world with Roma, affectionately known as Bubbles, his own girlfriend in Tunbridge Wells. She had been, literally, the girl next door in his childhood, though her parents had moved to a better part of town when their chemist shop prospered. Friendship with her older brother kept him in contact, and he and Roma eventually fell in love when she was 17, two years younger than Denis. Apart from long acquaintance and the fact that their mothers were both members of the local Women's Conservative Association, Denis and Roma seem to have had little in common. In 1939 she was an art student aiming at a career as a commercial artist, vaguely Tory in outlook, and interested neither in his politics nor his cultural life—as he quipped after she failed to enjoy Groucho and Harpo in 'Go West': 'She's no Marxist in either sense of the word.'[16] He thought her reading trivial, and he put up with trips to the local theatre to see silly comedies just for the sake of holding her hand. What held them together was sex, a mutual delight in hours spent using 'the language of lip and limb' (a phrase he borrowed from the American poet and novelist Frederic Prokosch) on rural grassy banks or the sofa in the 'lounge' (as her family called it, he remarked, when they went up in the world) after mum and dad had gone to bed.[17] The outbreak of war seemed to provide him with an excuse to escalate their sexual activity—if not now, when?—but, after a weekend of lengthy discussions, the condom he had overcome his embarrassment to purchase remained in his pocket with no more than a maybe about the possibility that his 'strictly dishonourable intentions' would be fulfilled next time they met.[18] Two weeks into the phoney war 'our feelings of Sept. 3rd about love in wartime seem to have evaporated. We talked it over at length and decided that, so far, there's nothing to justify our taking risks in sex just because there happens to be a state of war.'[19] Despite a further attempt on her virtue on Christmas Eve (they were up discussing it until four in the morning) it remained intact; and in April, when his call-up was imminent, he was still confiding cheekily to Mass-Observation that 'poking was not on the agenda'.[20] 'I'm more or less in love with a girl whom I've known for years', he had written in January, but, unlike his friends Stuart and Rosie who had married at once when evacuation separated them, Denis and Roma were 'not so deeply and ecstatically in love that we'd rush off and get married next week' just because of his call-up. Marriage, they 'sensibly' agreed, should wait until after the war, if they were still so inclined; and in the meantime the 'risks in sex' should be avoided.

Slebech

By the time he was called up, Denis' fears that being in khaki would put an end to his intellectual life had been assuaged by reassuring reports from friends and long conversations with an artillery man billeted in his lodgings. He even found himself, eavesdropping on 'cheerful noisy matey crowds' of soldiers, looking forward to the experience: 'what made me feel so happy', he wrote after one such encounter, 'was the fact that their conversation, bright, witty, heavily sarcastic at the expense of Army life in general . . . all showed how it's possible for intelligent people to continue to be intelligent in (and at the expense of) the Army'.[21] Drafted into the Non-Combatant Corps, newly established in March 1940 to provide a home for non-absolutist objectors, he was not disappointed. After basic training in Great Yarmouth the new company, NCC No. 1, was sent to Wales, initially to work on Barry Docks and then, from October 1940, to a decaying early nineteenth-century Pembrokeshire manor house, Slebech, earmarked as a future training centre where most of the 250 members were employed constructing a pipeline to bring water from Haverfordwest, six miles away. During the first year of his army life he wrote little for Mass-Observation, but from March 1941 the diary resumes, painting a vivid picture of life in the NCC, a life that Denis clearly enjoyed. He was, according to MO's wartime director, one of the few Army diarists who did 'not appear to be in a continuous recurrent state of browned offness'.[22]

This was not the real army. The NCOs, mainly middle-aged ex-building labourers in the Pioneer Corps, struggled to exert authority over the argumentative young clerks, schoolteachers, students, and assorted individualists in their charge.[23] Despite daily harassments from a much hated sergeant major, the men used industrial muscle—a go-slow on the pipeline construction—to ameliorate working conditions and force recognition of a representative mess committee to deal with food grievances. Displays of chronic disrespect drove the sergeant major to distraction: 'Stand to attention when you talk to me. I'm not a bloody lackey nor a servant!' 'The funny part about it', Denis commented, '. . . is that he *was* a lackey and servant. In civvy life he was a doctor's chauffeur-handyman . . . I'm sure that in no other unit but this one would you find a sergeant major talking to the men like that: *appealing* to be respected almost.'[24]

Although his first-aid training failed to get him into the Medical Corps, which had closed its doors to conscientious objectors by the time Denis was conscripted, it was sufficient to secure appointment as a medical orderly in the NCC, thereby avoiding the rigours of pick and shovel work. The work—dealing with sceptic fingers, scalds, burns, boils, cuts, rubbing liniments into sore backs, accompanying the more serious cases to the Army doctor in Haverfordwest—was 'pleasantly responsible, yet gives plenty of privileges and leisure'.[25] Never before had he had so much time for reading—highlights included Penguin New Writing, Auden, MacNeice, Graham Greene, Grassic Gibbon, George Orwell, Virginia Woolf, plus a steady diet of Left Book Club and other political tracts, war reportage, and half a dozen weekly magazines. Long summer afternoons reading, sunbathing, and swimming naked in the estuary bore witness to 'the sort of holiday-camp life that a medical orderly can lead'.[26]

And there was friendship. Denis had little time for the apolitical Christian pacifists—Plymouth Brethren, Christadelphians, etc.—narrow-minded 'good boys' who kept to themselves, worked needlessly hard to ingratiate themselves with authority and worried only about 'managing to wangle time off from fatigues on Sundays to attend the gatherings of their particular sects'.[27] But there were plenty of like-minded others, including Nobby, a dance-band trumpeter from an East End socialist family with whom he happily argued about both politics and jazz, and Bert, a communist bus conductor from Bristol who strove manfully, but unsuc-cessfully, to convince him of the validity of revolutionary defeatism and to 'bow the knee to Dutt' (Palme Dutt, the ideological pope of British communism).[28] Although there were up to thirty paying supporters of the Communist-led People's Convention in the corps, the party members were cautious about operating openly, and it was not until May 1941 that they admitted Denis (previously 'suspect . . . as being "not safe" on account of my too noisy Leftness') to the inner circle, a small Marxist Discussion Group whose secret meetings out in the fields were romantically described by the leader as 'getting useful experience in underground organisation'.[29] Everything changed, of course, when Hitler attacked the Soviet Union in June, removing for Denis 'my last lingering doubt about the fact that this war must be fought'; but he had been sufficiently impressed by the comrades to wait anxiously for the next issue of *Labour Monthly* and the 'sheet anchor' of a 'definite pronouncement [from] the prophet Dutt'.[30]

Ever since Hitler struck to the West in May 1940 Denis had been losing patience with those conscientious objectors who, he believed, failed to confront the question of how they personally would react to a Nazi invasion. Impressed by the tactics of guerrilla resistance advocated by Spanish War veteran Tom Wintringham, he became increasingly uncomfortable about the logic of his own non-combatant status:

> I am no longer a conscientious objector to killing [he wrote in December 1940] because I can envisage in an invasion circumstances when killing one enemy can be obviously and directly the means of saving the lives of civilian fellow-workers, and maybe even friends and family. In those circumstances the possession of an ability to use even a rifle (though preferably a tommy gun and grenades) are ... desirable ... I want above all to do medical work, but I want also to be able to fight when the necessity comes.[31]

By this time about a fifth of the company had transferred to combatant units, and a further fifth, including Denis, had put their names down for bomb-disposal work. When, in April 1941, the chance of transfer came, Denis hung back on the unconvincing grounds that it would mean missing his next leave, a lame rationalization, as he admitted to his diary, of his fear. Both his mother and his girlfriend pressed him not to volunteer for such dangerous work, and, unlike an artist friend who, ground down by seven months hard labour on the pipeline, chose bomb disposal in the belief that the threat of sudden death would 'quicken the pace of time', Denis was enjoying his leisurely life as a medical orderly. What finally persuaded him to leave this comfortable billet was the Nazi invasion of the Soviet Union on 22 June. Two days later Denis joined with other left-wing friends to request transfer to bomb disposal.

Luton

As things turned out the year he spent in bomb disposal posed little danger to Denis' life, if only because his unit had hardly any bombs to dispose of.

Their training, after an intensive three-week induction course in Bedford, was, at best, episodic and most of their working time was spent building Nissan huts, going on pointless route marches or, worst of all, scrubbing the floors of their billet. Not until April 1942, eight months after his transfer, did he get to dig up his first real bomb, and the sense of achievement—'today, at last, I felt really like a member of a Bomb Disposal Section'—soon palled as the digging became routine.[33] He was also increasingly irritated by the conchie blind spot, as he saw it, about the likely results of a Nazi victory, contrasting the 'fuck the war effort' attitude of his companions with the 'genuine concern and keenness' that his mother and her Tory friends in Tunbridge Wells put into the drive for salvage, savings, and other patriotic causes.[34] Patriotic sentiment was not something that Denis often expressed, but that he felt it is revealed by his response to an MO directive in April 1942 which asked 'what particular piece of music gives rise to strong feelings in you?':

the spacious Englishness of Elgar . . . holds more for me than any other composer . . . Beauty of melody, admiration for the marvellous way Elgar's orchestration weaves its patterns . . . pride in the fact that Elgar is English . . . these are the kinds of feelings that Elgar's large scale orchestral works give me.[35]

Elgar, however, did not go unchallenged in Denis' musical affections. English patriotism vied for primacy with Communist internationalism:

The International . . . still produces in me that quickening of the pulse, that pride of feeling that it's *our* song, that feeling of being a part of something worthwhile. It probably in fact has a greater *emotional* effect on me than even Elgar has . . . I experience when hearing or singing the International the kinds of emotions which I suppose the patriotic Englishman ought to receive from God Save the King.[36]

Fortunately, since 22 June 1941, there had been little difficulty in combining these two loyalties.

Despite the frustrations of the work, and a growing belief that he ought to be taking a more active part in the war effort than his continuing non-combatant status allowed, Denis found much to enjoy in a unit whose social mix provided nourishment for different, even contradictory, aspects of his personality—'a nice mixture of low companions and intellectual conversation'.[37] During the induction course he had emerged as a key figure mediating between the more unruly element and 'the good boys' prepared to knuckle down to an Army authority far more rigorous than anything they had known at Slebech. With friends in both camps, and in cooperation with a tough but intelligent and well-read NCO who respected the conchies for their independence of thought, Denis helped to defuse what had at first looked like a troublesome stand-off. When they moved on to their more permanent billet, a requisitioned house in a suburban area of Luton, he chose to share a room with the 'bad boys'—five working-class Londoners (lorry driver, upholsterer, French polisher, engineer, and Nobby the jazz trumpet player from the East End) all in their early twenties and all given to gambling, drinking, chasing 'tarts', and general insubordination. Most of them had little time for Denis' left-wing politics, though Harry, the South London engineering worker, had been a communist and the others could sometimes be persuaded to join them in attending rallies organized regularly by a vigorous local Communist Party. At one large rally addressed by the Communist leader Harry Pollitt, Denis and four others made a contribution announced to cheers from the audience as 'Ten shillings from a Bomb Disposal Squad'.[38] There was much rough horseplay in the 'noisy, matey comradeship of the billet'.[39] On one occasion Denis was tied up like a cocoon in a blanket, manhandled out of the window and parked on top of the privet hedge; on another they dared each other to piss on the fire with predictably unpleasant consequences. But there were limits to Denis' laddishness. A couple of times he joined the others in a bit of 'tawdry tarting', but soon got fed up with the local 'monkey parade', writing contemptuously about 'slouching round the streets trying to pick up silly little cows that I wouldn't touch with a barge pole'.[40] When he did bring himself to touch, he retreated behind literary references to explain his feelings:

stroking her breast . . . with a distaste that reminded me of sordid goings-on in a Graham Greene novel . . . This business of playing around with female factory workers . . . rather disgusts me. In fact, but for the fact that this may have some MO value, as an example of the 'typical soldier's' night out, I could scarcely have brought myself to write about it. It was a degrading sort of business . . . [41]

His distaste for casual sex was reinforced by the fact that it was, in his experience, only available with working-class women; 'respectable girls' took too long 'to wear . . . down and talk . . . into it'.[42] Two years later, when he had been moved to Huddersfield, he still succumbed occasionally to the temptations of 'going out on the beer' with his mates and picking up 'some rough bit of stuff', but he never went so far as 'poking a pick-up' due to fear of VD and because 'pretty faces lose their charms for me when they open their pretty mouths and emit "EE, it were lovely" noises'.[43] His taste for low companionship did not extend to women: class mixing was, for Denis, a strictly masculine affair.

Usually, when his roommates went out on the town, Denis stayed behind, welcoming the opportunity to read quietly, listen to music, or write up his diary.[44] He had chosen to room with the working-class lads because he found them 'more tolerant, helpful and unselfish than those slightly higher up the social scale',[45] who tended to be more fastidious in their personal habits and therefore less easy to live with. But for intellectual nourishment he turned to the middle-class types elsewhere in the house, a commercial artist, a bank cashier, an insurance agent, a solicitor's clerk, a man who had worked in the *Manchester Guardian*'s advertising department, and his closest companion, a London University science student, who shared his own doubts about pacifism but, like Denis, stayed in the NCC because he liked the intellectual company. His contentment was further enhanced by the fact that the move from rural isolation in Pembrokeshire to Luton made it possible to keep in touch with London's 'civilized amenities'—'music, ballet, art, libraries, good films, etc.'[46]—and to spend weekend leaves with his friends Stuart and Rosie, now living near Reading, where he happily talked politics, films, books, poetry, and went to bed at 3 a.m.

He was also able to see more of Roma. Since his call up in April 1940 their relationship had remained much the same, centred on country walks and lovemaking. No longer an art student she was doing a boring job in the local food office while hankering for a more useful role as a munitions worker or in the WAAF, which she finally joined in April 1942. Meanwhile her disapproval of Denis' politics—'my redness makes her see red'[47]—and his attitude to army life had led to a major breach between them:

Late at night chez my girl a long and bitter argument about ambition, or my lack of it. I am [hauled] over the coals very fiercely for the fact that I am content to remain a private and scorn NCOs and officers. (They are in fact to me always 'the enemy': to be resisted and fought against. This is *not* a People's Army; and in its present structure I find it's a sort of class struggle. And I know which side I'm on.) The fact that I'm not doing anything to 'get on' isn't everything—my MO activity is disapproved of too. I ought, she says, to be writing articles which would bring in some money. The fact that I would a hundred times rather do something so obviously *worth* doing as MO doesn't seem to concern her.[48]

Rocked by her attacks he went to bed with three of his favourite political tracts:

The idea was roughly this: after the heavy attack on all my dearest principles and ideals by the girl I loved, I wanted to restore my faith in them. So I re-read parts of those books which made me feel that there is something worth working for besides mere self-advancement and family ties.[49]

A protracted row followed 'with much letter-writing, bitter words and misunderstandings', no doubt deepened by the falseness of his own position 'of being a combatant at heart yet still in the NCC'.[50] For several weeks he was too disturbed to continue the diary. It took two months to patch things up, and by the time normal relations were restored—a country walk and 'the afternoon passed in the usual thrilling manner'[51]—her call-up into the WAAF was imminent. By the summer of 1942, responding to her pressure, Denis claimed to have forsworn the life of 'the carefree conchie private' and was applying himself to 'getting on' by learning German in an (unsuccessful) attempt to get into Intelligence.[52]

1942—4

We know less about Denis' life during the rest of the war. His diary was only briefly resumed after the crisis with Roma and stopped completely in May 1942. But the broad outlines can be pieced together from his continuing responses to the monthly directives. By the end of 1942, having abandoned his non-combatant status and anxious 'to penetrate into the *real* Army and the *real* war', he found himself in Huddersfield training as a wireless operator in the Royal Corps of Signals and expecting to be sent overseas to a fighting front during the next twelve months.[53] Things went well at first, and he rapidly reconstructed the combination of 'low companions and intellectual conversation' that he had enjoyed in Luton.[54] He joined the committee of the local Rhythm Club, and went to plays and the ballet in Bradford and Leeds at the weekends: 'I have always managed to keep a civilian mentality intact in the Army', he wrote in 1945.[55] But he showed no aptitude for the work, found it impossible to memorize Morse code, and after a dismal spring in an overcrowded training centre outside the town he collapsed, was briefly hospitalized, failed his trade test, and spent the summer doing menial tasks in the cookhouse while the Army wondered what to do with him. Several weeks on a physical development course at Skegness restored his health, but his hopes of resuming the training came to nothing. In March 1944, still in the Signals Corps in Huddersfield, he was doing clerical work and now expected to serve out the war without seeing any fighting, which he did, although he spent nearly two years in Burma and did not get back to civilian life until well into 1946.

Resilient as ever, Denis does not seem to have been overly dismayed by the failure of his attempt to get into 'the real war'. Even at his low point during the summer of 1943 he felt temperamentally so well suited to Army life that he toyed with the idea of staying on after the war, like Lawrence of Arabia in the RAF (a rather improbable role model) living 'at the Army level physically and the high level intellectually'.[56] Such thoughts were not unconnected with the attenuation of his relationship with Roma that followed her conscription and his move to the North. Although they continued to meet when their leaves coincided, they both had tentative relationships with other people, she with a US airman, he with a succession of those 'respectable girls' whose resistance to physical intimacy he never had time to wear down. By the spring of 1944 the ups and downs of their romance had, he believed, 'resolved themselves not in a clean break, but in an understanding (born of long intimacy) to remain very good friends'.[57] His own ambivalence about the prospect of marriage was reinforced by the pleasure he took in Army life which, he had long felt, freed him from the obligations and responsibilities of civilian existence. Although half his army pay went towards his mother's income, he relied on his elder sister to take care of the family finances, describing himself as a 'practised procrastinator' in financial matters:

I feel that at the moment . . . I am too irresponsible by temperament to take kindly to the many self-imposed responsibilities of family life . . . I don't like being hemmed in by obligations. And marriage, of course, is one long series of obligations . . . The Army has increased my old liking for pleasing myself. It may seem a strange thing; but even in the crowded communal life of the Army one is more at liberty . . . to live one's own personal life unhampered by social obligations, than one ever was in civil life . . . In a way the Army is an ideal bachelor existence.[58]

James Byron, one of the 'conchie heroes' who were parachuted as stretcher bearers into France on D-Day, remarked of his own time in a bomb-disposal unit how the 'vague adolescent team-love . . . the pleasant feeling of being liked, the absorption in the lives of other men, the merging

of self into community' served to 'undo the process of growing up'.[59]
Something like this happened to Denis, for whom Army life was in many
ways a repeat of his boarding-school years. Earlier in the war he had
noted that 'being able to enjoy myself in the ranks on a private's pay,
the temptation is not to worry about personal advancement at all'. Under
pressure from Roma—'I love her enough to want to "get on" for her
sake'—he had made an effort, but when this failed and his love cooled,
he settled happily enough for a life free from the responsibilities of civilian
existence.[60]

A similar detachment was apparent in his attitude to politics. In January
1943 he described himself as 'still a sort of borderline indecisive hanger-on
of the Communist Party'.[61] As in Slebech, where he had been much
impressed by Bert the Bristol bus conductor, he soon came under the
influence of a communist ex-laboratory assistant who not only shared
his love of classical music but was also 'properly expert in the whole
gospel of the prophet Marx'.[62] Struggling against 'my obstacle-making
individualism ... and tendencies towards bourgeois intellectualism', this
man did his best to turn Denis into 'heart and soul a Party man', but they
were posted apart in the spring 'maybe just in time ... a few more months
under his influence and my last inner ring of defences might have been
overcome'.[63] This seems an unlikely outcome: the inner defences of his
detachment were robust. Although he continued to read the *Daily Worker*,
Tribune, *New Statesman*, and was briefly enthused by the emergence of
Common Wealth, he found the local political life much less interesting
than in Luton: 'the whole area seems politically dead. The general trade
of the woollen industry seems to lead to woollen minds.' The Communist
Party had little presence in Huddersfield and the quasi-pacifist local ILP,
stirring up trouble among engineering apprentices, held no appeal for a man
who wanted to place his faith in the pro-war, productionist communist-led
shop-stewards' movement. Among his fellow soldiers Denis continued to
be known as a 'red' and scarcely a day passed without at least one argument
provoked by right-wing sentiments he could not abide. 'In this way', he
wrote in the autumn of 1943 in mitigation of his 'shamefully negative'
record of political activity, 'I can claim that politics play a considerable
part in my life ...'. Although, at this point, he still hoped to become
politically active after the war, he had a shrewd suspicion that 'some simple
human counter-interest' (e.g. marriage) might prevent this.[64] A year later

he seemed to have reconciled himself to a permanent position on the sidelines:

> I'm afraid idealistic politics always boil down to 'the flat ephemeral pamphlet and the boring meeting' and I always seem to 'stand outside' any political meeting...and can't get absorbed in it emotionally. I always seem to take my journalistic detachment with me...I shall move, I expect, on the fringe of political circles without ever wanting to throw my whole life into the struggle.[65]

When, in the summer of 1941, Denis had been waiting for his transfer to bomb disposal to come through he contracted a skin infection that put him in hospital for three weeks. This left him with what he described, using Virginia Woolf's title, as 'a kind of between-the-acts' feeling. That was before he had read the book, but when he did, the next day, it chimed precisely with the 'vaguely unreal feeling' that he had felt on and off ever since the day war was declared: 'Everything is somehow beautiful but doomed, the violence of war just round the corner, bombers fly over, personal relations are subtle yet clouded...I don't think I could have chosen a better book than *Between the Acts* to suit my mood.' Such was the impression that Virginia Woolf's last novel made on him that he read it twice more during the next two years.

What did a young pacifistic, fellow-travelling journalist making the best of life in the Army find so appealing in Virginia Woolf's novel about a group of well-heeled middle-aged and elderly people watching a village pageant? In real life he bristled at the very sight of the kind of woman who might be found organizing such an event (he would have hated Gertrude Glover!). Sitting opposite a tweedy lady on a train he imagined her:

> [as the] would-be dictator of some Suffolk village: on the committee of the Women's Institute and probably chairman of village Conservative Association...She wore tweeds and suede shoes, an ARP badge...She read *The Times* with disdain and infuriatingly methodically. And having read it, she started on the crossword...All the worst qualities of 'managing' women.[66]

But that was in October 1939. As his attitude to the war changed he came to appreciate the down to earth patriotism of his mother and her WVS friends, much as Virginia Woolf acquired a new-found admiration for the WI.[67]

Clearly the book spoke to his experience of Army life as marking time, a sense that the main current of his life—career, marriage, growing up, and accepting the responsibilities of adulthood—was held in suspension for the duration of the war. But perhaps he also sensed a deeper affinity between his own quest for meaning, and Virginia Woolf's character of Lucy Swithen, whose response to 'marking time' was to savour a present transcending time and history, glimpsing in the epiphanies offered by music or religious emotion 'the point of intersection of the timeless with time', as T. S. Eliot put it in the *Dry Salvages*, which Denis bought and read a few weeks after his first encounter with *Between the Acts*.[68] Denis found consolation for the ravages of contemporary history in culture, particularly poetry and in classical music: 'life is still worth living while the music of Beethoven can be heard…the most worthwhile thing which war can't take away.'[69] The Christian faith in which he had been brought up and which had provided the basis for his pacifism proved rather less resilient. His habit of regular churchgoing did not survive the outbreak of war, though still in the spring of 1941 he could take comfort in the occasional high-church service, suffused with the beauty, the sweetness and light, that, like Matthew Arnold, he found so lacking in the austere religiosity of the nonconformist sects. A year later, although he still claimed nominal membership of the Church of England and attended services at Christmas and Easter, his belief had become vestigial and he no longer prayed. 'For me nowadays,' he wrote, 'going to a Communist meeting on a Sunday evening has replaced churchgoing. I might even say that I attend the meetings in somewhat of the same spirit as the good Christian would attend Church.'[70] Despite his view that as a 'would-be Marxist materialist [he] shouldn't admit to an interest in matters on the spiritual plane', his continuing need for something more than his Marxist friends had to offer was apparent in his engagement with J. W. Dunne's reassuringly 'scientific' endorsement of the paranormal, *An Experiment with Time*, and Lin Yutang's popular distillation of Eastern wisdom, *The Importance of Living*.[71]

Denis was a young man finding his feet politically, socially, professionally, and sexually. The main effect of the war on his life appears to have been to enable him to postpone decisions about his professional and personal future. According to the (pacifist) historian of conscientious objection most members of the NCC came to regret the compromise with militarism involved and to realize 'the hollow values and the falseness of military life'.[72] Denis, by contrast, had found, much to his surprise, that the Army provided a kind of freedom from social pressures, a space of irresponsibility which he came to value. Although his interest in politics continued, life in the Army was not conducive to political activism and his wartime experience confirmed his detachment from active politics. It also helped him to resist pressures to settle down: by postponing the question of his future career it also postponed the question of marriage.

Despite their wartime ups and downs he and Roma did finally marry in September 1946, and within a few months Denis was again working on a local newspaper. His last pre-war holiday had been a 1,200 mile cycling tour of England, and his wartime experiences increased his desire to 'wander', perhaps as a 'roving reporter'. He was eventually to find his metier working on the magazine *Modern Caravan*, whose visionary founder had seen caravanning as serving 'a new social group living . . . a broader more interesting life'.[73] As technical editor Denis would have had no time for the prophetic gloom of cultural reactionaries like T. S. Eliot, who feared that 'our ancient edifices' would be bulldozed 'to make ready the ground upon which the barbarian nomads of the future will encamp in their mechanised caravans'.[74] By the 1970s, however, the barbarians had arrived and Denis himself was nostalgically deploring the swamping of enthusiastic hobbyists by ignorant newcomers attracted by the mass-marketing of caravans 'merely as a means of having a family holiday'.[75] For a time, however, the nomadic world of the caravanner seems to have provided him with an occupation well suited to the rather detached curiosity with which he approached his life and times.

Figure 7. Matthew Walton, circa 1925.
Courtesy Rita Lawson.

Figure 8. Bertha Walton, circa 1923.
Courtesy Rita Lawson.

9

The Waltons: A democratic marriage[1]

For Matthew and Bertha Walton, a school teacher and his wife living in a small town in the Durham coalfield, Mass-Observation was a joint enterprise. Among the reasons they gave for joining in 1937 was that it was something they could do together, and one of the pleasures of their diary is the insight it gives into a particularly companionate and democratic marriage. The fact that they read each other's diaries, may have made them less than frank at times, but it testifies to their closeness as a couple. Before the war they were equally involved, but from September 1939 Matthew wrote most of the diary, while Bertha added her own passages when she had something of special interest to contribute. By the summer of 1944, having written regularly throughout the war, Matthew was losing interest and Bertha took over, keeping the diary going until the end of 1946.

Bertha and Matthew were natural recruits for Mass-Observation, sharing many of the concerns of its founders, Tom Harrisson and Charles Madge. She had read extracts from *Savage Civilisation,* Harrisson's vivid account of his adventures in Melanesia, and relished the opportunity to turn an anthropological gaze on her own activity in public life. Matthew, a regular reader of *New Verse,* knew Madge's poetry and had been intrigued by his surrealist experiment with 'collective poetry'. They were both convinced of the social scientific value of the work: as Matthew put it, very much in line with MO's first statement of objectives, the organization would accumulate 'a vast repository of scientific data, hitherto unavailable, for the future use of students of psychology, anthropology, comparative religion, sociology, etc. when these become sciences'.[2]

When they joined MO in 1937 they were both intensely involved in left-wing politics. They organized fund-raising for Aid to Spain, did secretarial work for the unemployed workers' movement, and for several years Matthew ran a WEA class in one of the outlying mining villages where 80 per cent of the men were on the dole. Members of the Left Book Club, their sympathies were broadly communist, but they chose to work in the Labour Party where Matthew became chair of the local party. After the outbreak of war their paths diverged. Matthew, always inclined to deplore the 'sheep-like docility'[3] of the masses, became increasingly despondent about the efficacy of socialist politics in Britain, and sought solace in self-isolating literary and artistic pursuits. In contrast, Bertha's war, like Nella Last's, was a time of liberation (although she had suffered none of the repression in her marriage that afflicted Nella), and she wrote with delight about her new and unexpected experiences in wartime employment, and with stoical determination about her continuing Labour Party activism.

Matthew

Matthew, born in 1904, was much the same age as Ernest van Someren, and was the only other graduate among the diarists: he had read English at Durham University. But, as the son of a colliery official, he had none of Ernest's cultural capital, and he lived, not among fellow spirits in a wealthy suburb within easy reach of the cultural resources of the metropolis, but on a lower-middle-class housing estate in Bishop Auckland, an isolated town in the midst of what he saw as the cultural desert of the Durham coalfield. Matthew and Bertha both perceived themselves, in Matthew Arnold's terms, as cultured aliens struggling to survive among the philistines. Responding to a Mass-Observation questionnaire in 1939 Matthew described himself as:

completely alien to the [lower-middle] class to which, nevertheless, I feel I belong…Social values entirely different…I mix with individuals of a certain intelligence and political outlook—leading [he added dolefully] to an extremely restricted social environment.[4]

The immediate neighbours, George and Mabel Sands, were politically sympathetic and good friends, and Matthew enjoyed the company of a communist art teacher who lived a few doors away. But most of the neighbours they dismissed as the kind of people who aspired to buy cars, kept pets, listened to Radio Luxembourg, read pulp fiction, and busied themselves with home improvements. The Waltons, by contrast, spent their money on books, records, paints, culture-packed holidays in London and, once (in 1938), in France.

Matthew was unambitious in his job, and for seventeen years after graduating he remained at the same elementary school despite the fact that he appears to have gained little intrinsic reward from the teaching. 'Poetry is the only thing I teach with zeal', he wrote in August 1943.[5] Otherwise his diary comments are characteristically brief and downbeat: 'School started. Same grind'; 'School is so mechanical that it leaves nothing...in the memory'; 'foul wet windy day...The kind of day when you realise fully the misery of going on from day to day, year to year in the same bloody building teaching the same bloody things, subjected to the same bloody red tape and futilities...'. [6] It may be that he was using the diary as a dumping ground for his more negative feelings while keeping the positive to himself. His neighbour's son, who was one of Matthew's wartime pupils, remembers him as 'a good teacher...He had that ability to stimulate your interest in the subject being taught, rather than the more common method in those less enlightened days of beating the subject into you!'[7] As a graduate he might have expected a headship or a move into secondary education, but, according to Bertha, his political reputation and his refusal to kow-tow to members of the appointing committees ruled this out.[8]

Nevertheless the job had its advantages: above all that it gave him time for reading. Matthew attributed his own escape from lower-middle-class conformity not to his university education, which on his own account left him largely 'illiterate', but to his passion for buying books. Although he could not accommodate more than about 1,800 books in his house, he turned his stock over at regular intervals with the help of a second-hand book dealer from Darlington. These books, he insisted against the criticism of friends and relatives, were no extravagance: they constituted an alternative 'social and intellectual environment. They allow me to test my brain on finer brains and so develop it. They increase my worth as a human being...'.[9] And the job gave him time for his other great passion, painting. He painted in the evenings, at weekends, and during long summer holidays spent at home or with his uncle, a farmer in rural Cumberland who was himself also a painter. Matthew copied Velasquez, Renoir, Degas,

Van Gogh; struggled with a self portrait ('the arm won't come right'); produced surrealist compositions 'from "chance" designs'; sketched Bertha reading Stendhal; and had 'a luscious time splashing rose madder all over the canvass'. Painting was largely a solitary pleasure: the diary provides little evidence of an audience, apart from occasional conversations with the art teacher down the road. There were regular visits from an old friend, a freelance artist living in Coventry, but he 'sniffed' at Matthew's efforts, frowned on his 'fumbling Modernism,' and was seldom complimentary. Inspiration came mainly from books, since touring exhibitions rarely reached the North East. Excited by one such exhibition in December 1940, Matthew lectured Mass-Observation on the cultural deprivation of the provinces: 'I don't think you buggers in London have ever realised the burning lust for cultural "sensations" that those unfortunates in the outer world are possessed by.' When circumstances permitted he made up for lost time staying with friends in London, following a fierce schedule of art galleries, theatre and concerts interspersed with orgies of book-buying in the Charing Cross Road.

The political life, when he took it up in his early thirties, threatened to disrupt this calm and cultured existence. 'Stepping forward from thought to action,' as he put it later, enjoying the irony, 'I ceased reading and joined the Left Book Club.'[10] During the three years before war broke out he threw himself into political activity, until he was expelled from the Labour Party for organizing a public meeting for Stafford Cripps' Popular Front campaign early in 1939. For a time he remained active in the Left Book Club where his closest friendships now lay, but from the spring of 1940 even this involvement ceased and thereafter his only regular political commitment was to sell six copies of *Russia Today* each month. This intense but short-lived period of activism was deeply disillusioning for Matthew. While his interest in politics remained, his diaries are peppered with despairing comment on the futility of politics and the ignorance and apathy of the masses. Only the Soviet Union did not fail him.

During the early months of the war Matthew tried to make sense of the situation with his small circle of intellectual friends: 'Beer party tonight among the "intellectuals"—hiding their lost "raison d'etre" under a more than usual outburst of cynicism.'[11] The diaries are reticent about his analysis, deliberately so since he expected 'Imperialist War' to result in the persecution of communists and their sympathizers. Shortly after Dunkirk, alarmed by the internment of enemy aliens, including some German Jews he had befriended, he destroyed the previous month's diary; not because he feared for the safety of left-wingers following a Nazi invasion, but because (as he saw it) Britain's own crypto-fascists were (like their French equivalents) using fears of a pro-Nazi Fifth Column to:

cast suspicion on the erstwhile Left, with the result that the 'old-fashioned Anti-Fascists'...have felt the net closing around them (queer how in melodramatic circumstances, the clichés of melodrama suggest themselves)...This last month I have been through the house with a small tooth comb burning, ironically enough, evidence of past anti-fascist activity [old lecture notes, collections of cuttings, etc.]. 'Wait till you have to begin burning your beautiful books' said one enemy alien to me...I have begun.[12]

The paranoia quickly subsided, to be replaced by an attitude of detachment. In Cumberland on half-term holiday during the London blitz, he reflected on:

the agony of London's ordeal while we sit here in peace. And there's nothing to do. For three years up to the outbreak of war one could fight against it. Now we're helpless...Defeatist I suppose. But one grows weary of struggling for ever against the tide.[13]

Noting that 'life is a comedy to him who thinks, a tragedy to him who feels', Matthew opted for the comedy.[14] The suppression of the *Daily Worker* in January 1941 left him bereft of political guidance. The Nazi attack on the Soviet Union in June 1941 did little to change this attitude of detachment, despite the fact that 'defending Socialism as actualised in the Soviet Union' had always been the primary motive of his politics.[15] At a time when left-wingers of similar views threw themselves into campaigning for the opening of a second front and the maximization of war production, Matthew preferred to dwell on the comic aspects of establishment pro-Sovietism—the International on the BBC or the local anti-communist bigwigs out collecting for Russia on the street. With little faith in the capacity of the British masses and still less in the stability of their rulers' marriage of convenience with Russia, Matthew invested all his hopes for the future of civilization in the Soviet war effort, preferably unaided by the West: 'Eventually,' he wrote in the summer of 1942 as Stalingrad struggled to hold out, 'the less help they get from capitalist countries, the less dependent they are, the better for the future...Personally for the sake of the future of civilisation, I don't care a hoot whether we lose, as long as Russia wins.'[16] This total transfer of historical agency to the Soviet Union served to confirm his own political inactivity.

Talk of post-war reconstruction following the publication of the Beveridge Report at the end of 1942 left him similarly cold. Where other socialists were inspired by visions of a reformist, or even revolutionary, anti-fascist patriotism, Matthew had only cynicism to offer. He turned down an invitation to rejoin the Labour Party, retrospectively thankful that his expulsion had released him from the futilities of local politics, and declined to join the Communist Party. One aspect of his pre-war political life that he did sustain into the war years was his friendship with Jimmy, a full-time communist organizer who worked in the coalfield for the National Unemployed Workers' Movement. During the war Jimmy became an all-purpose poor man's lawyer representing workers at call-up tribunals, arbitration committees, pension appeals etc., and Matthew and Bertha were often called on to help with the paperwork. Matthew's admiration for Jimmy was unstinting: 'a real... old-time fighter. ... hated like the devil by local Union leaders, Labour Party councillors, etc. No wonder—he does single handed what they ought to do as organized bodies, fights single-mindedly for the workers.'[17] But (regretfully) he saw such militancy as an anachronism, out of kilter with a Communist Party which after Stalin's dissolution of the Comintern in May 1943 seemed to have lost its *raison d'être*: 'wonder how the Party will stumble along now, on its own. Joe sure is realistic, but it makes the future of social revolution in the capitalist world a very hazy affair.'[18] When, in September 1943, Mass-Observation asked its members what part politics played in their lives 'nowadays', Matthew responded: 'Nil... I shall remain inert', though he did concede that 'probably when the fun starts, as it will after the war, I'll be dragged out of my hole'.[19]

There had been one brief moment of optimism. When air raids began in the North East in July 1940 Matthew, in line with Communist Party policy, had persuaded George Sands, his friend next door, who was deputy to the chief ARP warden, to canvass the estate on the need for a communal shelter.[20] The response was overwhelming and within weeks construction had begun. Matthew, who had always felt something of a 'social misfit' in his political work, wallowed in the comradeship of manual labour:

A couple of joiners said 'We'll make these bloody schoolteachers work'. I determined I would show I could work with anyone and have made a point of coming on the job early and staying till the end. It was physical torture at first.

Now I can work in an eight hour shift and feel fresh at the end of it. Never having done any manual work (disliking even gardening), not being mechanically minded (beyond working a gramophone), I can now use a pick and shovel with professional ease, can mix and puddle cement, and use the mixer, erect shuttering, locate field drains, etc, etc . . . My neighbours have lost that air of suspicious respect for me as a schoolteacher, and grant me instead the friendly respect of a good worker . . .

Building the shelter, Matthew enthused: 'has turned us from an ill-sorted conglomeration of shifty suspicious railinged-off lower middle and skilled working class anti-social units, into a community . . . we are all on the intimate terms of men who work together'. He even swapped friendly abuse with the local policeman: 'It's going to be awkward for him when he comes to search the house for back copies of the *Daily Worker*.'[21]

Appointed secretary of the Shelter Committee, Matthew drafted rules and regulations. Despite the field drains the underground shelter quickly flooded, and he consolidated his new-found neighbourliness by joining the butcher and the coal merchant in evening trips around the coalfield ostensibly to scrounge old pumps but actually providing a good excuse for a pub crawl. In the absence of air raids many of the residents quickly came to favour sleep over safety, disregarded the sirens, and stopped using the shelter. As winter set in Matthew's initial hopes for a general democratic awakening faded in face of the tedium of the pumping rota and increasingly fractious meetings of the shelter committee. In April 1941 he took opportunity of the first AGM to resign. This was not an unusual trajectory. Excited speculation about the dawning of a new democratic spirit rooted in neighbourly responses to the threat of bombing was commonplace in the autumn of 1940—even *The Times* ran an enthusiastic leader on the subject—but the experience was too ephemeral to override the deeper sources of Matthew's political pessimism.[22]

Even before the romance of shelter democracy began to wane, Matthew remarked that the main effect of the war had been 'to take me back three or four years to my non-political days when I was a book-worm'. No longer distracted by the struggle to prevent the war, he 'reverted to reading'.[23] With a few exceptions (Rex Warner, Auden) contemporary literature held little appeal: history was moving too fast and 'the topical is dead before it is published'.[24] He read or reread the classics of the English, American, Russian, German, and French novel (the latter in French), some history (Gibbon, a biography of Napoleon), some Marxism (Lenin,

Engels), some literary criticism (I. A. Richards, Edmund Wilson), and Pepys' diary. Worried by the eclecticism of his reading he cast around for some more specialized 'line of study'.[25] Poetry was his first love and his 1941 new year resolution was to devote an hour each morning 'working on Auden ... You can't be fire-watching and warden-dutying all day. It's much more heartening surely to read and ponder "history to the defeated/May say Alas but cannot pardon".' [sic][26] The spring of 1941 saw him reading widely in anthropology. During 1942 he researched and wrote an essay on Elizabethan drama—'something to fasten on'—which was positively received by the Durham University academic to whom he sent it.[27]

His pleasure in all this was palpable, heightened by his belief that the time for culture might be short. 'Began my weekend's painting. Must get on as much as I can while the going's good. Christ knows how much longer my painting life will last and there's a Renoir nude I've always yearned to copy.'[28] This in May 1940 as blitzkrieg shattered the Netherlands. And a few days later: 'spent day in neighbour's orchard doing a Van Gough on the apple blossom ... all so idyllically peaceful while all around ... hell was raging.'[29] After another day painting, reading, and listening to a Beethoven quartet on the gramophone: 'Supremely selfish and unsocial, supremely enjoyable.'[30] And two years later: 'Nothing to report. Happy is the country that has no history ... Life flows on smoothly amidst world catastrophe ...'.[31] He felt himself personally suspended between Auden's era of the 'flat ephemeral pamphlet and the boring meeting' and 'the time for shooting and bombing and burrowing into the earth'. There was something desperate in his pleasure. He felt impelled to 'seize the last chance of culture and study. We may be the last to have that chance for generations.'[32] The war was destroying a 500-year-old way of living, 'and what way of living it will engender is past the wit of man to say'.[33] Virginia Woolf's suicide in May 1941 showed that 'the impasse was inescapable': he agreed with the tributes in Horizon which took her 'as a symbol—not of the "Eclipse of the Highbrow", but of the End of a Culture. Certainly there seems little room for intellectual and aesthetic values in modern Western European society. In fact culture has no place in our "culture" (anthropologically speaking).'[34] Suggestions that the war was spreading appreciation of high culture among the masses betrayed 'the rankest utopian idealism' among 'some of our Marxist intellectuals' (in this instance Day Lewis).[35] He was much impressed by Tom Harrisson's scorching account of the wartime tide of right-wing, anti-intellectual literature: 'to judge from most war books, Britain is fighting this war to protect the world against Auden and Picasso, the Jews and any form of collectivism.'[36] The reaction of the Bishop Auckland cinema audience to the *Grapes of Wrath* (boredom, indifference, disbelief) or to *Citizen Kane* (irritated incomprehension) confirmed his dim view of 'contemporary democratic standards of taste'.[37]

What role could there be for the intellectual in this climate? Before the war he had 'given [himself] to the struggle without reserve', but, he now realized, his experience had always been that of a 'fish out of water'. Unlike Jimmy, the communist organizer he so admired, Matthew was not a 'born rebel'.[38] Perhaps his working-class comrades in the Labour Party had been right to distrust the intellectuals. In any event there was no place for them and their 'individual values' in the totalitarian atmosphere of war, and Auden, he argued, had been right to leave the war zone for the safety of the United States: 'it is probably better (from the point of view of art) to have a live Auden than a dead Owen.'[39] Meanwhile the best to be said 'for the "cultured" [was that] their culture is useful for its escapist function', to 'keep [the] mind from entirely rotting away'.[40] By the end of 1940 Matthew's three closest friends had all been called up—a reporter on the Newcastle Chronicle ('we met over Lawrence and Dostoevsky; we graduated into ILP and Marxism together, and now the imperialist war has got him'); a teacher ('the only left-winger whose judgement I ever entirely relied on'); and Frank, a librarian with whom he had passionate arguments about Auden ('built like Dr. Johnson, eccentric, "classically" literary...oblivious of politics, though taking the *Worker* to oblige his militant friends...Loosing Frank...means another source of light stopped').[41] When it seemed likely, at the end of 1941 that teachers of his own age group would be called up he found himself '*hoping* I have to go, as preferable to mouldering here'. He had conceived 'an illogical desire' to 'run away to sea' and was green with envy when his friend and neighbour, George Sands, was passed A1 for naval service.[42] But the call-up never came. He was briefly amazed to discover when fire-watching that Bishop Auckland ('this miserable hole') contained another man who shared his 'secret vice' (a reader of Pepys, Havelock Ellis, Wordsworth).[43] More often, however, deprived of the coterie of intellectual friends who had sustained him, he felt isolated, left out, marginal, depressed: 'I am rapidly getting to the stage when I want to go nowhere and see no one. I slip out of this deadness into the artificial environment of books.'[44] Despite his protestations to 'you buggers in London'—those imagined MO readers who, he assumed, could not conceive of the cultural deprivations of the provinces—it is clear that Matthew rather enjoyed his sense of himself as a man of culture isolated among barbarians. Significantly, for example, he showed no interest in the pitman painters of the nearby Spennymoor Settlement or in their bohemian tutors, although he and Bertha did make occasional use of the Settlement's film club to see continental movies.[45]

Matthew Walton had a good deal in common with Denis Argent. Like Denis his sense of himself revolved around issues of culture and left-wing politics; both men were voracious readers of fiction, contemporary poetry, and political literature; both appreciated classical music and jazz; both were fellow-travellers close to the Communist Party but never willing to join. For Matthew, as for Denis the net effect of the war was depoliticizing. The trauma of the coming war, in the 1930s, and then of the actual one had dominated these men's lives for ten years. Matthew, no less than Denis, had felt himself to be 'between the acts'. Both men apologized for standing on the sidelines by saying that they would probably get drawn into political activity again in the struggles that would follow the war, although it is not clear that either really believed this. And when peace finally came both Denis and, as we shall see, Matthew turned with relief to the cultivation of home, family, and career. In the meantime what saved Matthew from retreating entirely into his private world was the continuing activism of his wife. Bertha's war, unlike Matthew's, was a liberating, at times exhilarating, experience. She grew politically, while he shrank.

Bertha

Bertha and Matthew had been a couple since their schooldays, and came from very similar backgrounds. Her father, like his, worked as a manager; her mother had been a teacher, and she herself taught in an elementary school until her marriage in 1929. During the 1930s she had sought relief from 'middle-class, new house estate boredom' by teaching needlework in adult education classes and social service centres; having some money of her own was more important to her than the work itself which she found tedious.[46] She also wrote articles on foreign cookery for the *Newcastle Chronicle*, donating the proceeds to a refugee charity. In the late 1930s she had been as active as Matthew in the Left Book Club and the Labour Party.

Although they jointly organized the offending Popular Front meeting for Cripps, she had not been expelled and she continued as Labour Party dues collector and ad hoc social worker among the Catholic housewives of the neighbouring slum clearance area.

The Bishop Auckland Labour Party was not a happy place for the middle-class teachers who made up its left wing. Ben Pimlott's biography of Hugh Dalton, the local MP, provides a portrait of the local party which fully bears out the Walton's view of it as both ineffective and corrupt.[47] While Bertha hung on, her accounts of the inner life of the party were hardly calculated to encourage Matthew to rejoin. In January 1941 Dalton addressed a delegate meeting of the constituency party in a 'bleak room of the church institute':

> Above the mantelpiece [the first work Bertha did for MO in 1937 had been to describe the contents of mantelpieces, including this one] . . . hung seven black cats cut out of paper with red neck-ribbons. God knows what meeting could have left these behind, and nothing more incongruous could I imagine, looking round the dull elderly gathering. On the opposite wall a row of pegs—at a height suited to giants—hung five head gears of delegates. Truly representative of the modern Labour Party—two caps, two trilbies, and one bowler. The cats looked at the hats and under both the meeting went on.

Dalton, currently Minister of Economic Warfare, 'gave the low down to the privileged', but in fact said nothing they didn't already know.[48]

It was not politics but war work that excited Bertha. Early in 1939, along with other members of the Labour Party Women's Section,[49] she had qualified as an ARP instructor, and subsequently occupied a responsible position as a warden. She toyed with the notion of applying for paid work in ARP, but was deterred by the usual stories of graft attached to public life in the town. When it seemed likely that Matthew would be called up, she cast around for work to occupy her, ready to consider anything but a return to teaching. Opportunity came when the next-door neighbour's lodger offered to find Bertha a managerial job in the NAAFI in which he held a senior position. Despite the fact that this would involve working away from home, what had begun as a contingency plan to follow Matthew's call-up became an immediate reality when Matthew, to Bertha's astonishment, urged her not to wait. He explained:

> My fundamental reason is a psychological one. If she can leave me temporarily and satisfy herself by mastering a new profession, then she'll return satisfied; if she turned it down, she'd be unsatisfied with herself, and unconsciously turn

that on to me. We've been in a dither and a daze all weekend, but things seem settled.[50]

Next door's lodger, it turned out, was looking for a furnished house with his wife and a curious deal was struck by which Matthew became a lodger in his own house catered for by his tenants: 'Our friends and neighbours would think us mad but that doesn't count. I think it would be good for B, and—provided I can visit her frequently—I can stick it here with a room on my own and my books.'[51] At the end of October 1941 Bertha left for the army camp at Catterick where she was to train as a manageress. It was the couple's first separation since their days at college twenty years earlier.

If the Labour Party was tedious, the NAAFI turned out to be a nightmare—exhaustingly long hours, responsibility for the bookkeeping (which was not Bertha's forte), filthy kitchens, and dormitories infested with rats. Her diary entries—the first sustained writing she did for Mass-Observation—provide a vivid picture of life behind the NAAFI counter: 'she finds it tough and sordid but interesting', wrote Matthew approvingly, 'my God is she finding out how the kitchen maid class live. It's made her more than ever on the side of the masses against the classes.'[52] At first Bertha rose to the challenge, fascinated by the attitudes of the working-class girls in her charge (their superstitions, their games, their tolerance of appalling conditions, the warmth of their affection for her) and ready to do battle on their behalf with the hierarchy over shocking low wages and conditions. But the pace was more than she could take. Following a clash with the authorities over a requirement for the girls to work on Christmas Day, and in poor health, she decided to quit.

Determined to find another job nearer home she badgered the Labour Exchange, but they could find nothing suitable. As with the NAAFI, it was through a chance encounter with a neighbour that in April 1942 she found the job of her dreams—working in a local engineering factory. Hans Stephan was a foreman in a button-making factory set up by two German Jewish refugees on the local trading estate in the late 1930s and partially converted to aircraft work during the war. The Waltons had known Stephan and his family, also German Jewish refugees, since 1937 and had lent their support when the family were separated by the internment of enemy aliens in 1940. Delighted to find an educated woman actually asking for work, the owner created a job for her as a trainee inspector, checking aircraft parts for accuracy. Bertha was excited by her introduction to factory life: 'It was thrilling to learn what a chaser, a reamer, a wrench, etc were', she wrote after a spell in the tool room, 'and how to measure taps and drills.' 'I like the dirt and grease and noise and working with others feels good ... more ... matey than anything else I've done ...'[53] The factory was small and she quickly got to know her fellow workers, mostly young girls and lads between 16 and 26, and a handful of older men. In common with a number of other female MO diarists newly engaged in factory work, Bertha quickly came to feel 'completely detached from my previous life and friends ... and ... lost all interest in the house and its welfare':

So now I am a factory worker on good terms with bosses and workers. My work is useful, satisfying and I am happy after a twelve hour shift to eat, sit dazed by the fire, dream of what I've learnt, relate more interesting happenings to Matthew, go to bed soon after nine o'clock ... I have never been happier. I have marriage and independence.[54]

After seven weeks: 'Every day is still thrilling, yet it all means so much to me that I find I can discuss it with no one except Matthew.' Thankfully, she also found the energy to supplement Matthew's diary with her own accounts of her life in the factory.

Within a month of her arrival the boss had her singled out to replace the chief inspector who was wanted on production work. She plied him with articles by Mass-Observation's Tom Harrisson diagnosing the pathology of factory life, and—when it resumed publication in September 1942—copies of the *Daily Worker*, full of constructive advice on how to increase production. Bertha identified with the other married women who coped with the stresses of factory life much more calmly than the younger girls and lads, and 'did not blame the boss for everything that goes wrong'.[56] She observed the frictions of factory life at first with some detachment, notably the short shrift given by all sides to the arrival of a new foreman who 'made a bad start by being efficient the first week ... salvaging rejects from worked materials so exposing slackness of workers, inspection and management ... an affront not easily forgiven'. Matthew quipped that she would soon replace the managing director. He should have known better where his wife's real loyalties lay.

When Bertha started there was no union organization in the factory, although a short strike during her first week had succeeded in reinstating a lad suspended by an unpopular foreman. Cuts in the workforce in July created 'great unrest, but I see no organised opposition'.[58] In the autumn, however, the men formed a branch of the AEU (until January 1943 an exclusively male union), and Matthew reported: 'Fun and games at B's factory—Union organisers, MAP [Ministry of Aircraft Production] reps, etc—but the men have won hands down and everyone's on top of the world.'[59] Six months later the management retaliated by sacking the shop steward, 'a peaceable, old trade unionist of thirty-five years experience', and all forty members of the union came out on strike.[60] The strike collapsed after a few days because the shop steward, acting on advice from union officials, asked to be released. With some difficulty the men found someone willing to take over his job, fully expecting to be victimized, and Bertha herself emerged as shop steward for the women: 'I was elected and gladly accepted being in the happy position of not caring how the fight ended personally, so long as I got the chance to fight.'[61] For a woman who had worked in industry for scarcely more than a year, Bertha's confidence was impressive: 'The workers were without a leader, inexperienced, and felt they had been sold, but by whom they were not very clear.' It was clear to her that the AEU official, wanting a quite life, had manipulated the sacked shop steward into accepting his fate. 'Now my great difficulty is going to be to keep the workers in the AEU and fight the bosses at the same time. I like the fight because I understand it, and I don't think anyone else among the workers does.'[62] No doubt class played a part in her confidence. We know of other middle-class women, from far more conventional, even conservative backgrounds, who volunteered for wartime factory work and found themselves pushed into positions of shop-floor leadership.[63]

During the summer and autumn of 1943 Bertha thoroughly enjoyed her role as a member of the firm's production committee, and the first woman ever to attend the AEU's regional shop-stewards' quarterly meeting in Darlington. When the reluctant male shop steward resigned in October, complaining that the job interfered with his dog-racing, Bertha made union history by agreeing to act for the men as well: 'she feels out of place', Matthew reported, 'representing men who've served a life time to the trade, but she's the only one at the factory who will fight and they know it. That's the advantage of being economically independent of it.'[64] The union was quick to find a token man to fill the breach, but it was to Bertha that the men in a neighbouring factory turned for advice when they

wanted to establish an AEU branch of their own. The owner must have
been regretting his earlier enthusiasm to employ an 'educated' woman, and
it was clear to Bertha that it was only a matter of time before he found a
pretext to get rid of her.

The pretext, as it turned out, was cancer. During February 1944 Bertha
spent three weeks in hospital having radiotherapy on a pituitary gland
tumour. In May, still convalescing, she was sacked. Although, as a shop
steward, her appeal was backed by the union, it was unsuccessful, she was
disappointed that her fellow workers did nothing to defend her: 'I . . . have
watched exploitation of the labour of young people to whom I became
very attached and have been let down by some of the same people who
could not take it when the struggle with the bosses came to a head.'[65]
In the summer, feeling fitter, she longed to get back into factory life.
Again the Labour Exchange had nothing to offer her except teaching, so
in desperation she marched into a local clothing factory, demanded to see
the bosses and:

told them how much they were missing in not appointing a coordinating labour
welfare officer. They're thinking it over and will let her know. Hopeful, if only
they don't get in touch with neighbouring factory and learn of her trade union
activities.[66]

But, of course, they did. Eventually, through a contact arising from
Matthew's bibliophilia, she landed a three-day a week job as supervisor
of a chain of lending libraries. Though 'homesick for my factory life', she
enjoyed the work, which took her away from home for days at a time
travelling around the North East. 'What a pleasant job mine is', she wrote,
'meeting people and passing on.'[67]

With the end of the European war, which also put an end to her job,
Bertha put her energies back into political life. Her detailed accounts of
the 1945 election campaign in Bishop Auckland show the Labour Party
at its worst. Bertha had persuaded her neighbour George Sands, after his
medical discharge from the Navy in the autumn of 1944, to take on the
secretaryship of the ward party, and between them they worked out a
programme of leafleting and canvassing, only to have it sabotaged by the
inaction of the agent for whom the town vote was relatively unimportant
given the solidity of the Labour vote in the outlying mining villages.
Bertha chaired a women's meeting addressed by Dalton and Alderman
Middlewood, the man responsible for Matthew's expulsion and against

whom she had once 'cried "Shame" ... when he called Cripps a Fascist'. (Middlewood was 'most surprised when he found me in the chair, but elaborately polite'.)[68] Even more problematic for Bertha were the tie-ups between Dalton and the owners of the factory in which she had worked. This became an issue in the election campaign when Dalton was accused of having given factory sites on the trading estate to German Jewish refugees in the 1930s while excluding local businessmen.[69] These allegations were vigorously denied by Middlewood, who had been president of the Development Board, but there was no denying the close links between local Labour leaders and the German Jewish factory owners, the wealthiest of whom threw a party for Dalton on election night.[70] During the day the candidate had been driven around by a former pit owner who had worked as an inspector alongside Bertha (for twice her salary) during the war. As a friend of the owners his incompetence had been overlooked; and during the strike he had spied on the union and blacklegged on the strikers.

Labour politics were, for Bertha, more duty than pleasure. After the election Matthew urged her either to give up politics altogether or to stand for election to the local council, but she could bring herself to do neither: 'I cannot work up any enthusiasm ... I hate all the local intrigues and yet I have a strong political conscience and would find it hard to give it up.'[71] A meeting of delegates from the women's sections in the constituency—all raffles and money raising, no politics, all elderly—did nothing to relieve the gloom. The meeting 'opened with a hymn "These Things Shall Be" which all the Methodists seemed to know and finished with the Red Flag which about four of us knew.' She left before tea:

> I always find it easy to be two-faced till it comes to eating, and then I feel sick ... So now I know the Women's Sections are just the same as the rest of the local organisations of the Labour Party. A handful of dumb folks genuinely working—people who work for their own class, but are used by unscrupulous people who wish to be in control of local affairs and a sprinkling of folks like myself who will not be used, therefore black balled if any attempt is made to further socialism and so I know I am utterly useless except to be a subscribing member and so help to keep the machinery running. A most disheartening job.[72]

She wondered whether to join the Communist Party, whose members had played a prominent part in Dalton's election campaign, but 'what more good could I do there? Less than I do now I think.'[73] And so she persevered. But the best was in the past. After one particularly dull Labour Party meeting in June 1945 she remarked:

As I came away I met a young lad from the factory (now in the air force) who once went with me to a Communist meeting and oh how refreshing he was. He takes no part in politics, but he wants to learn and he is alive. I am so grateful for the education I got among those young lads, factory life stands out for ever as something I did that really was worthwhile.[74]

Bertha's diary continues until the end of 1946, a year in which her frustration with inefficiency and corruption in local Labour Party increased; she joined the Business and Professional Women's Club (consisting mainly of Tory women, who, quixotically, she aspired to convert); and decided, aged 43, to adopt a baby. Thereafter, Norman, the adopted son, seems to have become her life.[75]

The couple

Matthew and Bertha experienced the war in very different ways: he the disillusioned intellectual retreating from politics into culture; she the frustrated housewife blossoming through her engagement in war work. But to take them simply as representatives of these two types would be to miss the significance of their symbiosis. The fact that both responses could occur, without contention, in the same household reminds us of those human qualities of understanding, toleration, and trust that make democracy possible. Historical agency belongs to individuals, but also to collectivities. Even at the elementary level of the couple, the sum was more than its constituent parts.

As a couple they were affectionate and mutually supportive. When separated she yearned for his calm, he for her liveliness and sociability. He depended on her to counteract his tendency to isolate himself in his books and his painting, although he also welcomed the solitude afforded by her frequent weekend visits to her parents. It had been Bertha, keen to expand their shared activities, who had persuaded Matthew to become a mass observer in the first place: 'Bertha is not only enthusiastic, but energetic and pushes me into situations ... which otherwise I would only use in daydreaming.'[76] They both suffered when she was at the NAAFI, though delighting in the intensity of their occasional weekends.

He reassured himself that 'parting like this has improved our relationship together—broken down the crust of habit, and shown us just how much together we are.'[77] Nevertheless her eventual return, he wrote lyrically, 'is as welcome as the flowers in May'.[78]

He understood and supported her need to escape from 'housewifely futility', and enjoyed her growing self-confidence.[79] After a visit to the factory he remarked: 'Funny to see B is self-assured and "at home" in a strange environment and so satisfying to know that 12 years of marriage has left her capable of striking out on her own.' His own father had died young, leaving his mother penniless: 'but I know now that she is capable of looking after herself economically'.[80] He gained vicarious pleasure from her daily accounts of her 'factory day', and from the fellowship of her workmates in the pub where they went to pay her union dues. Several were ex-pupils of his, one of whom 'insisted on telling the world how I'd warmed his arse for him'.[81] But the 'crack' (talk) was matey and the beer flowed.

He was supportive in more practical ways too. He had always helped out with the housework, and was capable of managing on his own when Bertha was ill or away visiting her parents. When the air raids threatened he got Bertha to teach him to fillet a herring: 'the beginning of carrying out a revolution to learn how to cook. It's as well to be prepared for any eventuality these days, and anyhow one cannot have knowledge of too many techniques.'[82] Later he learned to bake: 'my pastry,' he boasted proudly, 'is recognised by experts (as Northern women are) to be super'.[83] When Bertha started at the factory he took over the cooking, though he was relieved when after a few weeks she started having her main meal in the canteen; and Mabel, next door, looked after the cleaning. When Mabel became ill, Bertha got herself onto a shorter shift so that she and Matthew could do the chores together after school; but when Bertha herself went into hospital he struggled to cope, even though they had hired a cleaner. They both disliked housework, and neither of them wanted to waste time on home improvements, preferring to pay trade union rates rather than 'blackleg' on the work of skilled tradesmen.

George and Mabel Sands were close friends.[84] Both families had taken in refugee Spanish children before the war, and in 1941 Matthew agreed to take responsibility for the Sands' 7-year-old son if they were killed.[85] The two couples went to the cinema together, looked after each other when sickness struck, spent New Year's Eve together. Matthew and George shared regular nights out for beer and billiards at the workingmen's club. The women pooled their washing days. When in 1944 the Waltons could not find anyone to paint the outside of their house they put aside their principled objections to depriving skilled tradesmen of work sufficiently to allow George, whose hobby was house painting, to do it for them, with Bertha (temporarily unemployed) as his assistant. By the end of the war Bertha had persuaded George to take on the post of ward secretary for the Labour Party and it seems to have been Mabel's unexpected pregnancy in 1946 that triggered the Waltons' decision to adopt a baby of their own.

The diaries offer no explanation of the fact that they were childless. Responding to a 1943 MO directive which asked 'How important are children to family life?', Matthew wrote: 'Very little, if your wife satisfies you.'[86] A curious response, but one which suggests that he was not keen on the intrusion of children into the intimacy of their relationship. Similarly Bertha, in 1939, deploring her neighbours' fondness for pets, had written: 'I value my freedom above gratifying my possessive instincts.'[87] By 1946, however, these instincts had shifted, and a few months before the decision to adopt a baby she had already taken in a stray cat. Following her illness in 1944, when it was clear that she would not conceive, and without a secure job or career prospects, Bertha was keen to adopt, but, until reassured about her health by the doctor, felt it would be unfair to risk leaving Matthew with a baby to care for if the cancer were to return. During the later months of 1946 Bertha's diary recorded repeated frustration of their attempts to adopt; but her eventual success in January 1946 is the most likely explanation of the fact that MO received nothing further from her after the end of the year.

Despite the differences in their individual wartime trajectories, politics and culture were intimately woven in the texture of the Waltons' life together. In January 1944 Matthew wrote in his diary:

B and I spent a pleasant evening by the fire. She less tired than usual and even was able to tackle [I. A.] Richards' *Practical Criticism*, analysing her first example and talking it over together. Long time since the factory's left her with enough energy to tackle anything intelligent. And yet I know, it's the factory that's most satisfying to her—the work, the mixing with folk, the fighting for what she believes in.[88]

Bertha sometimes presented herself as a practical woman, not an intellectual. In contrast to her husband she 'never had any thirst for knowledge of no immediate use'.[89] But this was not strictly true. Matthew's diary reveals her not only engaging in practical criticism, but also writing the occasional poem or short story of her own, and her literary abilities are apparent in many of her own diary entries. Her tastes in music, film, theatre, and literature were similar to Matthew's, although she read much less than he did. The contrast drawn by Matthew between 'tackling anything intelligent' and 'fighting for what she believes in' perhaps says more about his own retreat from politics than it does about any dislocation between culture and politics in Bertha's life. The Waltons saw their home, with its books, its gramophone records, its paintings, as a resource not only for themselves but for others as well, a haven of enlightenment, culture, and intelligent left-wing talk in the wilderness of a new lower-middle-class housing estate in a small market town.

The chief beneficiaries of the Waltons' cultural resources were the colony of German Jewish refugees brought to Bishop Auckland to work in the trading estate factories. Moved by the plight of these young refugees, the Waltons had volunteered their services, finding lodgings for them, feeding them, helping them to cope with their displacement and 'the hatred they meet'.[90] Not that the refugees were simply victims. Bertha was irritated by some of the more well-heeled girls, including a 'spoiled' graduate from Berlin working in her uncle's factory while awaiting a visa to join her sister in the US; an irritation perhaps intensified by Matthew's obvious pleasure in 'comparing cultures' and arguing politics with the girl.[91] Matthew, who claimed to be emotionally unmoved by the larger catastrophes of war, was horrified by the internment of anti-Nazi German Jews, particularly when Stephan, the refugee foreman who was later to find Bertha a job in the aircraft factory, was separated from his wife and son: 'It's hateful to see a man with no roots, broken with loneliness, with no one to turn to in his fear . . . Our lack of imagination is even more dreadful than our lack of logic.'[92] 'I'm sorriest of all,' he wrote, for the German Jews because they have no nucleus round which to build their own salvation. [They] are the unhappiest people in the world—particularly those who were invited to this country as refugees, and then put into concentration camps side by side with their Nazi enemies.'[93]

Later in the war the Waltons befriended a group of German Jewish lads who Bertha met through her work in the factory, jazz lovers who came to listen to their records and who Matthew described as 'intellectually

mature and knowledgeable when compared with our kids'.[94] Invited back
to their lodgings 'it was pathetic the way they'd prepared to entertain us, as
though we'd done them a favour by inviting them. They certainly showed
imagination in their supper, and taste in their gramophone records.'[95] Their
closest friend among the refugees was Gerd, a boy 'of good family' (father
dead, mother disappeared, sister in Palestine) who had arrived in Leeds a
few days before war broke out from Berlin, trained as an engineer, but
then found himself forced to stay in Bishop Auckland making handbags
instead of joining his friends on aeroplane work in London. Despite the
intervention of the Waltons' poor man's lawyer friend, Jimmy, Gerd was
refused his release for more than two years by a National Service Officer
in the pockets of the trading-estate factory owners: 'a young boy' wrote
Bertha, 'already suffered enough and made to suffer more by cruel and
foolish people'.[96] While he waited for his release Gerd became one of
the family, joined them on trips to the cinema and theatre, and moved in
when evicted from his lodgings. When he eventually escaped to London he
kept in touch and helped to organize the Waltons' periodic culture-packed
holidays in the metropolis. It is clear from the way they wrote about these
young refugees that Matthew and Bertha derived as much pleasure as they
gave. They enjoyed the exoticism of their foreignness and found them
educationally and intellectually a cut above their English neighbours. The
same went for a young soldier they befriended, a friend of a friend stationed
nearby, a Jewish solicitor who came to borrow Marxist literature and stayed
to listen to classical music and play chess: 'we gave him what he wanted,
music, books and conversation'.[97]

There were powerful currents of anti-alien and anti-Semitic sentiment
in wartime Britain,[98] and the Walton household provided sanctuary for
some of the victims of these currents. But the Waltons' own attitude to the
Jews was far from straightforward. Writing in 1946 Bertha explained how
her pre-war 'sentimental outlook on Jewish refugees'—impelled, oddly
enough, by having identified with Shylock when she had acted him at
school—had been qualified by contact:

I . . . found them to be good and bad as other races, but they really do ask for trouble
and persecution . . . They are tactless, have strong inferiority complex which makes
them push themselves forward, they shout, quarrel among themselves and seem
to be always in a state of turmoil . . . There is something in the character of Jews
which will not let them rest and be content.[99]

Despite such racial stereotyping, class remained the Waltons' main category
of analysis. Matthew attributed rising anti-Semitism to the conspicuous
consumption of the Jewish factory owners and their relatives: 'Their dress
and manner is indiscrete, as is their display of opulence. They lack the
hypocritical "good taste" of your English wealthy.'[100] Not surprisingly,
given her experience in the factory, Bertha drew a sharp line between
'the refugees in a real sense' who she had befriended and 'the aggressive,
unpleasant "better-off" type' who had been able to set up in business on
the trading estate.[101] When, shortly after the war, a row blew up in the
Labour Party over a request from the Jews to build a synagogue in the
local cemetery, Bertha deplored equally those 'councillors who spend their
time "licking" (as the people here say) the Jewish capitalists', and others
'befogged by anti-semitism' who 'said some shocking things . . . against the
Jews—but not against Capitalist Jews'.[102] Her own 'hatred' was reserved
for the 'Jewish bosses' who 'buy all the houses at fabulous prices' and
for Labour councillors 'who allow themselves to be bribed'. Len Lewin,
Dalton's friend, had been able to arrange for electricity to be laid to his
rural mansion, 'while the [nearby] village for years has tried in vain'. By
granting unjustifiable favours to rich Jews, corrupt local politicians were
creating the anti-Semitism 'which hits the decent, hardworking Jews most
when trouble breaks out'.[103] Whatever racializing stereotypes they may
have entertained, the Waltons were not anti-Semites, and they made the
best of the influx of well-educated Jewish refugees to further their own
struggle to escape the drabness of their small-town environment.

Before the war Matthew and Bertha had turned to politics not only
to combat war, fascism, and unemployment but also, as Bertha put it,
to enable them to mix with 'alive people with minds sharpened on
intellectual and political problems'.[104] Cultural distinction and democratic
activism were thus seamlessly united. Popular Front politics with its stress
on the 'defence of culture' against fascism, lent purpose to their lives,
while helping them to sustain their sense of themselves as cultured and
intelligent people far removed from the philistinism of their lower-middle-
class neighbourhood.[105] The war disrupted this shared orientation, leading
each of them to renegotiate, in very different ways, the tensions between
distinction and democracy.

Political activism played a marginal role in the narrative that Matthew
constructed of his selfhood during the war. While his socialist commitment
remained undimmed, the form that it took (unreserved faith in the USSR

as the custodian of humanity's future) effectively let him off the hook
of active political engagement. Retrospectively, he saw himself as having
been a 'misfit' in left-wing politics.[106] He was unresponsive to the new
openings for the left created by wartime radicalism and sought fulfilment
in culture for culture's sake. By the closing years of the war some of the
energies he had previously devoted to politics were being redirected into
his work as a teacher. At beginning of 1944 he volunteered to move to
an understaffed elementary school closer to home, and found the change
'hard but refreshing, next best thing to being in the navy'.[107] His interest
in his work grew further when he was head-hunted for a temporary job
teaching English, history, and geography to 14- to 16-year-olds in a selective technical college in Stockton.[108] Eventually, in July 1945, he found
himself a job at the grammar school in Spennymoor, despite efforts to
block his appointment by the county education committee: 'the ... head is
reputed to be quite fearless, one of the few with no tie-ups of intrigue'.[109]
He stayed there for the rest of his career, becoming head of Latin. In later
life Ronald Sands, the neighbour's son, remembers him as something of
a hermit who looked up from his books only to watch cricket on the
television.

Bertha too had her share of disappointments, but politically she was made
of sterner stuff than her husband. What drove her, her 'political conscience',
was less a worked-out system of ideas, more a desire to be where the action
was—air-raid warden, social worker, shop steward, socialist activist in the
Labour Party. Experience had taught her that political will alone was not
sufficient to prevent a war or to unionize a factory. But, however obscure
the road ahead, the point was to position oneself to contribute when
opportunity arose:

I used to believe [she wrote in the autumn of 1944] that individual effort and more
so group effort could change the pattern of events. Now I believe that nothing I
can do will make any difference until the pattern begins to change. [But] then I
will be ready to pick up the new strand to weave my particular patch to suit my
ideas . . . I know just how much I can help others and have gained confidence in
my own powers.[110]

The war, which drove Matthew back to his books, provided Bertha with
new opportunities to deepen and extend the range of her civic activism.
What is most impressive about her account of her time in the factory is not
so much the qualities of leadership displayed—we lack the independent
evidence needed to assess these—but her confidence that she possessed

such qualities. For Bertha personal growth and political activism went hand in hand.

Divergent though their trajectories were, Matthew and Bertha lived happily together, respecting and supporting each other's needs, miserable when deprived for any time of each other's company. The ecological pressures of war did something to ameliorate their sense of alienation from the local community and their friendship with their closest neighbours blossomed. The Jewish refugees who they befriended were, the Waltons believed, even more unfortunate than the working-class girls in the NAAFI or the Irish Catholic housewives in the local slums; but they were also much better educated. By identifying with the Jews, who so conveniently combined in their persons both victimhood and culture, the Waltons had found a way of reconciling their democratic instincts with their own sense of cultural distinction. Here, unambiguously, it was possible both to value culture and to contribute to democratic life.

That both partners in this most democratic and companionate of marriages should move from a fierce commitment to political activism in the later 1930s, towards the satisfactions of parenthood and (for Matthew) his work as a teacher, may be emblematic of the broader shifts occurring in the culture of the British left between the 1930s and the 1950s. Revolutionary socialism as a goal to live by had always been hard to sustain in the placid waters of British political life. After Hitler came to power, revolutionary hopes were inescapably tempered by the need to defend the bad against the worse, and the disintegration of the Popular Front synthesis of opposition to 'fascism and war' after the Nazi–Soviet pact and the early triumphs of Hitler's war machine was as likely to lead to political despair as to renewed revolutionary fervour. Whatever hopes were subsequently inspired by the prospect of a Western European revolution emerging from an anti-fascist war fought in alliance with USSR, it quickly became apparent after 1945 (if not before) that the war in the West had been won by the forces of capitalist restoration, not by revolutionary popular upheaval. Few of those attracted to revolutionary socialist ideas in the 1930s could sustain such perspectives ten years later, when they found themselves having to come to terms not only with exhausted populations settling (at best) for the security offered by social democracy, but also by the difficulty of upholding any idea of progress at all in face of the exterminist horrors of Auschwitz and Hiroshima, and the probability that the future held a third world war, of even greater destructive power than those that had laid waste the first half of the twentieth century. In such circumstances it is not surprising that the Waltons, like many others, should have retreated from political commitment into private life. But the personal was also political, and how people lived their private lives was as important to the emergence of a more democratic society as was their participation in public affairs. Matthew may have been waiting for the sun to rise in the East, but in fact the gleam of the future was very much closer to home. In so far as the late twentieth century was to rediscover any idea of human progress it was the democratic nature of the Waltons' marriage, and the human fellowship they fostered around their home, that pointed the way forward, not the revolutionary dreams with which, in a dark time, they had sought to sustain faith in the future.

10

Conclusion

In a well-known essay, Robert Darnton used an account of the ritual massacre of cats by apprentice printers to explore popular mentalities in eighteenth-century France. Cats, he pointed out, are 'good to think' with because they hold an ambiguous position between nature and culture. Simultaneously domestic pets and wild animals, they resist categorization and in all cultures carry an overload of symbolic meanings.[1] The Mass-Observation diaries have also been good to think with. The diarists, writing as they felt from day to day, also resist categorization. They force us to attend to improbable mixtures of belief, to the incoherent, contradictory, as yet un-rationalized sources from which individuals construct meaning in their lives. An apparently apolitical guardian of conventional morality turns out to harbour utopian socialist ideas; one pacifist is reconciled to the manufacture of armaments by the allure of science, another embraces the army as a welcome release from the responsibilities of civilian life; an intellectually aspiring (and sexually predatory) housewife flips between visions of Armageddon and humanist rationalism. Eccentricity, the diaries remind us, is ordinary.

Engaging with the lives of others, provokes thoughts about one's own. Much of the appeal of biography lies in its stimulus to self-reflection, and it is my hope that this very diverse group of people will have struck chords among my readers, provoking them to reflect on their own selfhoods, as well as gaining a more vivid and nuanced picture of life in wartime Britain. All research, they say, is autobiography, and in the course of this work, I have found myself using these nine individuals as a sounding board for my own puzzles about 'the meaning of life'. The way these individual stories have been told no doubt reflects the unresolved muddles of my own selfhood: nine biographies standing in, catlike, for the nine lives of their author. But in summing up what has been said in this book, I will not attempt to disinter the tenth life, the buried autobiography. Nor will I try to assemble the kaleidoscopic fragments into a coherent account of subjectivity in wartime Britain: my point throughout has been to resist the cultural historian's tendency to reduce individual subjectivities to collective identities. My purpose here is simply to place side by side some of the characteristics of the nine diarists as a way of reprising the three main themes identified in the Introduction—the impact of war on active citizenship; the process of democratization in private life; and the search for meanings that could transcend the wartime context of limitless violence.

The popular memory of national unity and purpose during the second world war has long served in British culture as a nostalgic refuge from the challenge of finding an identity appropriate to the world of late modernity and post-imperial globalization. Looking back from the individualism of their own times, successive post-war generations have found in the comforting solidarities of wartime a seemingly solid and reliable point of reference; an anchor in the maelstrom of modernity; reassurance that ethical community is a viable human possibility. The imagined community at war was real enough at the time, and several of the diaries testify to the effective fusion of national purpose with individual identity. For Nella Last the war provided legitimate opportunity to put nation before husband and deploy her talents beyond the domestic sphere. Her story, uniting national mobilization with personal emancipation, accords well with dominant narratives of the impact of war (which may help to account for the popular resonance of her diaries). The same could be said of Mary Clayton, stoically 'bombed out and keeping going' through the London blitz, and Gertrude Glover, uplifted in her relentless public activity by a utopian sense of reformist momentum.

But while the experience of these three older women exemplifies a wartime enhancement of active citizenship, the other diarists tell a different story. Bertha Walton, like Nella, found freedom and personal satisfaction in her war work, but in her case this had as much to do with the opportunities it gave her to pursue class struggle against the bosses as it did with any patriotic identification with a unified nation at war. Moreover her joy was short-lived; as, even more so, was Matthew's brief engagement with the communal democracy of the air-raid shelter. For him the larger reality was a modernity which had failed, leading him and (later) Bertha to turn away from public engagement and seek affirmation in work and private life. Eleanor Humphries, struggling for self-esteem under the weight of serving Horace, found momentary satisfaction in staying put (and conscientiously reporting to Mass-Observation) during the blitz. But what was more central to her experience of war was that it deprived her of the daily domestic service without which she found it impossible to establish a satisfactory balance between domesticity, voluntary work, and the writing which sustained her fragile sense of self. Although her voluntary work expanded during the war, she undertook it less in a spirit of national service than as a way of evading conscription. For Denis Argent, who *was* conscripted, the satisfactions of army life were real enough, but he understood his participation in the war effort as an interlude, a welcome evasion of growing up, not as a character-building rite of passage to maturity as a responsible citizen. Lillian Rogers, wide open to the limitless unanchored possibilities of modernity, pursued her flamboyantly unconventional quest for personal emancipation and the ethical life with little concern as to how this might contribute to the defeat of Nazi Germany. And Ernest van Someren, although his sources of satisfaction were many and various, experienced few of the joys of wartime national unity. Indeed it was his involvement in the war effort that constituted the one flaw in an otherwise idyllic existence.

For Ernest, the most secure and reliable sources of selfhood (outside his work) were the every-day rewards of companionate marriage and the company of like-minded friends. Much the same was true for the Waltons, although Matthew, however much he valued these things, could not but see his pleasure in them as something of a sideshow to the world-historic issues being settled on the Eastern front. Ernest, on the other hand, whose attitude to politics was informed by John Macmurray's insistence on 'the primacy of the personal nexus of community over the functional nexus of organized society', could savour family, fellowship, and the interlocking networks of Quaker, pacifist, and WEA activity as themselves prefigurative, contributing to the building of the good society from the margins, behind the backs of History's big players. While Roosevelt, Stalin, and Churchill deployed mechanized violence on an inconceivable scale, sowing with their necessary murders the seeds of God-knew-what future catastrophes, the gleam of a desirable future was, he believed, to be found in the quiet pursuit of kindness, equality, and good fellowship

in whatever islands of peace survived in a brutalized world. The fact that
Ernest's privileged existence depended on his continuing participation in
the production of the means of violence, did not in itself invalidate his
socialist pacifism, although it did serve to remind him of the Christian truth
that sin and an uneasy conscience were inescapable components of human
existence.

If the political is personal; if, as Virginia Woolf insisted, the tyrannies
and servilities of the intimate sphere underwrite the tyrannies and servilities
of the public world, then it is in the struggle of the women diarists
to establish their autonomy that we have come closest to encountering
the front line of progressive social change. Mary Clayton, who had
known what it was to be a subordinate wife, had subsequently built a
thoroughgoing personal independence running her own business and in
a free union with her partner. In the absence of her diaries, Gertrude
Glover might be glimpsed by a historian researching the archives of her
various committees as a conventional guardian of traditional morality, but
the diaries show her successfully combining marriage and motherhood
with a degree of autonomy and independence that could normally be
aspired to in her generation only by spinsters with private means or a
professional career. While she operated in the public world with the
condescension (and to some extent the deference) appropriate to her class
position, there was an egalitarianism in her outlook apparent both in
her critique of the unreflective authoritarianism of Coventry's industrial
managers, and in her admiration for the democratic aspirations of youth.
Among the married women, Gertrude's unproblematic independence was
unmatched. Even Bertha Walton, partner in the most companionate of
marriages, felt a frisson of freedom when her war work gave her a degree
of independence that she had not previously enjoyed. Others were not so
fortunate. Nothing that Eleanor Humphries tried—her voluntary work,
her flirtations, her writing—seems to have done anything to alleviate her
wifely subordination. Nella Last, for all the vigour of her self-assertion,
remained trapped in her unsuitable marriage, fearful that whatever gains
she had made would not outlast the war. It would be, she believed,
for the next generation to establish the autonomy which her 'weak
streak' had prevented her from laying down earlier in her own marriage.
Lillian Rogers acknowledged no such weak streak in herself, and her
pursuit of autonomy tested her marriage (probably) to destruction. Living
dangerously in her restless search for knowledge and power, she did more

than any of the other diarists to explore the possibilities of modernity, promiscuously criss-crossing the boundaries between intimate relationships and public life.

The war raised existential questions that encouraged the diarists to look for sources of meaning beyond the rewards of either active citizenship or private life. Shame and horror at the violence and what it portended for the future were not far from the minds of even the most patriotic of them. Nella's sense of wartime emancipation was haunted not only by anxiety about the safety of her son, but also by her acute awareness of the problems that even victory would bring; the difficulty of putting the genie of violence back into its bottle. One reaction to the context of violence was to look to religion. Nella, Gertrude, and Lillian all invoked Armageddon as the key to contemporary history, though only Lillian took this very seriously, coping with her fear during the blitz by turning to her father's eccentric beliefs and his promise of supernatural protection. It was not long, however, before her 'everlasting question mark' took her from the Book of Revelation to the humanists. For Nella, the unknowable mysteries of God's plan for mankind provided existential consolation for her fears and disappointments, while Gertrude, by contrast, was able to use her do-it-yourself religion to conjure the promise of a bright tomorrow, carried forward on an optimistic tide of a social Christianity. Ernest, though holding back from the life changes that a wholehearted commitment to his Christian pacifist beliefs would have demanded, was nevertheless able to pursue an approximation to God's kingdom in civilized fellowship with wife, children, and friends in an affluent London suburb. Eleanor, the most oppressed of wives, might have found comfort in religion, but she could not imagine embracing beliefs that would have earned nothing but contempt from her rationalist husband.

The other four diarists were more inclined to look to left-wing politics than to religion to cure the ills of the world, but they all looked in one way or another for something beyond politics. Mary Clayton's matter-of-fact faith in social work and a reformist Labour Party left her hankering after 'something, something, something' more. Denis Argent, though toying with communism as a substitute for religion, found himself unable to take the plunge, and looked to the cultural epiphanies offered by high church services or Beethoven symphonies to enhance his spiritual life. The Waltons had no interest in Christianity, and Matthew would probably have subscribed to Lenin's view that too much Beethoven was bad for the revolutionary will.[2] Nevertheless he made a religion not only of his communism, but also of the cultural inheritance which, he feared, was being systematically destroyed in the death throes of bourgeois civilization. While Matthew's epiphanies, whether in Soviet communism or in high culture, took him away from active participation in the life of the community, there were others (Gertrude, Nella, and Ernest) who found in their religious beliefs a source of sustenance for their active citizenship.

At every turn, the personal intersected with the political. The dutiful active citizenship espoused by people like Nella Last, Gertrude Glover, or Mary Clayton, which played such a significant role in Britain's wartime mobilization, was intimately linked to their capacity to establish a degree of personal independence and autonomy in their private lives. Their stories can be read as testimony either to the long after-life of Victorian notions of 'character', or as skirmishes in a struggle for female equality in the intimate sphere which was to become so central to later twentieth-century processes of democratization. Similarly with Lillian Rogers, whose search for the ethical life took her among earnest post-Victorian secularists, while her bold adventures in the Casino dance hall could be seen as anticipating a sexual revolution whose time had not yet come. Matthew Walton, inspired by the vision of October 1917, struggled against the grain of his personality to shape himself as an instrument of the revolution, but it may be that where his talents were most productively employed on behalf of the dispossessed was in giving succour and companionship to cultured refugees from Hitler's Germany. In the era of the Second World War it was pacifists like Ernest van Someren who, fearing that military victory could only prepare the way for new confrontations, were most explicit in seeking ways to outflank the operations of centralized power by pursuing democratic and egalitarian fellowship in the interstices of organized society. From the 1960s, under the influence especially of feminism, the notion that the personal is political became a vital part of any progressive politics.

I said that this book was an experiment in historiography. Biographies of the powerful have always played a central role in historical writing, but in moving beyond 'great man' approaches, historians, influenced by the dominant modes of social scientific thinking, have usually looked to impersonal, structural explanations of change, and/or sought to locate historical agency in organized collectivities such as nation, class, or party. The 'cultural turn' in the writing of history has done much to enlighten us about the power of discourse to shape experience. But we have yet to discover satisfactory ways of integrating the study of the subjectivities of ordinary people into the history of social and cultural change. Perhaps the time is ripe for a 'biographical turn', for attention to the moment in which individuals make their own history.

A book based on biographies of a handful of individuals cannot pretend to offer a rounded history of the war years, or even of the active citizenship whose sources I set out to identify. Rather, engagement with the Mass-Observation diaries has helped me to place questions about wartime citizenship within the much broader context of the making of a modern democratic selfhood. I am not casting the war as a central driver of this longer-term process of democratization, but it does provide a context within which—because of the existence of the MO diaries—it has been possible to probe various aspects of the broader process. None of the diarists were creatures of habit unthinkingly reproducing received cultural norms. Their self-reflexivity helps us to think about the ways in which people seeking to answer the question of who they are and how they should live might contribute to larger processes of social change. As active citizens some of the diarists set out deliberately to engineer social change; but even as private individuals, muddling through, buffeted by forces beyond their control, they were at the same time historical agents. In using the resources of the culture to make meaning of their lives each of these nine diarists contributed, however modestly, to molecular processes of change both in the intimate sphere and in the conduct of public life. By paying attention to their self-fashioning we may have come closer to glimpsing those deeply personal processes from which history's vast impersonal forces are, in the end, constructed.

Notes

CHAPTER 1

1. James Hinton, *Shop Floor Citizens: Engineering democracy in 1940s Britain* (Aldershot, 1994); James Hinton, *Women, Social Leadership and the Second World War: Continuities of class* (Oxford, 2002).

2. For a brief account of MO see my entry in the 'themes' section of the *Dictionary of National Biography*. The fullest account of MO's foundation and early goals is in Nick Stanley, 'The extra dimension: A study and assessment of the methods employed by Mass-Observation in its first period, 1937–1940' (CNAA PhD thesis, 1981). Tom Jeffery, *Mass-Observation: A short history* (Birmingham, 1978) remains of value. Stimulating recent discussions include Ben Highmore, *Everyday Life and Cultural Theory: An introduction* (London, 2002), 75–112, Tony Kushner, *We Europeans? Mass-Observation, 'race' and British identity in the twentieth century* (Aldershot, 2004), and Nick Hubble, *Mass-Observation and Everyday Life: Culture, history, theory* (Basingstoke, 2006).

3. Charles Madge and Tom Harrisson, *Mass-Observation* (London, 1937), 47–8.

4. Bob Willcock, who ran MO after Tom Harrisson was called up in 1942, characterized the observers as people either already involved in various kinds of voluntary public activity, or those 'whose interest in MO shows a desire for such activity'. Bob Willcock, 'Polls apart', ch. 7, 2, Unpublished MS, MO archive, cited in Stanley, 'The extra dimension', 164. See also the MO survey of voluntary action commissioned by Beveridge: Lord Beveridge and A. F. Wells, *The Evidence for Voluntary Action* (London, 1949), 33–4, 42–3, 45.

5. DRs Jan. 1942, Jan. 1943, Jan. 1944, Dec. 1944–Jan. 1945.

6. DR Aug. 1944.

7. Charles Taylor, *Sources of the Self: The making of the modern identity* (Cambridge, 1989), 54–5. Taylor's magisterial exploration of the sources of the modern

self is rooted in the discipline of philosophy, but it pays some attention to historical work on mentalities, on everyday lived experience.

8. The most important influences on my understanding of modern selfhood have been Taylor, *Sources of the self*; Alisdair MacIntyre, *After Virtue: A study on moral theory* (London, 1985); Anthony Giddens, *Modernity and Self-identity: Self and society in the late modern age* (Cambridge, 1991); Anthony Giddens, *The Transformation of Intimacy: Sexuality, love and eroticism in modern societies* (Cambridge, 1992).

9. Norbert Elias, *The Society of Individuals* (Oxford 1991), 14. For a critique of Giddens' writing along similar lines see Matthew Adams, 'The reflexive self and culture: A critique', *British Journal of Sociology*, 54/2 (2003), 221–38.

10. For a valuable discussion of social interactionist models of the self see Ian Burkitt, 'The shifting concept of the self', *History of the Human Sciences*, 7/2 (1994). Also Trevor Butt and Darren Langdridge, 'The construction of self: The public reach in to the private sphere', *Sociology*, 37/3 (2003), 477–92.

11. Penny Summerfield, *Reconstructing Women's Wartime Lives: Discourse and subjectivity in oral histories of the Second World War* (Manchester, 1998); Paul Thompson, *The Voice of the Past: Oral history* (Oxford, 2000).

12. Erving Goffman, *The Presentation of Self in Everyday Life* (London, 1990), 63, 114–16, 236. On Montaigne's *arriere-boutique* see Peter Goodall, 'The author in the study: Self-representation as reader and writer in the medieval and early modern periods' in R. Bedford, L. Davis, and P. Kelly (eds.), *Early Modern Autobiography: Theories, genres, practices* (Michigan, 2006), 112–13.

13. Certainly the historical evolution of conceptions of selfhood provides no clue to where, ultimately, the true self may be found. Thus Goffman's account, and the sociological role theory that informed it, rested on a rejection of Romantic conceptions of authenticity and inwardness and had much in common with the performative understanding of the self described in Dror Wahrman's discussion of the eighteenth-century regime of identity (*The Making of the Modern Self: Identity and culture in 18th-century England* (London, 2004). See also E. J. Hundert, 'The European Enlightenment and the history of the self' in Roy Porter (ed.), *Rewriting the Self: Histories from the Renaissance to the present* (London, 1997).

14. Diarist 5390, 19 May 1942.

15. Some diarists, struggling to fulfil what they took to be the brief, found themselves apologizing for the absence of the war from their diaries. 'I keep trying to drag the war into the diary,' wrote Gertrude Glover, 'but it won't come . . . I think if lids could be lifted off all heads, very little war would be noticed inside most' (18 Oct. 1944). Another diarist, Mary Clayton, solved the problem by opening most entries with a one-line summary of

the war news before getting down to the serious business of her day: a practice that resulted in some surreal juxtapositions: 'Russians . . . have started offensive . . . towards Karkov. Mrs S. kept her appointment with dentist yesterday' (14 May 1942). The outcome of the former was uncertain. But this diarist's campaign to persuade her cleaner to get her sadly neglected teeth seen to was definitely succeeding.

16. The mass observers tended to be people with a high degree of self-knowledge, and, as Tony Kushner has suggested, writing for MO served further to enhance this (Kushner, *We Europeans*, 136–8, 164, 238–43). By comparison with Gertrude Glover's MO diaries (see Ch. 3), those kept by another Warwickshire WI activist are bland and uninformative: Peter Donnelly (ed.), *Mrs Milburn's Diaries: An Englishwoman's day-to-day reflections, 1939–45* (London, 1979). And the often-cited account of the London blitz in Vere Hodgson, *Few Eggs and No Oranges* (London, 1999) is driven by relentless cheerfulness and grit derived from its origins as letters to her sister in Rhodesia, more morale-boosting war propaganda than a genuinely self-reflective diary. Jenny Shaw notes that one advantage of the directive replies is that they provide the depth of unstructured interviewing, without the dangers of 'embarrassment, leading questions, over-identification or desire to please' (Jenny Shaw, *Intellectual Property, Representative Experience and Mass-Observation*, MO Archive, Occasional Papers, 9, 1998, 4.)

17. However, the fact that most diarists did not retain a copy of what they sent to MO means that these diaries cannot have served what one examination of diary writing found to be a major function of diary writing—a means of 'managing time', as an address to the future self, or an archive of the younger self. Wendy J. Weiner and George C. Rosenwald, 'A moment's monument: The psychology of keeping a dairy' in R. Josselson and A. Lieblich (eds.), *The Narrative Study of Lives* (London, 1993), 48–52.

18. Michael Roper, 'Splitting in unsent letters: Writing as a social practice and a psychological activity', *Social History*, 26/3 (2001), suggests that for the management guru Lyndall Urwick, writing (unsent) confessional letters, 'the typewriter provided a technology through which emotions could be captured, rendered in the clear and consistent form of the typeface, and exposed to a cool gaze. Paper acted as a container as much as a conduit for his feelings.' While this rings true for at least one of the diarists discussed in this book (Ernest van Someren), the use of the typewriter seems to have no such effect on the writing of another (Eleanor Humphries). In these two cases gender was more significant than technology in determining the relationship of the written text to the author's feelings.

19. Writing about eighteenth-century England, Felicity Nussbaum points out that 'the diary serves the social/historical function of articulating a multiplicity of contestatory selves, of unstable and incoherent selves at an historical moment when that concept is itself the object of contest' ('Towards conceptualizing diary' in James Olney, *Studies in Autobiography*, (Oxford 1988), 132). She has in mind Locke's and Hume's questioning of the existence of a continuous subject, an essential self; but a similar problematic is apparent in twentieth-century thinking about selfhood. In my approach to the diaries, I have tried to follow Nausbaum's advice, resisting the 'urge is to stalk the coherent selves hiding beneath the surface of these self-reflective writings' and to read instead for 'the subject's fragmentations and discontinuities, repetitions and revisions'. Felicity Nussbaum, *The Autobiographical Subject: Gender and ideology in 18th-century England* (London 1989), 15.

20. Virginia Woolf, *Mr Bennett and Mrs Brown* (London, 1924), 4–5. The *Daily Herald* originated as a printers' strike sheet in January 1911.

21. A. J. P. Taylor, *English History, 1914–45* (Oxford, 1965), 600.

22. Richard Sennett, *The Fall of Public Man* (London, 1977); Christopher Lasch, *The Culture of Narcissism: American life in an age of diminishing expectations* (London, 1991); Jurgen Habermas, *The Structural Transformation of the Public Sphere* (Cambridge, 1992); MacIntyre, *After Virtue*.

23. M. R. J. Higonnet, et al., *Behind the Lines: Gender and the two World Wars* (New Haven, 1987); Susan Pedersen, *Family: Dependence and the origins of the Welfare State. Britain and France, 1914–1945* (Cambridge, 1993); M. Pugh, 'Domesticity and the decline of feminism, 1930–50', in H. L. Smith, *British Feminism in the Twentieth Century* (Aldershot, 1990); Sheila Jeffreys, *The Spinster and her Enemies: Feminism and sexuality 1880–1930* (London, 1985).

24. Brian Harrison, *Prudent Revolutionaries* (Oxford, 1987); Pat Thane, 'The women of the British Labour Party and feminism, 1906–1945' in H. Smith (ed.), *British Feminism in the Twentieth Century* (Aldershot, 1990); Judy Giles, *Women, Identity and Private Life in Britain, 1900–50* (Basingstoke, 1995); Maggie Andrews, *The Acceptable Face of Feminism: The Women's Institute as a social movement* (London, 1998); P. M. Graves, *Labour Women: Women in British working-class politics, 1918–1939* (Oxford, 1994); Gillian Scott, *Feminism and the Politics of Working Women: The Women's Co-operative Guild, 1880s to the Second World War* (London, 1998); Alison Light, *Forever England: Femininity, literature and conservatism between the wars* (London, 1991); David Jarvis, 'The Conservative Party and the politics of gender, 1900–1939' in Martin Francis and Ina Zweiniger-Bargielowska (eds.), *The Conservatives and British Society, 1880–1990* (Cardiff, 1996); Caitriona Beaumont, 'Citizens not feminists: The boundary negotiated between citizenship and feminism by mainstream

women's organisations in England, 1928–39', Women's History Review, 9/2 (2000), 411–29; Hinton, *Women and Social Leadership*; Mathew Hilton, 'The female consumer and the politics of consumption in twentieth-century Britain', *Historical Journal*, 45/1 (2002), 103–28.

25. Marcus Collins, *Modern Love: An intimate history of men and women in twentieth-century Britain* (London, 2003), 4–5. On Carpenter and the 'new life' see Sheila Rowbotham, 'In search of Carpenter', *History Workshop Journal*, 3 (1977), and Sheila Rowbotham and Jeffrey Weeks, *Socialism and the New Life: The personal and sexual politics of Edward Carpenter and Havelock Ellis* (London, 1977).

26. Virginia Woolf, *Three Guineas* (London, 1943, first published 1938), 206, 258–9.

27. John Macmurray, *Reason and Emotion* (London, 1962, first published 1935), 30; John Macmurray, 'Freedom in the personal nexus' in R. N. Anshen (ed.), *Freedom, its Meaning* (New York, 1940), 192, cited in Frank G. Kirkpatrick, *John Macmurray: Community beyond political philosophy* (New York, 2005), 83.

28. Macmurray, *Reason and Emotion*, 102. Macmurray's thinking was influenced by Marion Milner's compelling autobiographical account of her own search for 'emotional rationality', for a resolution of the conflict between the feminine and masculine aspects of her psyche: Joanna Field (pseud.), *A Life of One's Own* (London, 1986, first published 1934). The echo of Virginia Woolf's 1928 title is unlikely to have been an accident.

29. Macmurray, *Reason and Emotion*, 118.

30. Anthony Giddens, *The Transformation of Intimacy: Sexuality, love and eroticism in modern societies* (Cambridge, 1992), 56–7, 181–2, 188–90, and *passim*.

31. R. W. Connell, *Masculinities* (Cambridge, 2005), 226–8.

32. Joan Scott, *Gender and the Politics of History* (New York, 1988), 6, 44–7.

33. Marcel Mauss, 'The category of the human mind: The notion of person, the notion of self' in *Sociology and Psychology: Essays* (London, 1979). This essay was first published in the *Journal of the Royal Anthropological Institute*, 68 (1938), 263–81.

34. Carole Pateman, *The Disorder of Women: Democracy, feminism and political theory* (Cambridge, 1989).

35. Taylor, *Sources of the Self*, 13, 23, 211 ff.

36. Leonore Davidoff and Catherine Hall, *Family Fortunes: Men and women of the English middle class, 1780–1850* (London, 1987); A. James Hammerton, *Cruelty and Companionship: Conflict in 19th-century married life* (London, 1992), 150–1.

37. Richard Titmuss, *Problems of Social Policy* (London, 1950), 508.

38. Angus Calder, *The People's War: Britain 1939–1945* (London, 1971), 21.

39. For an insightful discussion of this phenomenon see Stuart Macintyre, 'British Labour, Marxism and working-class apathy in the 1920s', *Historical Journal*, 20/2 (1977), 479–96.

40. The doubts were analysed most effectively in MO's 1944 report on attitudes to reconstruction, *The Journey Home*. For divergent appropriations of this MO analysis see Steven Fielding, Peter Thompson, and Nick Tiratsoo, *England Arise! The Labour Party and popular politics in 1940s Britain* (Manchester, 1995), and James Hinton, '1945 and the Apathy School', *History Workshop Journal*, 43 (1997), 266–73.

41. Mass-Observation, *The Journey Home* (London, 1944), 48.

42. Angus Calder, *The Myth of the Blitz* (London, 1991); Macolm Smith, *Britain and 1940: History, myth and popular memory* (London, 2000).

43. For these 'counter-narratives of war' see Stephen Brooke, 'War and the nude: The photography of Bill Brandt in the 1940s', *Journal of British Studies*, 45/1 (2006), 118–38; Adam Piette, *Imagination at War: British fiction and poetry, 1939–1945* (Basingstoke, 1995); Lyndsey Stonebridge, 'Anxiety at a time of crisis', *History Workshop Journal*, 45 (1998), 171–98.

44. Elizabeth Bowen, *The Heat of the Day* (Harmondsworth, 1979), 275. We know Titmuss had read Bowen's novel because he quotes with approval her characterization of social solidarity among civilians caught up in the London Blitz: 'the wall between the living and the living became less solid as the wall between the living and the dead thinned' (*Social Policy*, 347) using it to buttress his own argument that, despite pre-war expectations, civilian bombing turned out to be far less damaging either to social solidarity or to individual psychological health than mass unemployment had been in the 1930s. This remark of Bowen's is, however, open to far darker readings; and the main thrust of her account was quite the reverse of Titmuss's optimistic picture of wartime social progress. On Bowen see Heather Bryant Jordan, *How Will the Heart Endure: Elizabeth Bowen and the landscape of war* (Ann Arbor, 1992); Maud Ellman, *Elizabeth Bowen: The shadow across the page* (Edinburgh, 2003).

45. For a discussion of gender differences in attitudes to the war, based on Mass-Observation sources, see Lucy Noakes, *War and the British: Gender, memory and national identity* (London, 1998).

46. T. S. Eliot, *Four Quartets* (London, 1959), 44.

47. Callum G. Brown, *The Death of Christian Britain: Understanding secularisation 1800–2000* (London, 2001).

48. Stephen Parker, *Faith on the Home Front: Aspects of church life and popular religion in Birmingham, 1939–1945* (Oxford, 2005); Matthew Grimley, 'The religion of Englishness: Puritanism, providentialism and "national character", 1918–45', *Journal of British Studies*, 46 (2007), 884–906.

49. James Olney presents a Christian essentialist account of selfhood along these lines: *Metaphors of Self: The meaning of autobiography* (Princeton, 1972), 327–9 and *passim*.

50. Diarist 5399, DR May 1942.

51. Mass-Observation, *Puzzled People: A study in popular attitudes to religion, ethics, progress and politics in a London Borough* (London, 1947), 29 ff.; Parker, *Faith on the Home Front*, 87; Jenny Hazelgrove, *Spiritualism, and British Society between the Wars* (Manchester, 2000).

52. Taylor, *Sources*, 376–7, 422.

53. James Hinton, 'The "class" complex': Mass-Observation and cultural distinction in pre-war Britain', *Past and Present*, 198/2 (2008).

54. James Byrom, *The Unfinished Man*, (London, 1957), 135. Contrast Pierre Bourdieu, *Distinction: A social critique of the Judgement of Taste* (London, 1984), 18–19. Bourdieu's sociological critique of high culture identifies taste in music, not as the doorway to a higher spirituality, but as the false consciousness of class par excellence, precisely because music appears to be pure art, abstract and non-referential, the most radical and absolute form of the negation of the social. There is, of course no reason why great music, or any other supreme achievements of the human spirit, should not play a role in the reproduction of social inequality. But one can observe this without devaluing its spiritual power.

55. Taylor, *Sources*, writes of 'the heroism of unbelief' (404), 'facing a disenchanted universe with courage and lucidity . . . those who hold this view have a sense of the dignity of human beings, which consists precisely in their ability to stand unschooled and uncowed in the face of the indifferent immensity of the world and to find the purpose of their lives in understanding it and transcending in this way by far their own insignificant locus and being . . . Man can be annihilated by the universe, but his greatness in relation to it consists in his going down knowingly. Something inspires our respect here, and this respect empowers' (93–5).

56. Taylor, *Sources*, 314–19, 355, 383, 390.

57. The term 'life writing' was coined by Virginia Woolf to encompass the full range of ways in which individuals put the bewildering complexity of their experiences and feelings down on paper—diaries, letters, memoirs, autobiographical fiction, etc. Hermione Lee, *Virginia Woolf* (London, 1997), 4; Suzette A. Henke, *Shattered Subjects: Trauma and testimony in women's life-writing* (New York, 2000), pp. xiii, xvi.

58. An edited version of the diary of Nella Last (the subject of Ch. 2 below) was first published in 1981 and has recently been republished in the wake of Victoria Wood's TV dramatization of her (substantially fictionalized) life.

Richard Broad and Suzie Fleming (eds.), *Nella Last's War: A mother's diary, 1939–45* (Bristol, 1981); Richard Broad and Suzie Fleming (eds.), *Nella Last's War: The Second World War diaries of housewife, 49* (London, 2006). Dorothy Sheridan, the MO archivist, edited *Among You Taking Notes: The wartime diary of Naomi Mitchison* (London, 1985). Edward Stebbing published his own MO diary, *Diary of a Decade 1939–50* (Lewis, 1998). More recently the diaries of three young women have been published: Robert Malcolmson and Peter Searby (eds.), *Wartime Norfolk: The diary of Rachel Ddonau, 1941–42* (Norwich, 2005); Olivia Cockett, *Love and War in London: A woman's diary, 1939–1942*, ed. Robert Malcolmson (Waterloo, 2005); Patricia and Robert Malcolmson (eds.), *A Woman in Wartime London: The diary of Kathleen Tipper, 1941–1945* (London, 2006). A second volume of extracts from Nella Last's diary has now been published, taking the story to the end of 1948, Patricia and Robert Malcolmson, *Nella Last's Peace: The post-war diaries of housewife, 49* (London, 2008); and the same authors have published a section of the diary of Denis Argent, the subject of Ch. 7: *A Soldier in Bedfordshire: The diary of Private Denis Argent 1941–1942* (Bedford, 2009).

59. Angus Calder and Dorothy Sheridan (eds.), *Speak for Yourself: A Mass-Observation anthology, 1937–49* (London, 1984); Dorothy Sheridan (ed.), *Wartime Women: An anthology of women's wartime writing for Mass-Observation, 1937–45* (London, 1990); Sandra Koa Wing (ed.), *Our Longest Days: A people's history of the Second World War* (London, 2007); Simon Garfield's trilogy in which entries by eleven different diarists are woven into an evocative portrait of life in wartime (and immediate post-war) Britain: *Our Hidden Lives: The remarkable diaries of post-war Britain* (London, 2004); *We Are at War: The remarkable diaries of five ordinary people in extraordinary times* (London, 2005); *Private Battles: How the war almost defeated us* (London, 2006).

60. Celia Fremlin, one of Mass-Observation's most able investigators and a talented writer, abandoned her attempt (in 1944) to write a history of the war based on the diaries, concluding: 'The longer I work on the diaries the more definite becomes my opinion that they should <u>not</u> be used on their own. They are essentially <u>supplementary</u> to more detailed investigations. Used thus they provide invaluable quotations, sidelights, etc. But when you try to use them by themselves you continually come up against the fact that you can't prove anything from them.' Celia Fremlin to Bob Willcock, 14 Sept. 1944, MO File Report 2181.

61. Margaretta Jolly, 'Historical entries: Mass-Observation diarists 1937–2001' in *New Formations*, 44/Autumn (2001) is a pioneering essay in this vein,

though based only on the few diaries that had been published when she wrote.

62. Tom Harrisson, *Living Through the Blitz* (Harmondsworth, 1978), 254.

63. One could make the case that the mass observers as a group 'represented' a vanguard of modern reflexive selfhood, as I suggested in Hinton, 'The "class" complex', *Past and Present*, 198/2 (2008).

64. Michael Rustin, 'Reflections on the biographical turn in the social sciences' in Prue Chamberlayne, Joanna Bornat, and Tom Wengraf (eds.), *The Turn to Biographical Methods in the Social Sciences* (Abingdon, 2000). See also Ken Plummer, *Documents of Life 2: An invitation to a Critical Humanism* (London, 2001).

65. 'In memory of Sigmund Freud' in W. H. Auden, *Selected Poems*, ed. Edward Mendelson (London, 1979), 93.

66. Mathew Thomson, *Psychological Subjects: Identity, culture and health in twentieth-century Britain* (Oxford, 2006), 13. For an alternative view see Graham Richards, 'Britain on the couch: The popularization of psychoanalysis in Britain, 1918–1940', *Science in Context*, 13/2 (2000) and Michael Roper, 'Between manliness and masculinity: The war generation and the psychology of fear in Britain, 1914–1950', *Journal of British Studies*, 44/2 (2005), 348–50. On Victorian ideas of character see S. Collini, *Public Moralists: Political thought and intellectual life in Britain 1850–1930* (Oxford, 1993), chs. 2 and 3. Nikolas Rose, *Governing the Soul: The shaping of the private self* (London, 1999) has argued that British people became, during the later decades of the twentieth century, 'psychological selves', internally colonized at the deepest levels of their self-awareness by the armies of psychological specialists whose expertise established the norms by which they lived 'a subjection that is more profound because it appears to emanate from our autonomous quest for ourselves' (260). See also 'Assembling the modern self' in Roy Porter (ed.), *Rewriting the Self: Histories from the Renaissance to the present* (London, 1997). Mathew Thomson, *Psychological Subjects*, 6–8 and *passim* rehearses some of the implausibilites of this top-down argument. In any case, any such a regime of psychological governance was, in the 1940s, still in its infancy.

67. Much the same goes for the dreams that MO, in search of a collective unconscious, encouraged its diarists to send it. As Tyrus Milner points out ('In the Blitz of Dreams: Mass-Observation and the historical uses of dream reports', *New Formations*, 44/Autumn (2001)) the meaning of these dreams was much too individual to be understood outside a therapeutic situation. But for an interesting attempt to put dead people on the couch see Roper, 'Splitting in unsent letters'.

68. M. Foucault, *The Order of Things* (London, 1970), 387. But for a more or less humanist reading of Foucault's later writing see Patrick Hutton, 'Foucault, Freud and the technologies of the self' in Luther H. Martin, et al. (eds.), *Technologies of the Self: A seminar with Michel Foucault* (Massachusetts, 1988).

69. This point has been particularly well made by Michael Roper, 'Slipping out of view: Subjectivity and emotion in gender history', *History Workshop Journal*, 59/1 (2005), 70: 'To conceive of subjectivity primarily in terms of representation, however, is to endorse a profoundly lifeless notion of human existence, in which we deny to history the rich depth of emotional experience that surely animates us in our own lives.' He describes how much cultural history leaves the reader with a 'sensation of abstraction' (62), confronted by claims for the meaning of public discourses for subjectivity advanced without encountering in any depth any individual human agent.

70. Field, *A Life of One's Own*, 208.

71. Michael Roper, 'Slipping out of view', 65–6.

72. T. S. Eliot, 'The Love Song of J. Alfred Prufrock', *Collected Poems, 1909–1935* (London, 1958), 13.

CHAPTER 2

1. Richard Broad and Suzie Fleming (eds.), *Nella Last's War: A mother's diary, 1939–45* (Bristol, 1981); Richard Broad and Suzie Fleming (eds.), *Nella Last's War: The Second World War diaries of housewife, 49* (London, 2006). A second volume has now been published, taking the story to the end of 1948. Patricia and Robert Malcolmson, *Nella Last's Peace: The post-war diaries of housewife, 49* (London, 2008). I am grateful to the Malcomsons for allowing me pre-publication access to this volume.

2. Roger Bromley, *Lost Narratives: Popular fictions, politics and recent history* (London 1988), 163–9 points out how the marketing of Nella's wartime diaries has followed a conservative agenda in emphasizing the personal, familial dimensions of her wartime experience. But he himself largely ignores the public dimension of her life—perhaps because, seeing voluntary work as conventionally allotted public space for middle-class women, he assumed that her involvement in WVS was not capable of providing a significant challenge to the patriarchal structure of her marriage. His discussion of Nella's (published) text turns on an interesting distinction between the 'mental space' created by her status as a mass observer and the 'conventional space' she inhabited as a member of her 'class-fraction and generation'. But the distinction is overdrawn, in ways which tend to exaggerate the degree,

and misidentify the causes, of Nella's distance from the conventions of her milieu. Bromley's view of the diaries as themselves a form of 'breakdown' entirely neglects their role as a therapeutic response to the real nervous breakdown which, as we will see, she had suffered in 1937–8.

3. 6 Apr. 1948.

4. DR, Jun. 1939.

5. 6 Nov. 1940, 31 Jan. 1940.

6. DR, Jun. 1939.

7. 9 Jan. 1942.

8. 28 Jul. 1943.

9. Arthur's intellectuality and wide reading are apparent in the few DRs that he did for Mass-Observation in the autumn of 1943.

10. 14 Aug. 1941.

11. 1 May 1943.

12. DR Jun. 1944.

13. 24 May 1945.

14. 24 Sep. 1945.

15. 27 Oct. 1945.

16. Max Dimmack, *Clifford Last* (Melbourne, 1972), 6.

17. The literature is extensive. See in particular M. R. J. Higonnet, et al., *Behind the Lines: Gender and the Two World Wars* (New Haven, 1987); Susan Pederson, 'Gender, welfare and citizenship in Britain during the Great War', *American Historical Review*, 94 (1990); P. Summerfield, 'Women in World War Two', in A. Marwick (ed.), *Total War and Social Change* (Basingstoke, 1988); P. Summerfield, *Reconstructing Women's Wartime Lives: Discourse and subjectivity in oral histories of the Second World War* (Manchester, 1998); M. Pugh, 'Domesticity and the decline of feminism, 1930–50', in H. L. Smith (ed.), *British Feminism in the Twentieth Century* (Aldershot, 1990); Pat Thane, 'The women of the British Labour Party and feminism, 1906–1945', in Smith (ed.), *British Feminism in the Twentieth Century*; David Jarvis, 'The Conservative Party and the politics of gender, 1900–1939', in Martin Francis and Ina Zweiniger-Bargielowska (eds.), *The Conservatives and British Society, 1880–1990* (Cardiff, 1996).

18. 28 Aug. 1941.

19. Sam Davies and Bob Morley, *County Borough Election Results, England and Wales, 1919–1938: A comparative analysis*, i: *Barnsley—Bournemouth* (Aldershot, 1999), 58.

20. DR Jan. 1945; Stephen Taylor, 'The suburban neurosis', *Lancet*, 26 Mar. 1938, 759–61.

21. 31 May 1940.

22. Day Survey Oct. 1938, reproduced in Dorothy Sheridan (ed.), *Wartime Women: An anthology of women's wartime writing for Mass-Observation, 1937–45* (London, 1990), 41.

23. On WVS, see James Hinton, *Women and Social Leadership in the Second World War: Continuities of class* (Oxford, 2002).

24. 28 Dec. 1942. This was another ambition which Will had crushed: 'I was not let take advantage of my father's offer to put me into a little shop of whatever line I chose' (2 Oct. 1947), cited in Malcolmson, *Nella Last's Peace*, 186.

25. 28 Aug. 1941.

26. 5 Oct. 1942.

27. 17 Aug. 1940.

28. 11 Nov. 1942.

29. 7 Dec. 1939.

30. 1 Oct. 1959.

31. 13 Oct. 1941; 1 Sep. 1940; DR Dec. 1943.

32. Davies and Morley, *County Borough Election Results*, 60–2.

33. Vera Dart report of visit to Barrow, 6 Feb. 1939; Regional Organizer report on Barrow, 24 Oct. 1941; Regional Organizer to Miss Willan, 12 Apr. 1951—all in Region 10/2/Barrow in Furness, Women's Royal Voluntary Services archive.

34. Hinton, *Women and Social Leadership*, 86–8, and see Gertrude Glover's MO diary, 30 May 1942. Before the war, warned by the Town Clerk that they would have difficulty recruiting in Barrow unless 'the Labour element was represented on our staff', the WVS regional organizer had asked him to nominate suitable Labour women, but nothing came of this. Vera Dart, Report on Barrow 6 Feb. 1939, Region 10/2/Barrow in Furness, Women's Royal Voluntary Services archive.

35. 1 Aug. 1940.

36. 6 Nov. 1942.

37. 25 Jul. 1945.

38. 27 Jul. 1945.

39. 3 Jan. 1947, cited in Malcolmson, *Nella Last's Peace*, 141.

40. DR Apr. 1942.

41. 27 Aug. 1945.

42. 18 Feb. 1947, cited in Malcolmson, *Nella Last's Peace*, 142.

43. James Hinton, 'Conservative women and voluntary social service, 1938–1951', in Stuart Ball and Ian Holliday (eds.), *Mass Conservatism: The Conservatives and the public since the 1880s* (London, 2002), 100–19.

44. 17 Oct. 1939.

45. 13 Feb. 1940.

46. 28 Nov. 1939.

47. 17 Oct. 1939.

48. 2 May 1940.

49. 29 Apr. 1941.

50. Foster Jeffrey, 'Report on Barrow', 8 May 1941; Foster Jeffrey to Mrs Huxley, 8 May 1941; Foster Jeffrey, 'Report on Barrow', 10 Jun. 1941, Region 10/2/Barrow in Furness, Women's Royal Voluntary Services archive.

51. 5 May 1942.

52. 18 Dec. 1943.

53. 17 Dec. 1942.

54. 2 Dec. 1943.

55. 21 Apr. 1942; 5 Jan. 1943.

56. 31 Aug. 1939; 23 Nov. 1939.

57. DR Dec. 1943.

58. 30 Dec. 1940.

59. 19 Jul. 1943.

60. 1 Nov. 1939; 1 Sep. 1942.

61. 10 Dec. 1939.

62. 22 Jan. 1941.

63. 25 Sep. 1939.

64. 30 Apr. 1940.

65. 31 Aug. 1942; 19 Aug. 1943.

66. 14 Sep. 1939.

67. DR Jan. 1940.

68. MO file report 2; Ian McLaine, *Ministry of Morale: Home front morale and the Ministry of Information in World War II* (London, 1979), 49–50; Angus Calder, *The People's War: Britain 1939–1945* (London, 1971), 71.

69. 28 Aug. 1941; 24 Nov. 1943.

70. 19 Aug. 1942; 27 Apr. 1941.

71. 8 Oct. 1942. While Nella was, no doubt, unusually thoughtful about these issues, her changed attitude to reprisals was, according to Mass-Observation, characteristic of those who experienced bombing. Tom Harrisson, *Living Through the Blitz* (Harmondsworth, 1978), 149, 315–16.

72. 15 May 1940.

73. 30 Oct. 1942.

74. 5 Jun. 1940.

75. 31 Jul. 1945.

76. 1 Aug. 1940.

77. 16 Jun. 1942.

78. DR Apr. 1942.

79. 29 Nov. 1939.

80. 10 May 1940; Stephen Parker, *Faith on the Home Front: Aspects of church life and popular religion in Birmingham, 1939–1945* (Oxford, 2005), 110.

81. 6 Apr. 1948, cited in Malcolmson, *Nella Last's Peace*, 228.

82. DR Feb. 1942.

83. DR Dec. 1940.

84. 8 Jan. 1943; 5 Oct. 1941.

85. 9 Feb. 1940.

86. 4 Feb. 1941.

87. 6 Sep. 1940; 9 Feb. 1940; 29 Aug. 1945.

88. 13 Sep. 1945.

89. 2 Aug. 1947, cited in Malcolmson, *Nella Last's Peace*, 169.

90. 21 Apr. 1948, cited in ibid. 245.

91. 25 Jul. 1945.

92. 25 Jul. 1945.

93. 14 Mar. 1940.

94. 14 Mar. 1940.

95. 15 Jun. 1945; 17 Nov. 1943; 19 Jan. 1942. Marion Jolly wrongly attributes this separation to Nella's initiative: 'Historical Entries: Mass-Observation diarists 1937–2001', *New Formations*, 44 (Autumn 2001), 118.

96. 17 Nov.1943.

97. 4 Oct. 1940.

98. 10 May 1945.

99. 2 Oct. 1947, cited in Malcolmson, *Nella Last's Peace*, 185.

100. 10 May 1945.

101. 2 Oct. 1947, cited in Malcolmson, *Nella Last's Peace*, 186.

102. 8 Aug. 1940.

103. 1 Oct. 1938, cited in Sheridan, *Wartime Women*, 41.

104. 10 Jun. 1940.

105. 3 Mar. 1941.

106. 22 Sep. 1939. 'William Hickey' was written by Tom Driberg, later a Labour MP. As a close friend of Tom Harrisson he used his column in the *Express* to promote MO. Judith M. Heimann, *The Most Offending Soul Alive: Tom Harrisson and his remarkable life* (Honolulu, 1997), 133.

107. 17 Sep. 1947, cited in Malcolmson, *Nella Last's Peace*, 182.

108. 10 Mar. 1943.

109. 7 May 1945.

110. 30 Dec. 1940. She knew about 'montage' from her brother, a professional photographer working for the railways.

111. 2 Nov. 1942; 30 Apr. 1948, cited in Malcolmson, *Nella Last's Peace*, 248.

112. Bromley, *Lost Narratives*, 169.
113. DR Feb. 1945.
114. 17 Feb. 1966.
115. 5 Oct. 1948, cited in Malcolmson, *Nella Last's Peace*, 261; 7 Feb. 1950.
116. This is the judgement of Jennifer Purcell, to whom I am grateful for letting me read draft chapters of her D.Phil. thesis, since completed as 'Beyond Home: Housewives and the nation, private and public identities 1939–1949' (D.Phil., University of Sussex, 2008). Her book, *Domestic Soldiers: Women in wartime Britain*, will be published by Constable and Robinson in 2010.

CHAPTER 3

1. James Hinton, *Women, Social Leadership and the Second World War: Continuities of class* (Oxford, 2002).
2. 14 Jan. 1942.
3. Gertrude F. Glover, *A False Note: A play for women in one act* (London, 1937). This is a comic tale set in a village shop. Appropriately for the WI, the cast range in age and class—from Mrs Wilde a 'down-at heel, resigned' woman facing eviction for non-payment of rent (because her father drinks his pension money instead of giving it to her), to a 'young lady' ('young, active') with a car waiting outside who is going on a picnic. The landlady eviction threatening ('impoverished spinster') is not unsympathetic, and everyone acknowledges she has to live. Another character bets money on the horses (and wins on this occasion) but she herself agrees with the rest that gambling is bad and a waste of money and explains that she only does it to keep her husband happy: 'I got to live peaceable with Joe. He don't drink, and he's good in a number of ways, but, lummy, I do grudge the money as goes on horses.' The plot revolves cleverly around the (accidental) passing of a fake pound note, which Mrs Wilde (in a moment of desperation) steals from the till, and, later, contrives to replace (having been given an advance payment for domestic work by another character) in the till. So Wilde's crime is never discovered.
4. W. B. Stephens (ed.), *The Victoria History of the County of Warwick*, viii: *The City of Coventry and Borough of Warwick* (London, 1969), 77–83.
5. 3 Nov. 1944.
6. DR Mar. 1943.
7. 13 Feb. 1942.
8. 14 Mar. 1942.
9. 15 May 1942.
10. 28 Oct. 1943.
11. 31 Dec. 1942.

12. Maggie Andrews, *The Acceptable Face of Feminism: The Women's Institute as a social movement* (London, 1998). In an excellent recent article Helen McCarthy shows how organizations like the WI can be read 'in at least three different ways: as the basis for a liberal project of inclusion and integration, a conservative vehicle for fostering hierarchy and deference, or a social democratic struggle to transform the prevailing relations of power within civil society. At different times and in different places, one can glimpse all three agendas at work...', 'Parties, voluntary associations, and democratic politics in interwar Britain', *The Historical Journal*, 50/4 (2007), 910.

13. 28 Mar. 1943.

14. 2 Mar. 1943.

15. 11 Nov. 1941.

16. 17 Nov. 1942.

17. 23 Oct. 1941; 3 Jan. 1942.

18. 30 Aug. 1944.

19. 8 May 1944.

20. 23 Oct. 1941.

21. Miss Fletcher Moulton, report on Warwickshire, 8 Jul. 1938, Region 9, office papers, Women's Royal Voluntary Service archive.

22. 30 Sep. 1942.

23. 1 Jul. 1943.

24. 3, 7 Apr. 1944.

25. 4 Nov. 1941.

26. DR Nov. 1943. Peter Ackers and Jonathan Payne comment on the relatively peaceful character of industrial relations in the prosperous Warwickshire coalfield: 'Before the storm: The experience of nationalization and the prospects for industrial relations partnership in the British coal industry, 1947–1972—rethinking the militant narrative', *Social History*, 27/2 (2002), 194.

27. Mass-Observation, *People in Production: An enquiry into British war production* (London, 1942); James Hinton 'Coventry communism: A study of factory politics in the Second World War', *History Workshop Journal*, 10 (1980), 90–118; James Hinton, *Shop Floor Citizens: Engineering democracy in 1940s Britain* (Aldershot, 1994), ch. 3.

28. 19 Feb. 1944.

29. 12 Nov. 1941.

30. DR Mar. 1944.

31. 12 Nov. 1941; 5 Dec. 1941.

32. 12 Jan. 1944; 3 Mar. 1943.

33. Matthew Thomson, *Psychological Subjects: Identity, culture and health in twentieth-century Britain* (Oxford, 2006), 160.

34. 28 Jan. 1949.

35. H. Smith, 'The problem of equal pay for equal work in Great Britain during World War Two', *Journal of Modern History*, 53 (1981), 655, 661–3; Olive Banks, *The Politics of British Feminism, 1918–1970* (Aldershot, 1993), 100–1; P. Brooks, *Women at Westminster* (London, 1967), 136–9; Alison Oram, '"Bombs don't discriminate!" Women's political activism in the Second World War', in C. Gledhill and G. Swanson (eds.), *Nationalising Femininity: Culture, sexuality and British cinema in the Second World War* (Manchester, 1996), 55–8.

36. DR Nov. 1943; 17 Apr. 1943.

37. DR Sep. 1943.

38. 11 Mar. 1947.

39. Banks, *Politics of British Feminism*; S. Pedersen, *Family: Dependence and the origins of the welfare state. Britain and France, 1914–1945* (Cambridge, 1993); M. Pugh, *Women and the Women's Movement in Britain, 1914–1959* (Basingstoke, 1992).

40. Dale Spender, *There's Always Been a Women's Movement this Century* (London, 1983); Andrews, *Reasonable Feminism*; Pat Thane, 'The women of the British Labour Party and feminism, 1906–1945', in H. Smith (ed.), *British Feminism in the Twentieth Century* (Aldershot, 1990)

41. Hinton, *Women, Social Leadership*, 180.

42. DR Apr. 1944.

43. DR Jan. 1943.

44. DR Jan. 1944.

45. DR Apr. 1944.

46. Hera Cook, *The Long Sexual Revolution: English women, sex and contraception, 1900–1975* (Oxford, 2004), 205.

47. 17 Aug. 1943.

48. 21, 25 Apr. 1944.

49. DR Apr. 1944.

50. Sonya O. Rose, *Which People's War?: National identity and citizenship in Britain 1939–1945* (Oxford, 2003), 69, 72–4, 92.

51. Ibid. 79.

52. To be fair to Sonya Rose, she herself insists on the fragility of the discourses she analyses.

53. DR Nov. 1944.

54. DR Mar. 1942.

55. 25 Oct. 1942.

56. DR Oct. 1942; 8 Aug. 1943.

57. DR Mar. 1943.

58. DR Mar. 1942.

59. DR May 1942.

60. DR Aug. 1944.

61. For a contemporary analysis along these lines see Peter Drucker, *The End of Economic Man: A study of the new totalitarianism* (London 1939), ch. 20. Gertrude was impressed by this book.

62. On the evolution of the quietist pacifism characteristic of many Second World War conscientious objectors see Martin Ceadel, *Pacifism in Britain, 1914–1945: The defining of a faith* (Oxford, 1980).

63. DR Mar. 1942.

64. 7 Oct. 1943.

65. Graham Dawson, *Soldier Heroes: British adventure, empire and the imagining of masculinities* (London, 1994), 4.

66. 5 May 1945.

67. DR Nov. 1944.

68. H. G. Wells, *God the Invisible King* (London, 1917), 170–1.

69. 23 Oct. 1942.

70. DR Jan. 1943.

71. DR Oct. 1942.

72. DR Jan. 1942.

73. DR Sep. 1943.

74. DR Jan. 1945.

75. DR Aug. 1945.

76. For poll figures showing a surge of middle-class female support for Labour in the months following the 1945 election see James Hinton, 'Women and the Labour vote, 1945–50', *Labour History Review*, 57 (1993), 64; see also Hinton, *Women, Social Leadership*, 189–92.

77. 20 Jun. 1947; 17 Jan. 1948.

78. 28 Feb. 1945.

79. 28 Jan. 1948.

80. 24 Jan. 1949.

81. 12 Jan. 1949. The Berlin crisis, which she had expected to lead to war, put a damper on her usual optimism. Both sides, she thought, were behaving 'just about as boys of 10 would handle it', 6 Apr. 1948.

82. DR Oct. 1942.

83. 7 Jan. 1948.

CHAPTER 4

1. For example, when asked directly by MO, she was prepared to divulge the most intimate details of her married life: see her response to the March 1944 directive on attitudes to birth control reproduced in Angus Calder and Dorothy Sheridan (eds.), *Speak for Yourself: A Mass-Observation anthology, 1937–49* (London, 1984), 172–7.
2. DR Dec. 1937.
3. DR Aug. 1944; Dina Copelman, *London's Women Teachers: Gender, class and feminism, 1870–1930* (London, 1996).
4. DR Jun. 1939.
5. DR Mar. 1944.
6. DR Mar. 1944; DR Jun. 1939.
7. DR Mar. 1944.
8. On the marriage bar see Copelman, *Women Teachers*, 192.
9. DR Dec. 1942.
10. 4 Mar. 1940.
11. 2 Sep. 1945; 26 Mar. 1940.
12. DR Feb. 1939.
13. DR Dec. 1937.
14. 15 May 1943.
15. 24 Feb. 1940.
16. 6 Jun. 1945.
17. 4 Feb. 1940.
18. 17 Dec. 1942.
19. 19 Feb. 1940.
20. 8 Jun. 1943
21. DR Mar. 1943.
22. 23 Feb. 1944.
23. 10 May 1945. In 1934 she stood for Springfield Ward in Wandsworth Borough Council elections, got 2,824 votes, the top scoring of 6 Labour candidates in a Tory ward, Essex Data Archive, Local election results.
24. DR Aug. 1944. Her attitude was very similar to that of Vera Dart, a leading WVS full-timer, who stood as a Labour candidate in the 1945 general election. James Hinton, *Women, Social Leadership and the Second World War: Continuities of class* (Oxford, 2002), 89 n. 131, 178–9, 206.
25. DR Nov. 1945.
26. 21 Sep. 1942.

27. DR Sep. 1943.

28. DR Dec. 1942.

29. DR Jan. 1942.

30. DR Jul. 1942.

31. DR Feb. 1945.

32. DR Sep. 1943

33. 10 May 1945.

34. DR Sep. 1943. In one of these sessions a film strip of her own dealing with local government provided the main talking point.

35. DR Jun. 1942.

36. DR Oct. 1942.

37. 19 Aug. 1945.

38. 21 Jan. 1940.

39. DR Oct. 1942; DR Apr. 1942.

40. DR Mar. 1942.

41. 24 Jan. 1944.

42. Kate Fisher, *Birth Control, Sex and Marriage in Britain 1918–1960* (Oxford, 2006), 121, points out that women of this generation often presented themselves as 'undersexed'—but this testifies more to the cult of innocence and passivity than to any reliable notion of what 'normal' might be.

CHAPTER 5

1. 28 Jul. 1940.

2. Life Story, 1939.

3. Lane, according to his daughter, led a vigorous social life after he came to London, aged 16, in April 1919 to work for his uncle at The Bodley Head. (Jeremy Lewis, *Penguin Special: The life and times of Allen Lane* (London, 2005), 28–9; Clare Morpurgo, 'Allen Lane and his Foundation', Allen Lane Lecture, 2006, <www.allenlane.org.uk/2006_lecture.htm>). A few months older than Lane, Eleanor recalled teaching him how to dance and 'guiding and comforting him for a year or two . . . not that there were any sentimental relations between us'. The one concrete memory she records was of a Mansion House dance where he dumped her in favour of one of the many beautiful girls who ran after him: 'such a good looking boy' (23 May 1942; 19 Jun. 1942). Their friendship survived this incident however, but they lost touch after her marriage. In 1942, reading about the birth of his first child, she renewed contact and he invited her to his country house for the weekend. Horace refused, and nothing came of this.

4. Life Story, 1939.

5. DR Nov. 1943.

6. Life Story, 1939.

7. 21 Oct. 1939.

8. Celia Fremlin, MO File Report 2181 , Nov. 1944, ch. 1, 'The generation that has no time'.

9. 'Other people seem to get done around here—by 11, so they say. Their husbands may not need much waiting on and perhaps help at night and in the mornings' (17 Jul. 1941). In 1952, however, MO reported that the average housewife had no more than two hours leisure time a day, and diaries kept by middle-class women suggest that the time they spent on household tasks nearly doubled in the quarter century following 1937, reaching 7.5 hours per day by 1961. Claire Langhamer, *Women's Leisure in England, 1920–60* (Manchester, 2000), 31; J. Gershuny, *Social Innovation and the Division of Labour* (Oxford, 1983), 149–51; S. Bowden and A. Offer, 'Household appliances and the use of time: The United States and Britain since the 1920s', *Economic History Review*, 7/4 (1994) 734–5. On contemporary advice see, for example, P. L. Garbutt, 'The housewife her own housemaid', *Good Housekeeping*, Jan. 1940, 49.

10. 7 Feb. 1940; 11 Oct. 1941.

11. 1 Mar. 1942.

12. 4 May 1941.

13. 13 May 1943. Compare the aspiring woman writer cited by Chris Hilliard, *To Exercise Our Talents: The democratisation of writing in Britain* (London, 2006), 42–3, who ascribed her husband's scorn of her writing 'not only [to] the time I gave to it, but also the demands that writing made on my inner self. (I think the latter is a commoner form of grievance than one might suppose.)'

14. 6 Apr. 1941.

15. 3 May 1941.

16. 5 Jul. 1941.

17. 2 Mar. 1942. Gertrude Stein's *Autobiography of Alice B. Toklas*, with its mastery of rambling conversational prose, had been published by Eleanor's old friend Allen Lane in 1933. Stein of course was a 'genius'—like Horace—though she said it herself.

18. 2 Mar. 1942.

19. 18 May 1941.

20. 7 Jun. 1941.

21. 22 Jun. 1941.

22. 16 Nov. 1940. Some of this diary entry is reproduced Tom Harrisson, *Living Through the Blitz* (Harmondsworth, 1978), 92–3.

23. DR Jul. 1939.

24. 28 Jul. 1941.

25. 26 Feb. 1942.

26. 5 Mar. 1941.

27. DR Jun. 1939.

28. 25 Jun. 1941.

29. DR Jun. 1939.

30. 9 May 1941.

31. Life Story, 1939; 4 Mar. 1941.

32. 26 Aug. 1941.

33. DR Apr. 1939.

34. 9 Apr. 1940.

35. DR Jul. 1939.

36. T. F. C. Lawrence, 'Boswell, Robert William McGregor (1911–1976)', *Australian Dictionary of Biography*, xiii (Melbourne, 1993), 225–6.

37. 20 Sep. 1940.

38. 30 Sep. 1941.

39. 16 Apr. 1941.

40. 22 Feb. 1941.

41. 2 Jan. 1943.

42. 15 Apr. 1940.

43. 27 Jul. 1940.

44. 20 Sep. 1940.

45. 18 Oct. 1940.

46. 11 Nov. 1940.

47. 29 Nov. 1940.

48. 3 Jul. 1941.

49. 7 Jun. 1941; 8 Jun. 1941.

50. 8 Jul. 1941.

51. 6 Sep. 1941; 1 Jan. 1942.

52. 26 Feb. 1942.

53. 24 Dec. 1942.

54. 12 Apr. 1942.

55. 19 Apr. 1941; 12 Jul. 1940.

56. 19 Apr. 1941; 25 Mar. 1943.

57. 14 Mar. 1941.

58. 2 Jan. 1943.

59. 28 Mar. 1942.

60. 7 Mar. 1943.

61. 8 May 1941.

62. 23 Apr. 1941.

63. 20 Mar. 1940.

64. 21 Oct. 1940.

65. DR Mar. 1942.

66. 2 Aug. 1942. Other middle-class couples made similar economies: see 'A family budget in wartime', *Housewife*, May 1942. This article was written by Ernest van Someren, on whom see Ch. 7 below.

67. DR Nov. 1944.

68. M. Coubrough, 'Profile: Invalid Children's Aid Association', *Child Care Health Development*, 4/1 (1978), 59–66.

69. F. K. Prochaska, *Women and Philanthropy in Nineteenth-century England* (Oxford, 1980); Ann Summers, 'A home from home: Women's philanthropic work in the nineteenth century', in S. Burman (ed.), *Fit Work for Women* (London 1979); Jane Lewis, 'The working-class wife and mother and state intervention', in J. Lewis (ed.), *Labour and Love: Women's experience of home and family, 1850–1940* (Oxford, 1986); Ellen Ross, *Love and Toil: Motherhood in outcast London, 1870–1918* (Oxford, 1993).

70. 10 Feb. 1943.

71. 6 Aug. 1940; 29 Apr. 1941.

72. 19 Dec. 1939.

73. 24 Aug. 1942. On Lady Reading and 'nation before husband' see Hinton, *Women, Social Leadership*, 30.

74. On these changes see Jane Lewis, *The Voluntary Sector, the State and Social Work in Britain* (Aldershot, 1995).

75. 23 Mar. 1942.

76. 16 Mar. 1943.

77. 4 Mar. 1942.

78. 25 Mar. 1943.

79. 8 Jul. 1942.

80. Life Story, 1939; 5 Apr. 1942.

81. DR Nov. 1944; Life Story, 1939.

82. 9 Jul. 1942.

83. Herbert Grey, *Successful Marriage* (1941), 113, 114, cited in Marcus Collins, *Modern Love: An intimate history of men and women in twentieth-century Britain* (London, 2003), 118.

84. 18 Oct. 1940.

85. Self Report, Nov. 1941.

86. 21 Jul. 1940.

87. 30 Jul. 1941; 26 Mar. 1941; 21 Jul. 1940.

88. 28 Feb. 1940.

89. 18 Feb. 1943.

90. Nella Last diary, 2 Oct. 1947; 25 Dec. 1947.

91. DR Jul. 1939.

CHAPTER 6

1. Lillian had a daughter who is probably still alive, but I have been unable to trace her. Because of this I have not used her real name. (Mass-Observation catalogued her as diarist 5420.) I have also changed the names of her daughter and husband, but not of other acquaintances, some of whom were public figures about whom I have made use of information derived from other sources.

2. Online 1901 Census of England and Wales, National Archives.

3. 12 Oct. 1945; 18 Apr. 1941.

4. J. H. Baron, and A Sonnenberg, 'The wax and wane of intestinal autointoxication and visceroptosis: Hstorical trends of real *versus* apparent new digestive diseases', *The American Journal of Gastroenterology*, 97/11 (2002) 2695-9.

5. 28 Aug. 1940; DR Mar. 1943.

6. 18 Mar. 1940.

7. 20 Oct. 1942; DR May 1944.

8. DR Oct. 1943; DR Jun. 1943.

9. 4 Oct. 1940; DR Oct. 1940; DR Mar. 1943.

10. DR Aug. 1944; 14 Mar. 1941; 18 May 1941.

11. 1 Jul. 1941; 8 Mar. 1943.

12. 22 Feb. 1940.

13. 19 Feb. 1940.

14. 22 Feb. 1940.

15. Carl Chinn, *Brum Undaunted: Birmingham during the blitz* (Studley, 2005), 4-5.

16. 4 Dec. 1943.

17. DR Sp 1947.

18. 26 Nov. 1941.

19. 16 Jun. 1940.

20. 9 Jan. 1946.

21. 7 Apr. 1942.

22. 2 Jan. 1941.

23. 13 Jun. 1940; and her answer to the question about the main points of friction in family life: 'I can better describe the points of friction in my family life before marriage, as I have so little to work on now I am married' (DR Jul. 1939).

24. 7 Jan. 1940.

25. 11 Nov. 1943; 11 Mar. 1942; DR Sep. 1944; Norman Haire (ed.), *Encyclopaedia of Sexual Knowledge* (London, 1936).

26. 11 Nov. 1943; DR Apr. 1944; 11 Jan. 1946.

27. DR Apr. 1944.

28. For discussion of these issues see Kate Fisher, *Birth Control, Sex and Marriage in Britain 1918–1960* (Oxford, 2006); Hera Cook, *The Long Sexual Revolution: English women, sex and contraception, 1900–1975* (Oxford, 2004).

29. 18 Jan. 1941.

30. 17 Jan. 1941.

31. 29 Apr. 1941.

32. 15 Sep. 1941; 26 Jul. 1941.

33. 6 Mar. 1942.

34. 11 Mar. 1942.

35. 10 Aug. 1940.

36. 11 Mar. 1942.

37. 27 Jul. 1942; 13 Mar. 1942.

38. 27 Jul. 1942.

39. 12 Feb. 1943.

40. 13 May 1941. Like Lillian, these women were unusual. Marriage usually put an end to visits to the dance hall. Claire Langhamer, *Women's Leisure in England, 1920–60* (Manchester, 2000), 136–7, 165–9.

41. 14 Sep. 1942.

42. 18 May 1942.

43. 21 May 1942.

44. 1 Sep. 1942.

45. DR Sep. 1944.

46. Mathew Thomson, *Psychological Subjects: Identity, culture and health in twentieth-century Britain* (Oxford, 2006).

47. 12 Oct. 1943.

48. 29 Dec. 1939.

49. 11 Feb. 1940.

50. Tom Harrisson, *Living Through the Blitz* (Harmondsworth, 1978), 203, 249–50. She also relayed to MO horror stories told by her friend Esther's brother, an undertaker dealing with the corpses: 'but I wouldn't tell anyone else, the panic it could cause would be awful' (19 Nov. 1940).

51. 9 May 1945.

52. 21 Mar. 1941; DR Aug. 1944.

53. 4 Aug. 1942.

54. 25 Mar. 1942.

55. 11 Mar. 1942.
56. 1 Jun. 1942.
57. Though definitions of what constitutes adultery are notoriously flexible (and not only in the Clinton White House). Claire Langhamer ('Adultery in post-war England', *History Workshop Journal*, 62 (2006) 98) cites divorce court denials that adultery had taken place on the grounds that intercourse took place in the daytime, or that the woman concerned was over fifty!
58. 9 Sep. 1942.
59. 26 Sep. 1942.
60. She sent a copy of this to MO but unfortunately it has not survived. After his election in 1945 Usborne was to launch the Parliamentary Group for World Government.
61. 14 May 1945.
62. *The Ethical Societies Chronicle*, 24/165 (May 1944) 1–2.
63. L. H. C. Thomas, 'Clair Baier', in A. D. Best and Rex W. Last (eds.), *Essays presented to Dr. Baier* (Hull, 1976), pp. vii–x. From his early years in Hull after 1946, if not before, Baier was a Quaker.
64. 12 Oct. 1945.
65. DR Jan. 1945.
66. DR May 1944.
67. DR Jan. 1945.
68. 13 Feb. 1943.
69. 17 Jun. 1940.
70. S. Fielding, 'The Second World War and popular radicalism: The significance of the "movement away from party"', *History*, 80/1 (1995); George Orwell, *The Lion and the Unicorn* (Harmondsworth, 1982).
71. 19 Jun. 1940.
72. DR Jun. 1944.
73. DR May 1944.
74. 18 Apr. 1941.
75. 10 Oct. 1939. The book was J. F. Rutherford, *Fascism or Freedom* (New York, 1939). Gertrude Glover was also impressed by Rutherford, who made her 'wonder whether the Jehovah's Witnesses might not be right and the world wrong' (DR May 1942). Nella had a rather more down to earth approach: 'The shop has stacks of Rutherford's . . . books which people were persuaded to buy in a series and never read—never sold one, all for salvage' (7 Jun. 1945). The salvage was all too successful and *Fascism or Freedom* did not make it into the British Library.
76. 24 Jun. 1940.
77. 11 Aug. 1940.

78. 18 Apr. 1941.
79. 18 Apr. 1941.
80. 21 Mar. 1941.
81. DR Sep. 1944. This evolution rather undermines Stephen Parker's use of Lillian as evidence for his argument that the war served to strengthen popular religious belief, a striking example of how fragmentary evidence from the MO diaries can be used to lend plausibility to any proposition one cares to advance. (Stephen Parker, *Faith on the Home Front: Aspects of church life and popular religion in Birmingham, 1939–1945* (2005), 72, 79, 86, 92, 100.) Compare Mass-Obervation's own scepticism about the long-term impact of blitz-induced religiosity in reversing religious decline: Mass-Observation, *Puzzled People: A study in popular attitudes to religion, ethics, progress and politics in a London Borough* (London, 1947), 59–60. Lillian did, however, retain a lingering respect for her father's faith: 'I trust with all my heart that Dad is right, I cannot visualise how it can happen and yet greater things have happened' VE Day report, May 1945.
82. DR May 1944.
83. 10 Aug. 1945. The 'heroism of unbelief' is from Taylor, *Sources*, 404.
84. *The Ethical Societies Chronicle*, 24/161 (Jan. 1944) 2; 165 (May 1944) 2.
85. Mass-Observation, *Puzzled People*; I. D. MacKillop, *The British Ethical Societies* (Cambridge, 1986), 146–7.
86. DR Sep. 1944.
87. DR Apr. 1944.
88. 10 Aug. 1945.
89. 14 Sep. 1942.
90. Aug. 1943 (no date given).
91. 2 Dec. 1943.
92. 12 Oct. 1943.
93. 19 Oct. 1943.
94. 29 Oct. 1943.
95. Aug. 1943 (no date given); 13 Mar. 1943.
96. 30 Jul. 1945.
97. VE Day report, May 1945.
98. DR Jun. 1944.
99. 25 Jun. 1945. I have taken a few liberties with this quotation—translating some passages in indirect speech back into direct speech. There was no such journal as *Monthly Psychology*, but *You*, the successor to *Practical Psychology*, with which Lillian was familiar, came out monthly.
100. 4 Jul. 1945.
101. 10 Nov. 1946.

102. 15 Dec. 1945.

103. 25 Nov. 1945.

104. 26 Jun. 1945.

105. 25 Nov. 1945.

106. 25 Jan. 1946.

107. Best and Last, *Essays presented to Dr. Baier*, p. vii.

108. Oct. 1946 (no date given).

109. Aug. 1946 (no date given).

110. 22 Sep. 1946.

111. 6 May 1947.

112. 25 Dec. 1946.

113. Aug. 1947 (no date given); 6 May 1947.

114. Aug. 1947 (no date given).

115. 6 May 1947.

116. 21 Mar. 1941.

117. DR Jun. 1944. It would have been a depressing text. Her recent experience of 'mixing and talking' had shown her that '75% to 80% of men have no conception of morals, ideals or of decent living. The only thing likely to keep them straight is fear. Fear of disease, fear of results through not being able to have a woman wholly, fear of epileptic fits, fear of being found out, etc. etc.'

118. Dec. 1947 (no date given).

119. Diarist 5311, DR Mar. 1944.

120. 18 Dec. 1946.

121. 24 Feb. 1947; Aug. 1947 (no date given).

122. On the writers' groups see Chris Hilliard, *To Exercise Our Talents: The democratisation of writing in Britain* (London, 2006).

123. Thomson, *Psychological Subjects*, 6–9.

124. DR Jul. 1939.

125. Marshall Berman, *All That Is Solid Melts Into Air: The experience of modernity* (1983), 35.

126. Ibid. 226.

CHAPTER 7

1. Horace Fletcher, *Fletcherism: What it is; or how I became young at sixty* (London, 1913); Martin Gardner, *Fads and Fallacies in the Name of Science* (Dover, 1957); A. G. Christen and J. A. Christen, 'Horace Fletcher (1849–1919): "The Great Masticator"', *Journal of the History of Dentistry*, 45/3 (1997) 95–100; Osbert Sitwell, *The Scarlet Tree* (Boston, 1946), 258.

2. Donald Weeks, *Corvo* (London, 1971), 295–301; Ivy van Someren, 'Barron Corvo's quarrels', *Life and Letters and the London Mercury* (Feb. 1947), 104–9.

3. I am grateful to Laurie van Someren for giving me a copy of this memoir, which I have used extensively in the following description of Ernest's early years.

4. Cited in Miriam Benkovitz, *Frederick Rolfe: Baron Corvo. A biography* (London, 1977), 264.

5. Interview with Laurie van Someren, 4 Sep. 2008.

6. Simon Garfield, *Private Battles: How the war almost defeated us* (London, 2006), 540.

7. 30 Nov. 1941.

8. Ernest H. S. van Someren, *Spectrochemical Abstracts* (London, 1938–51).

9. 1 May 1941.

10. DR Sep. 1943.

11. 1 Jan. 1942.

12. 27 Jan. 1940.

13. 'A family budget in wartime', *Housewife* (May 1942).

14. Jack Edwards, *Broxbourne Past* (Waltham Cross, 1984), plate 60.

15. DR Jun. 1939.

16. 16 Dec. 1942.

17. DR Apr. 1943.

18. 26 Mar. 1942.

19. As well as being an accomplished folk dancer, John W. Strange was on the radical wing on Quaker thinking on colonies, condemning equally 'collective security' as the defence of imperial power and colonial appeasement as 'treating vast populations of human beings as so many head of live stock'. Pacifist Research Bureau, *War and the Colonies: A policy for socialist and pacifists* (London, 1939).

20. 5 Jun. 1940.

21. 13 Oct. 1940.

22. On the links between Carpenter and Lawrence see Sheila Rowbotham, 'In search of Carpenter', *History Workshop Journal*, 3 (1977) 130.

23. DR Nov. 1944.

24. Frank G. Kirkpatrick, *John Macmurray: Community beyond political philosophy* (2005), 18, 80.

25. A. Giddens, *Modernity and Self-identity: Self and society in the late modern age* (Cambridge, 1991), 87–8, 97.

26. 'Spain' in W. H. Auden, *Selected Poems*, ed. Edward Mendelson (London 1979), 54.

27. She was sacked by the newspaper after twenty-one years because she could not accept its support for appeasement. During the war she worked for the Ministry of Information on the censorship of dispatches to foreign newspapers.

28. 9 Sep. 1942.

29. DR Oct. 1940.

30. DR Dec. 1937.

31. Maurice B. Reckitt, 'The Christian Social movement in England: Its aims and its organization', *The Journal of Religion*, 4/2 (Mar. 1924), 167. At the beginning of 1945 Ernest renewed contact with the Auxiliary movement, establishing a discussion group at the Murex factory.

32. DR Nov. 1944. Macmurray ranked them in ascending order as forms of knowledge—science, art, religion—but saw science as the highest form of knowledge *yet* achieved by any society (Kirkpatrick, *John Macmurray*, 71).

33. DR Nov. 1944.

34. 17 Sep. 1939; 24 Oct. 1940.

35. Stephen Hobhouse, *Forty Years and an Epilogue: An autobiography, 1881–1951* (London, 1951).

36. 19 Sep. 1943.

37. 18 Jan. 1942.

38. Hobhouse had invited Davies to talk, and lent Ernest a copy of an article by Davies, 'Why are Christians concerned in politics?', *Theology* (Oct. 1942). For Davies' own voyage, a fascinating account of one man's struggle to reconcile Christianity and socialism, see his autobiography: D. R. Davies, *In Search of Myself* (London, 1961).

39. On Fairchild see James Hinton, *The First Shop Steward's Movement* (London, 1972), 302–4; Walter Kendall, *The Revolutionary Movement in Britain* (London, 1969) 245, 406–7.

40. DR Sep. 1943. His engagement with Common Wealth was stimulated by an old friend Tom Sargant, a member of the Common Wealth executive who stood for Parliament unsuccessfully in 1945. D. L. Prynn, 'Common Wealth: A British "Third Party" of the 1940s', *Journal of Contemporary History*, 7/1 (1972), 176.

41. Toc H, a Christian service club active in community and youth work, originated during the First World War.

42. 2 Oct. 1943; 3 Jan. 1944; 1 May 1944.

43. DR Jan. 1940; 15 Sep. 1941.

44. 'One of his projects produced the huge steel spools required to wind pipe for the cross-channel fuel supply (PLUTO pipe line under the ocean) for D-day' (Garfield, *Private Battles*, 4).

45. 1 Sep. 1940.

46. 15 Sep. 1941.

47. Martin Ceadel, *Pacifism in Britain 1914–1945: The defining of a faith* (Oxford, 1980), 307; Denis Hayes, *Challenge of Conscience: The story of the conscientious objectors of 1939–1949* (London, 1949), 76, 207, 241.

48. 28 Dec. 1941.

49. DR Sep. 1942.

50. 7 Apr. 1943.

51. 12 Oct. 1939.

52. Interview with Laurie van Someren, 4 Sep. 2008.

53. 9 Aug. 1942; DR Oct. 1942.

54. 19 May 1944.

55. He did make a few rather half-hearted attempts after the war to find employment more in keeping with his principles—as a scientific liaison officer in France, or at the Institute of Medical Research, but these came to nothing and he turned down the one ethically irreproachable job that he was offered, with Scott Bader, a Quaker-run firm making polyester resins.

56. DR Mar. 1943.

57. Aldous Huxley, *Ends and Means* (London, 1937), 3–4.

58. DR Sep. 1942.

59. 26 May 1940; 1 Sep. 1940.

60. DR Sep. 1942.

61. DR Dec. 1940.

62. DR Dec. 1937.

CHAPTER 8

1. Sheila Ferguson and Hilde Fitzgerald, *Studies in the Social Services* (London, 1954), 4.

2. Mass-Observation, *The Journey Home* (London, 1944), 59–63.

3. Part of his diary has been edited for publication by Patricia and Robert Malcolmson, *A Soldier in Bedfordshire: The diary of Private Denis Argent 1941–1942* (Bedford, 2009).

4. Jeremy A. Crang, *The British Army and the People's War 1939–1945* (Manchester, 2000).

5. DR Feb. 1940.

6. 28 Jan. 1940.

7. 7 Nov. 1939; 16 Jan. 1940; 15 Jun. 1941.

8. 8 Dec. 1939.

9. 4 Feb. 1940.

10. 9 Sep. 1939.

11. 19 Sep. 1939.

12. 20 Oct. 1939.

13. 24 Nov. 1939.

14. 24 Nov. 1939; 9 Mar. 1940.

15. 14 Apr. 1940.

16. 5 May 1941.

17. 7 Apr. 1940; 25 Dec. 1939.

18. 3 Sep. 1939.

19. 17 Sep. 1939.

20. 7 Apr. 1940. Later, after he had visited MO HQ he wrote: 'The one point which subsequently occurred to me was whether I ought not to bowdlerize these chronicles somewhat out of consideration for the girls of MO staff who may have to wade through verbatim Army obscenity' (2 Mar. 1942).

21. 24 Dec. 1939; 25 Feb. 1940.

22. 2 May 1941.

23. Denis Hayes, *Challenge of Conscience: The story of the Conscientious Objectors of 1939–1949* (London,1949), 122–3.

24. 26 Jun. 1941.

25. DR Dec. 1940.

26. 3 Jul. 1941.

27. May 1940. On tensions between quietist religious objectors and trouble-making political objectors within NCC, see Hayes, *Challenge of Conscience*, 130 and James Byrom, *The Unfinished Man* (London, 1957), 130–1.

28. 14 Mar. 1941.

29. 19 May 1941.

30. 30 Jun. 1941; 3 Jul. 1941.

31. DR Dec. 1940.

32. 20 Aug. 1941.

33. 2 May 1942.

34. 26 Feb. 1942.

35. DR Apr. 1942.

36. DR Apr. 1942.

37. DR Jan. 1943.

38. DR Sep. 1943.

39. 24 May 1942.

40. DR Feb. 1942. Did such things happen, he wondered, in Russian or German towns or 'is the monkey parade a purely English institution, a product of pluto-democracy?' (3 May 1942). On dating rituals and the 'monkey parade' see Andrew Davies, *Leisure, Gender And Poverty: Working-class culture in Salford and Manchester, 1900–1939* (Buckingham, 1992), 102–8; Claire Langhamer,

'Love and courtship in mid-twentieth century England', *The Historical Journal*, 50/1 (2007), 183. Langhamer's suggestion that 'parades of this nature were untenable during the war' appears to be contradicted by Argent's accounts.

41. 10 Oct. 1941.
42. DR Jun. 1944.
43. DR Jan. 1943; DR Jun. 1944.
44. DR 4307. On Friday nights he attended gramophone evenings provided for the troops by a local musical family.
45. DR Jan. 1943.
46. DR Jun. 1942.
47. 13 Dec. 1941.
48. 12 Dec. 1941. His mother had much the same attitude: 'She still feels its rather crazy to spend so much of my spare time on something that I don't make any money out of!' (10 Feb. 1940).
49. 13 Dec. 1941.
50. 19 Jan. 1942; 26 Feb. 1942.
51. 19 Apr. 1942.
52. DR Sep. 1942.
53. DR Aug. 1942.
54. DR Jan. 1943.
55. MO archive, TC 27/3/E: Forces' attitudes: demobilization 1945. Reports sent in by Panel members in the Forces, Oct. 1945 Most of this response in reproduced in Angus Calder and Dorothy Sheridan, *Speak for Yourself: A Mass-Observation anthology, 1937–49* (London, 1984), 148–50.
56. DR Aug. 1943.
57. DR Mar. 1944.
58. DR Mar. 1943.
59. Byrom, *Unfinished Man*, 135.
60. DR Jan. 1941.
61. DR Jan. 1941.
62. DR Sep. 1943.
63. DR Sep. 1943.
64. DR Sep. 1943.
65. DR Aug. 1944.
66. 30 Oct. 1939.
67. Marina Mackay, *Modernism and World War II* (Cambridge, 2007), 22–3.
68. Virginia Woolf, *Between the Acts* (London, 2000), 51. For a discussion of the affinities between Woolf's last novel and Eliot's *Four Quartets*, see Richard S. Lyons, 'The intellectual structure of Virginia Woolf's *Between the Acts*', in Eleanor McNees, *Virginia Woolf: Critical assessments*, iv (Mountfield, 1994).

69. 12 Sep. 1939.
70. DR Mar. 1942.
71. 15 Aug. 1941.
72. Hayes, *Challenge of Conscience*, 131–2.
73. Peter Warwick, *Berkley Magazine*, Aug. 1950; Denis Argent, *Modern Caravan*, Jun. 1970.
74. T. S. Eliot, *Notes Towards the Definition of Culture* (London, 1948), 108.
75. *The Times*, 27 Jan. 1972. In 1951 the Caravan Club had 7,000 members—compared with 60,000 in the 1970s and 250,000 in the 1980s:<http://www.caravanclub.co.uk/About+Us/History/>.

CHAPTER 9

1. An earlier version of this chapter was published as 'Middle-class socialism: Selfhood, democracy and distinction in wartime County Durham', *History Workshop Journal*, 62 (Autumn 2006).
2. Matthew, DR Dec. 1937.
3. Matthew, DR Dec. 1937.
4. Matthew, DR Jun. 1939.
5. Matthew, 10 Aug. 1943.
6. Matthew, 24 Jul. 1941; 25 Aug. 22 Oct. 1942; 22 Aug. 1943.
7. Letter from Ronald Sands, Apr. 2007.
8. Bertha's perception of nepotism and corruption in the appointment of school teachers in Bishop Auckland is borne out by Ben Pimlott, *Hugh Dalton* (London, 1985), 179.
9. Matthew, DR Jan. 1939.
10. Matthew, DR May 1942.
11. Matthew, 14 Apr. 1940.
12. Matthew, 19 Jul. 1940. Tony Kushner quotes a pacifist office worker who helped internees but censored his report of this in his MO diary for fear of being suspected of being a fifth columnist himself: *We Europeans? Mass-Observation, 'race' and British identity in the twentieth century* (Aldershot, 2004), 198.
13. Matthew, 15 Oct. 1940.
14. Matthew, 20 Jan. 1941.
15. Matthew, 3 Dec. 1939.
16. Matthew, 14 Jul. 1942.
17. Matthew, 31 May 1943.
18. Matthew, 23 May 1943.

19. Matthew, DR Sept. 1943. The post-war prospect that he had in mind was either a Soviet-led liberation of all Europe, or a neo-fascist reaction.

20. On the Communist Party's shelter campaign see Kevin Morgan, *Against Fascism and War: Ruptures and continuities in British communist politics* (Manchester, 1989), 288 ff.; and, in the North East, James Hinton, *Women, Social Leadership* (Oxford, 2002), 119–20.

21. Matthew, 20 Jul. 1940.

22. *The Times*, 19 and 20 Sept. 1940; R. Calder, articles in *New Statesman*, 21 Sept. 1940, 8 Mar. 1941; R. Calder, *Carry on London* (London, 1941); J. Strachey, *Post D* (London, 1941); 'The New Pattern', *Planning*, 178 (30 Sept. 1941), and see Hinton, *Women, Social Leadership*, 83–4.

23. Matthew, 7 Oct. 1940.

24. DR May 1942.

25. Matthew, 17 Nov. 1940.

26. Matthew, 1 Jan. 1941. Auden actually wrote: 'cannot help or pardon'.

27. Matthew, 26 Dec. 1941; 18 Jan. 1943.

28. Matthew, 11 May 1940.

29. Matthew, 18 May 1940.

30. Matthew, 15 Dec. 1940.

31. Matthew, 9 Jun. 1942.

32. Matthew, 1 Jan. 1941.

33. Matthew, 23 Oct. 1940.

34. Matthew, 29 May 1941.

35. Matthew, 20 Dec. 1940.

36. Tom Harrisson, 'War Books', *Horizon*, Dec. 1941.

37. Matthew, 18 May 1942; 23 Oct. 1940.

38. Matthew, 15 Jan. 1941; DR Jun. 1939.

39. Matthew, 8 Nov. 1940.

40. Matthew, 1 Jan. 1941.

41. Matthew, 19 Oct. 1940; 5 Nov. 1940; 30 Oct. 1940.

42. Matthew, 19 Dec. 1941; 30 Oct. 1940; 31 Oct. 1942.

43. Matthew, 27 Oct. 1941.

44. Matthew, 12 Nov. 1941.

45. On Spennymoor see N. Vall, 'Cultural improvers in North-East England, 1920–1960: "Polishing the Pitmen"', *Northern History*, 41 (2004); N. Vall, 'Bohemians and "Pitmen Painters" in North-East England, 1930–1970', *Visual Culture in Britain*, 5/1 (2004). I am grateful to Bill Lancaster for drawing my attention to these articles.

46. Bertha, DR Jan. 1945.

47. Pimlott, *Dalton*, 175–81, 559, 563.

48. Bertha, 12 Jan. 1941.

49. Bishop Auckland Labour Party Women's Section, *Minutes*, 29 Feb. 1939.

50. Matthew, 12 Oct. 1941.

51. Matthew, 17 Oct. 1941.

52. Matthew, 8 Nov. 1941. Substantial extracts from Bertha's NAFFI diaries are reproduced in Angus Calder and Dorothy Sheridan (eds.), *Speak for Yourself: A Mass-Observation anthology, 1937–49* (London, 1984), 136–43.

53. Bertha, 19 Apr. 1942; 3 May 1942.

54. Bertha, 3 May 1942. For the other diarists see Celia Fremlin: 'it is interesting to read through diaries which up to 1941 are entirely domestic—and then, quite suddenly, there is not one single word more about home or family for months', MO File Report 2181, Sept. 1944.

55. Bertha, 3 May 1942.

56. Bertha, 17 May 1942.

57. Bertha, 22 Jun. 1942.

58. Bertha, 1 Jul. 1942.

59. Bertha, 13 Nov. 1942.

60. Matthew, 25 May 1943.

61. Bertha, 28 May 1943.

62. Bertha, 28 May 1943.

63. Sue Bruley, 'A new perspective on women workers in the Second World War', *Labour History Review*, 68/2 (Aug. 2003).

64. Matthew, 20 Oct. 1943.

65. Bertha, DR Sept. 1944.

66. Matthew, 31 Aug. 1944.

67. Bertha, 30 Jan. 1945; 14 Mar. 1945.

68. Bertha, DR Jul. 1945.

69. Bertha enclosed a letter from 'Briton' in *Northern Echo* (letter dated Jul. 1945) alleging that Dalton was lying when he said that the factories on the St Helen's estate had been awarded to German Jews because no British entrepreneurs had applied. 'Briton' had applied, and been turned down. In August 1943 Matthew had met 'a little old local tailor, who talked of music and the Jews who are ruining his business, combined with fulminations against local MP and Councillors (he has a grievance, dating back from Depressed Area days, when the Council handed over new factory to the Jewish firm, when he had applied for it, a local firm of many years standing', Matthew, 17 Aug. 1943).

70. And Dalton was sufficiently worried to note in his diary: 'it is most important that we should have only Gentiles now' (B. Pimlott (ed.), *The Political Diary*

of Hugh Dalton (London, 1986), 358). On the close links between Dalton and the German Jewish factory owners see ibid., 178–9, 404–5, 559–60, 563.

71. Bertha, DR Jul. 1945.
72. Bertha, DR Jul. 1945.
73. Bertha, DR Jul. 1945.
74. Bertha, DR Jun. 1945.
75. I am grateful to Rita and Ronald Sands, offspring of the next-door neighbours, for sharing with me their memories of the Waltons in later life.
76. Matthew, DR Dec. 1937.
77. Matthew, 30 Nov. 1941.
78. Matthew, 27 Jan. 1942.
79. Matthew, 15 Apr. 1943.
80. Matthew, 13 Sept. 1942; DR May 1942.
81. Matthew, 10 May 1943.
82. Matthew, 28 Dec. 1940.
83. Matthew, 7 Nov. 1943.
84. After publishing an article on the Waltons (annonymized as the Brittains) in *History Workshop Journal*, I tracked down the Sands' two children, who generously shared with me their memories of Matthew and Bertha. Among other things they pointed out that, misreading the diary, I had quite wrongly asserted that the Sands 'had been dismissed in June 1939 as prime examples of the lower-middle class "property complex"'. The reference was in fact to the neighbours on the other side.
85. Much later, following Bertha's death and the death of his own adopted son, Matthew left his house to the Sands' daughter. In 2007 she was still living there.
86. Matthew, DR Nov. 1943.
87. Bertha, DR Jun. 1939.
88. Matthew, 24 Jan. 1944.
89. Bertha, DR Jan. 1945.
90. Matthew, 20 May 1940.
91. Bertha, DR Jul. 1946; Matthew, 21 Dec. 1939.
92. Matthew, 21 Jul. 1940.
93. Matthew, DR Oct. 1940.
94. Matthew, 24 Jun. 1942.
95. Matthew, 19 Jul. 1942.
96. Bertha, 2 Oct. 1945.
97. Matthew, 3 Aug. 1943.
98. Kushner, *We Europeans?*; M. Berghahn, *Continental Britons: German-Jewish refugees from Nazi Germany* (Oxford, 1988).

99. Bertha, DR Jul. 1946.
100. Matthew, 10 Jun. 1941. Similarly Bertha on the pre-war influx of Jews who 'regularly paraded in all their continental splendour in the drab streets of out-of-work Bishop Auckland'. Bertha, DR Jul. 1946. Conspicuous consumption was a frequent trope of anti-Jewish feeling in wartime Britain. Tony Kushner, *The Persistence of Prejudice* (Manchester, 1989), 115, 127.
101. Bertha, DR Jul. 1945.
102. Bertha, 16 Nov. 1945.
103. Bertha, DR Jul. 1946.
104. Bertha, DR Jun. 1939.
105. For an interesting anti-humanist Marxist critique of the Popular Front embrace of 'culture' as the reconciler of proletarian and bourgeois interests in the common struggle against fascist inhumanity, see Francis Mulhern, *Culture/Metaculture* (London, 2000).
106. Matthew, DR Jun. 1939.
107. Matthew, 12 Jan. 1944.
108. Bertha, 14 Sept. 1944.
109. Bertha, 6, 9, 30 Jul. 1945.
110. Bertha, DR Sept. 1944.

CHAPTER 10

1. Robert Darnton, *The Great Cat Massacre, and Other Episodes in French Cultural History* (Harmondsworth, 1985), 89–90. 'Good to think' is Levi Strauss's phrase.
2. Alisdair MacIntyre, *After Virtue: A study on moral theory* (London, 1985), 201: Gorki reported Lenin as saying: 'I know nothing that is greater than the Appassionata. I'd like to listen to it every day. It is marvellous superhuman music. I always think with pride—perhaps it is naive of me—what marvellous things human beings can do! But I can't listen to music too often. It affects your nerves, makes you want to say stupid nice things, and stroke the heads of people who could create such beauty while living in this vile hell. And now you must not stroke anyone's head: you might get your hand bitten off. You have to hit them on the head, without any mercy, although our ideal is not to use force against anyone. Hm, hm, our duty is infernally hard.'

Bibliography

Ackers, Peter, and Payne, Jonathan, 'Before the storm: The experience of nation-alization and the prospects for industrial relations partnership in the British coal industry, 1947–1972—rethinking the militant narrative', *Social History*, 27/2 (2002), 184–209.

Adams, Matthew, 'The reflexive self and culture: A critique', *British Journal of Sociology*, 54/2 (2003).

Addison, Paul, *Road to 1945* (London, 1977).

Andrews, Maggie, *The Acceptable Face of Feminism: The Women's Institute as a social movement* (London, 1998).

Auden, W. H., *Selected Poems*, ed. Edward Mendelson (London, 1979).

Banks, Olive, *The Politics Of British Feminism, 1918–1970* (Aldershot, 1993).

Baron, J. H., and Sonnenberg, A., 'The wax and wane of intestinal autointoxication and visceroptosis: Historical trends of real *versus* apparent new digestive diseases', *The American Journal of Gastroenterology*, 97 (2002), 11.

Beaumont, Caitriona, 'Citizens not feminists: The boundary negotiated between citizenship and feminism by mainstream women's organisations in England, 1928–39', *Women's History Review*, 9/2 (2000).

Benkovitz, Miriam, *Frederick Rolf: Baron Corvo. A biography* (London, 1977).

Berghahn, Marion, *Continental Britons: German-Jewish refugees from Nazi Germany* (Oxford, 1988).

Berman, Marshall, *All That Is Solid Melts Into Air: The experience of modernity* (London, 1983).

Beveridge, Lord, and Wells, A. F., *The Evidence for Voluntary Action* (London, 1949).

Bourdieu, Pierre, *Distinction: A social critique of the judgement of taste* (London, 1984).

Bowden, S., and Offer, A., 'Household appliances and the use of time: The United States and Britain since the 1920s', *Economic History Review*, 7/4 (1994).

Bowen, Elizabeth, *The Heat of the Day* (Harmondsworth, 1979).

Broad, Richard, and Fleming, Suzie (eds.), *Nella Last's War: A mother's diary, 1939–45* (Bristol, 1981).

——(eds.), *Nella Last's War: The Second World War diaries of housewife, 49* (London, 2006).

Bromley, Roger, *Lost Narratives: Popular fictions, politics and recent history*, (London, 1988).

Brooke, Stephen, 'War and the nude: The photography of Bill Brandt in the 1940s', *Journal of British Studies*, 45/1 (2006).

Brooks, P., *Women at Westminster* (London, 1967).

Brown, Callum G., *The Death of Christian Britain: Understanding secularisation 1800–2000* (London, 2001).

Bruley, Sue, 'A new perspective on women workers in the Second World War', *Labour History Review*, 68/2 (2003).

Burkitt, Ian, 'The shifting concept of the self', *History of the Human Sciences*, 7/2 (1994).

Butt, Trevor, and Langdridge, Darren, 'The construction of self: The public reach into the private sphere', *Sociology*, 37/3 (2003).

Byrom, James, *The Unfinished Man* (London, 1957).

Calder, Angus, and Sheridan, Dorothy (eds.), *The People's War: Britain 1939–1945* (London, 1969).

——, *Speak for Yourself: A Mass-Observation anthology, 1937–49* (London, 1984).

——, *The Myth of the Blitz* (London, 1991).

Calder, Ritchie, *Carry on London* (London, 1941).

Ceadel, Martin, *Pacifism in Britain, 1914–1945: The defining of a faith* (Oxford, 1980).

Chinn, Carl, *Brum Undaunted: Birmingham during the blitz* (Studley, 2005).

Cockett, Olivia, *Love and War in London: A woman's diary, 1939–1942*, ed. Robert Malcolmson (Waterloo, 2005).

Collini, S., *Public Moralists: Political thought and intellectual life in Britain 1850–1930* (Oxford, 1993).

Collins, Marcus, *Modern Love: An intimate history of men and women in twentieth-century Britain* (London, 2003).

Conekin, Becky, Mort, Frank, and Waters, Chris (eds.) *Moments of Modernity: Reconstructing Britain 1945–1964* (London, 1999).

Connell, R. W., *Masculinities* (Cambridge, 2005).

Cook, Hera, *The Long Sexual Revolution: English women, sex and contraception, 1900–1975* (Oxford, 2004).

Copelman, Dina, *London's Women Teachers: Gender, class and feminism, 1870–1930* (London, 1996).

Coubrough, M., 'Profile: Invalid Children's Aid Association', *Child Care Health Development*, 4/1 (1978).

Crang, Jeremy A., *The British Army and the People's War 1939–1945* (Manchester, 2000).

Darnton, Robert, *The Great Cat Massacre, and Other Episodes in French Cultural History* (Harmondsworth, 1985).

Davidoff, Leonore, and Hall, Catherine, *Family Fortunes: Men and women of the English middle class, 1780–1850* (London, 1987).

Davies, Andrew, *Leisure, Gender and Poverty: Working-class culture in Salford and Manchester, 1900–1939* (Buckingham, 1992).

Davies, D. R., *In Search of Myself* (London, 1961).

Davies, Sam, and Morley, Bob, *County Borough Election Results, England Wales, 1919–1938: A comparative analysis*, i: *Barnsley–Bournemouth* (Aldershot, 1999).

Dawson, Graham, *Soldier Heroes: British adventure, empire and the imagining of masculinities* (London, 1994).

Dimmack, Max, *Clifford Last* (Melbourne, 1972).

Donnelly, Peter (ed.), *Mrs Milburn's Diaries: An Englishwoman's day-to-day reflections, 1939–45* (London, 1979).

Drucker, Peter, *The End of Economic Man: A study of the new totalitarianism* (London 1939).

Edwards, Jack, *Broxbourne Past* (Waltham Cross, 1984).

Elias, Norbert, *The Society of Individuals* (Oxford 1991).

Eliot, T. S., *Notes Towards the Definition of Culture* (London, 1948).

Ellman, Maud, *Elizabeth Bowen: The shadow across the page* (Edinburgh, 2003).

Ferguson, Sheila, and Fitzgerald, Hilde, *Studies in the Social Services* (London, 1954).

Field, Joanna (Marion Milner), *A Life of One's Own* (London, 1986).

Fielding, S., 'The Second World War and popular Radicalism: The significance of the "movement away from party" ', *History*, 80/1 (1995).

——, Thompson, Peter, and Tiratsoo, Nick, *England Arise! The Labour Party and popular politics in 1940s Britain* (Manchester, 1995).

Fisher, Kate, *Birth Control, Sex and Marriage in Britain 1918–1960* (Oxford, 2006).

Fletcher, Horace, *Fletcherism: What it is; or how I became young at sixty* (London, 1913).

Foucault, M. *The Order of Things* (London, 1970).

Garbutt, P. L. 'The housewife her own housemaid', *Good Housekeeping*, January 1940.

Gardner, Martin, *Fads and Fallacies in the Name of Science* (Dover, 1957).

Garfield, Simon, *Our Hidden Lives: The remarkable diaries of post-war Britain* (London, 2004).

——, *We Are at War: The remarkable diaries of five ordinary people in extraordinary times* (London, 2005).

——, *Private Battles: How the war almost defeated us* (London, 2006).

Gershuny, J., *Social Innovation and the Division of Labour* (Oxford, 1983).

Giddens, Anthony, *Modernity and Self-identity: Self and society in the late modern age* (Cambridge, 1991).

——, *The Transformation of Intimacy: Sexuality, love and eroticism in modern societies* (Cambridge, 1992).

Giles, Judy, *Women, Identity and Private Life in Britain, 1900–50* (Basingstoke, 1995).

Glover, Gertrude F., *A False Note: A play for women in one act* (London, 1937).

Goffman, Erving, *The Presentation of Self in Everyday Life* (London, 1990).

Goodall, Peter, 'The author in the study: Self-representation as reader and writer in the medieval and early modern periods', in R. Bedford, L. Davis, and P. Kelly (eds.), *Early Modern Autobiography: Theories, genres, practices* (Michigan, 2006).

Graves, P. M., *Labour Women: Women in British working-class politics, 1918–1939* (Oxford, 1994).

Grimley, Matthew, 'The religion of Englishness: Puritanism, providentialism and "national character", 1918–45', *Journal of British Studies*, 46 (2007).

Habermas, Jurgen, *The Structural Transformation of the Public Sphere* (Cambridge, 1992).

Haire, Norman (ed.), *Encyclopaedia of Sexual Knowledge* (London, 1936).

Hammerton, A. James, *Cruelty and Companionship: Conflict in 19th-century married life* (London, 1992).

Harrison, Brian, *Prudent Revolutionaries* (Oxford, 1987).

Harrisson, Tom, 'War books', *Horizon*, December 1941.

——, *Living Through the Blitz* (Harmondsworth, 1978).

Hayes, Denis, *Challenge of Conscience: The story of the conscientious objectors of 1939–1949* (London, 1949).

Hazelgrove, Jenny, *Spiritualism and British Society between the Wars* (Manchester 2000).

Heimann, Judith M., *The Most Offending Soul Alive: Tom Harrisson and his remarkable life* (Honolulu, 1997).

Henke, Suzette A., *Shattered Subjects: Trauma and testimony in women's life-writing* (New York, 2000).

Highmore, Ben, *Everyday Life and Cultural Theory: An introduction* (London, 2002).

Higonnet, M. R. J., et al., *Behind the Lines: Gender and the two World Wars* (New Haven, 1987).

Hilliard, Chris, *To Exercise Our Talents: The democratisation of writing in Britain* (London, 2006).

Hilton, Mathew, 'The female consumer and the politics of consumption in twentieth-century Britain', *Historical Journal*, 45/1 (2002).

Hinton, James, *The First Shop Steward's Movement* (London, 1972).

——, 'Coventry communism: A study of factory politics in the Second World War', *History Workshop Journal*, 10 (1980).

——, 'Women and the Labour vote, 1945–50', *Labour History Review*, 57(1993).

——, *Shop Floor Citizens: Engineering democracy in 1940s Britain* (Aldershot, 1994).

——, '1945 and the apathy school', *History Workshop Journal*, 43 (1997).

——, 'Conservative women and voluntary social service, 1938–1951', in Stuart Ball and Ian Holliday (eds.), *Mass Conservatism: The Conservatives and the public since the 1880s* (London, 2002).

——, *Women, Social Leadership and the Second World War: Continuities of class* (Oxford, 2002).

——, 'Middle-class socialism: Selfhood, democracy and distinction in wartime County Durham', *History Workshop Journal*, 62 (2006).

—— 'The "class" complex: Mass-Observation and cultural distinction in pre-war Britain', *Past and Present*, 198/2 (2008).

Hobhouse, Stephen, *Forty Years and an Epilogue: An autobiography, 1881–1951* (London, 1951).

Hodgson, Vere, *Few Eggs and No Oranges* (London, 1999).

Hubble, Nick, *Mass-Observation and Everyday Life: Culture, history, theory* (Basingstoke, 2006).

Hundert, E. J., 'The European Enlightenment and the history of the self', in Roy Porter (ed.), *Rewriting the Self: Histories from the Renaissance to the present* (London, 1997).

Hutton, Patrick, 'Foucault, Freud and the technologies of the self', in Luther H. Martin, et al. (eds.), *Technologies of the Self: A seminar with Michel Foucault* (Massachusetts, 1988).

Huxley, Aldous, *Ends and Means* (London, 1937).

Jarvis, David, 'The Conservative Party and the politics of gender, 1900–1939', in Martin Francis and Ina Zweiniger-Bargielowska (eds.), *The Conservatives and British Society, 1880–1990* (Cardiff, 1996).

Jeffery, Tom, *Mass-Observation: A short history* (Birmingham, 1978).

Jeffreys, Sheila, *The Spinster and her Enemies: Feminism and sexuality 1880–1930* (London, 1985).

Jolly, Margaretta, 'Historical entries: Mass-Observation diarists 1937–2001', in *New Formations*, 44 (2001).

Jordan, Heather Bryant, *How Will the Heart Endure: Elizabeth Bowen and the landscape of war* (Ann Arbor, 1992).

Kendall, Walter, *The Revolutionary Movement in Britain* (London, 1969).

Kirkpatrick, Frank G., *John Macmurray: Community beyond political philosophy* (New York, 2005).

Koa Wing, Sandra, (ed.), *Our Longest Days: A people's history of the Second World War* (London, 2007).

Kushner, Tony, *The Persistence of Prejudice* (Manchester, 1989).

——, *We Europeans? Mass-Observation, 'race' and British identity in the twentieth century* (Aldershot, 2004).

Langhamer, Claire, *Women's Leisure in England, 1920–60* (Manchester, 2000).

——, 'Adultery in post-war England', *History Workshop Journal*, 62 (2006).

——, 'Love and courtship in mid-twentieth century England', *The Historical Journal*, 50/1 (2007).

Lasch, Christopher, *The Culture of Narcissism: American life in an age of diminishing expectations* (London, 1991).

Lawrence, T. F. C., 'Boswell, Robert William McGregor (1911–1976)', *Australian Dictionary of Biography*, xiii (Melbourne, 1993).

Lee, Hermione, *Virginia Woolf* (1997).

Lewis, Jane, *The Voluntary Sector, the State and Social Work in Britain* (Aldershot, 1995).

——, 'The working-class wife and mother and state intervention', in J. Lewis (ed.), *Labour and Love: Women's experience of home and family, 1850–1940* (Oxford, 1986).

Lewis, Jeremy, *Penguin Special: The life and times of Allen Lane* (London, 2005).

Light, Alison, *Forever England: Femininity, literature and conservatism between the wars* (London, 1991).

Lyons, Richard S., 'The intellectual structure of Virginia Woolf's *Between the Acts*', in Eleanor McNees (ed.), *Virginia Woolf: Critical assessments*, iv (Mountfield, 1994).

McCarthy, Helen, 'Parties, voluntary associations, and democratic politics in interwar Britain', *The Historical Journal*, 50/4 (2007).

MacIntyre, Alisdair, *After Virtue: A study on moral theory* (London, 1985).

Macintyre, Stuart, 'British Labour, Marxism and working-class apathy in the 1920s', *Historical Journal*, 20/2 (1977).

Mackay, Marina, *Modernism and World War II* (Cambridge, 2007).

MacKillop, I. D., *The British Ethical Societies* (Cambridge, 1986).

McLaine, Ian, *Ministry of Morale: Home front morale and the Ministry of Information in World War II* (London, 1979).

Macmurray, John, 'Freedom in the personal nexus', in R. N. Anshen (ed.), *Freedom its Meaning* (New York, 1940).

——, *Reason and Emotion* (London, 1962).

Madge, Charles, and Harrisson, Tom, *Mass-Observation* (London, 1937).

Malcolmson, Patricia, and Malcolmson, Robert (eds.), *A Woman in Wartime London: The diary of Kathleen Tipper, 1941–1945* (London, 2006).

—— (eds.), *Nella Last's Peace: The post-war diaries of housewife, 49* (London, 2008).

—— (eds.), *A Soldier in Bedfordshire: The diary of Private Denis Argent 1941–1942* (Bedford, 2009).

Malcolmson, Robert, and Searby, Peter, (eds.), *Wartime Norfolk: The Diary of Rachel Dhonau, 1941–42* (Norwich, 2005).

Marcus, Laura, *Auto/biographical discourses* (Manchester, 1994).

Mass-Observation, *People in Production: An enquiry into British war production* (London, 1942).

——, *The Journey Home* (London, 1944).

——, *Puzzled People: A study in popular attitudes to religion, ethics, progress and politics in a London Borough* (London, 1947).

Mauss, Marcel, 'The category of the human mind: The notion of person, the notion of self', in *Sociology and Psychology: Essays* (London, 1979).

Milner, Tyrus, 'In the blitz of dreams: Mass-Observation and the historical uses of dream reports', *New Formations*, 44 (Autumn 2001).

Morgan, Kevin, *Against Fascism and War: Ruptures and continuities in British communist politics* (Manchester, 1989).

Morpurgo, Clare, 'Allen Lane and his Foundation', Allen Lane Lecture, 2006, <www.allenlane.org.uk/2006_lecture.htm>.

Mulhern, Francis, *Culture/Metaculture* (London, 2000).

Noakes, Lucy, *War and the British: Gender, memory and national identity* (London, 1998).

Nussbaum, Felicity, 'Towards conceptualizing diary', in James Olney (ed.), *Studies in Autobiography* (Oxford 1988).

——, *The Autobiographical Subject: Gender and ideology in 18th-century England* (London 1989).

Olney, James, *Metaphors of Self: The meaning of autobiography* (Princeton, 1972).

Oram, Alison, '"Bombs don't discriminate!" Women's political activism in the Second World War', in C. Gledhill and G. Swanson (eds.), *Nationalising Femininity: Culture, sexuality and British cinema in the Second World War* (Manchester, 1996).

Orwell, George, *The Lion and the Unicorn* (Harmondsworth, 1982).

Pacifist Research Bureau, *War and the Colonies: A policy for socialist and pacifists* (London, 1939).

Parker, Stephen, *Faith on the Home Front: Aspects of church life and popular religion in Birmingham, 1939–1945* (Oxford 2005).

Pateman, Carole, *The Disorder of Women: Democracy, feminism and political theory* (Cambridge, 1989).

Pedersen, Susan, *Family: Dependence and the origins of the welfare state. Britain and France, 1914–1945* (Cambridge, 1993).

——, 'Gender, welfare and citizenship in Britain during the Great War', *American Historical Review*, 94 (1990).

Piette, Adam, *Imagination at War: British fiction and poetry, 1939–1945* (Basingstoke, 1995).

Pimlott, Ben (ed.), *Hugh Dalton* (London, 1985).

——, *The Political Diary of Hugh Dalton* (London, 1986).

Plummer, Ken, *Documents of Life 2: An invitation to a critical humanism* (London, 2001).

Prochaska, F. K., *Women and Philanthropy in Nineteenth-century England* (Oxford, 1980).

Prynn, D. L., 'Common Wealth: A British "Third Party" of the 1940s', *Journal of Contemporary History*, 7/1 (1972).

Pugh, Martin, 'Domesticity and the decline of feminism, 1930–50', in H. L. Smith (ed.), *British Feminism in the Twentieth Century* (Aldershot, 1990).

——, *Women and the Women's Movement in Britain, 1914–1959* (Basingstoke, 1992).

Purcell, Jennifer, 'Beyond home: Housewives and the nation, private and public identities 1939–1949', D.Phil., University of Sussex, 2008.

Reckitt, Maurice B., 'The Christian Social Movement in England: Its aims and its organization', *The Journal of Religion*, 4/2 (1924).

Richards, Graham, 'Britain on the couch: The popularization of psychoanalysis in Britain, 1918–1940', *Science in Context*, 13/2 (2000).

Roper, Michael, 'Splitting in unsent letters: Writing as a social practice and a psychological activity', *Social History*, 26/3 (2001).

——, 'Between manliness and masculinity: The war generation and the psychology of fear in Britain, 1914–1950', *Journal of British Studies*, 44/2 (2005).

——'Slipping out of view: Subjectivity and emotion in gender history', *History Workshop Journal*, 59/1 (2005).

Rose, Nikolas, 'Assembling the modern self', in Roy Porter (ed.), *Rewriting the Self: Histories from the Renaissance to the present* (London, 1997).

——, *Governing the Soul: The shaping of the private self* (London, 1999).

Rose, Sonya O., *Which People's War? National identity and citizenship in Britain 1939–1945* (Oxford, 2003).

Ross, Ellen, *Love and Toil: Motherhood in outcast London, 1870–1918* (Oxford, 1993).

Rowbotham, Sheila, 'In search of Carpenter', *History Workshop Journal*, 3 (1977).

——, and Weeks, Jeffrey, *Socialism and the New Life: The personal and sexual politics of Edward Carpenter and Havelock Ellis* (London, 1977).

Rustin, Michael, 'Reflections on the biographical turn in the social sciences', in Prue Chamberlayne, Joanna Bornat, and Tom Wengraf (eds.), *The Turn to Biographical Methods in the Social Sciences* (Abingdon, 2000).

Scott, Gillian, *Feminism and the Politics of Working Women: The Women's Co-operative Guild, 1880s to the Second World War* (London, 1998).

Scott, Joan, *Gender and the Politics of History* (New York, 1988).

Sennett, Richard, *The Fall of Public Man* (London, 1977).

Shaw, Jenny, *Intellectual Property, Representative Experience and Mass-Observation*, Mass-Observation Archive, Occasional Papers, 9, 1998.

Sheridan, Dorothy (ed.), *Among You Taking Notes: The wartime diary of Naomi Mitchison* (London, 1985).

——(ed.), *Wartime Women: An anthology of women's wartime writing for Mass-Observation, 1937–45* (London, 1990).

Sitwell, Osbert, *The Scarlet Tree* (Boston, 1946).

Smith, H., 'The problem of equal pay for equal work in Great Britain during World War Two', *Journal of Modern History*, 53 (1981).

Smith, Macolm, *Britain and 1940: History, myth and popular memory* (London, 2000).

Spender, Dale, *There's Always Been a Women's Movement this Century* (London, 1983).

Stanley, Liz, *The Auto/Biographical I: The theory and practice of feminist auto/biography* (Manchester, 1992).

Stanley, Nick, 'The extra dimension: A study and assessment of the methods employed by Mass-Observation in its first period, 1937–1940' (CNAA Ph.D. thesis, 1981).

Stebbing, Edward, *Diary of a Decade 1939–50* (Lewes, 1998).

Stephens, W. B. (ed.), *The Victoria History of the County of Warwick*, viii: *The city of Coventry and Borough of Warwick* (London, 1969).

Stonebridge, Lyndsey, 'Anxiety at a time of crisis', *History Workshop Journal*, 45 (1998).

Strachey, John, *Post D* (London, 1941).

Summerfield, Penny, 'Women in World War Two', in A. Marwick (ed.), *Total War and Social Change* (Basingstoke, 1988).

——, *Reconstructing Women's Wartime Lives: Discourse and subjectivity in oral histories of the Second World War* (Manchester, 1998).

Summers, Ann, 'A home from home: Women's Philanthropic work in the nineteenth century', in S. Burman (ed.), *Fit Work for Women* (London, 1979).

Taylor, A. J. P., *English History, 1914–45* (Oxford, 1965).

Taylor, Charles, *Sources of the Self: The making of the modern identity* (Cambridge, 1989).

Taylor, Stephen, 'The suburban neurosis', *The Lancet*, 26 March 1938.

Thane, Pat, 'The women of the British Labour Party and feminism, 1906–1945', in H. Smith (ed.), *British Feminism in the Twentieth Century* (Aldershot, 1990).

Thomas, L. H. C., 'Clair Baier', in A. D. Best and Rex W. Last (eds.), *Essays Presented to Dr. Baier* (Hull, 1976).

Thompson, Paul, *The Voice of the Past: Oral history* (Oxford, 2000).

Thomson, Mathew, *Psychological Subjects: Identity, culture and health in twentieth-century Britain* (Oxford, 2006).

Titmuss, Richard, *Problems of Social Policy* (London, 1950).

Vall, N., 'Bohemians and "Pitmen Painters" in North East England, 1930–1970', *Visual Culture in Britain*, 5/1 (2004).

——, 'Cultural improvers in North-East England, 1920–1960: "Polishing the Pitmen"', *Northern History*, 41 (2004).

van Someren, Ernest, *Spectrochemical Abstracts* (London, 1938–51).

van Someren, Ernest, 'A family budget in wartime', *Housewife*, May 1942.

van Someren, Ivy, 'Barron Corvo's quarrels', *Life and Letters and the London Mercury*, February 1947.

Wahrman, Dror, *The Making of the Modern Self: Identity and culture in 18th-century England* (London, 2004).

Weeks, Donald, *Corvo* (London, 1971).

Weiner, Wendy J., and Rosenwald, George C., 'A moment's monument: The psychology of keeping a diary', in R. Josselson, and A. Lieblich (eds.), *The Narrative Study of Lives* (London, 1993).

Wells, H. G., *God the Invisible King* (London, 1917).

Woolf, Virginia, *Mr Bennett and Mrs Brown* (London, 1924).

——, *Three Guineas* (London, 1943).

——, *A Room of One's Own* (Harmondsworth, 1972).

——, *Between the Acts* (London, 2000).

Zeldin, Theodore, *France 1848–1945: Politics and anger* (Oxford, 1979).

Index

Lightning Source UK Ltd.
Milton Keynes UK
UKOW06f1505120217
294177UK00017B/481/P